How to
Survive Spiritually
in Our Times

ALSO BY HAROLD KLEMP

How to Survive Spiritually in Our Times

HAROLD KLEMP

MAHANTA TRANSCRIPTS
BOOK 16

ECKANKAR
Minneapolis

How to Survive Spiritually in Our Times, Mahanta
Transcripts, Book 16

Copyright © 2001 ECKANKAR

The terms ECKANKAR, ECK, EK, MAHANTA, SOUL TRAVEL, and
VAIRAGI, among others, are trademarks of ECKANKAR, P.O. Box
27300, Minneapolis, MN 55427 U.S.A.

Printed in U.S.A.

Compiled by Mary Carroll Moore
Edited by Joan Klemp and Anthony Moore
Text illustrations by Ann Hubert
Text photo (page xiv) by Robert Huntley
Cover photos by Stan Burgess, Terry Cermola, Kevin Harrington,
Robert Huntley, Bree Renz, Sarah Sanderson

Library of Congress Cataloging-in-Publication Data

Klemp, Harold.
    How to survive spiritually in our times / Harold Klemp.
        p. cm. — (Mahanta transcripts ; bk. 16)
    Includes index.
    ISBN 1-57043-167-1 (alk. paper)
    1. Eckankar (Organization)—Doctrines. 2. Spiritual life—Eckankar
(Organization) I. Title. II. Series: Klemp, Harold, Mahanta transcripts ;
bk. 16.
BP605.E3K558 2001
299'.93—dc21

                                2001033279

∞ The paper used in this publication meets the minimum requirements of
the American National Standard for Information Sciences —Permanence
of Paper for Printed Library Materials, ANSI Z39.48-1984.

CONTENTS

FOREWORD

The teachings of ECK define the nature of Soul. You are Soul, a particle of God sent into the worlds (including earth) to gain spiritual experience.

The goal in ECK is spiritual freedom in this lifetime, after which you become a Co-worker with God, both here and in the next world. Karma and reincarnation are primary beliefs.

Key to the ECK teachings is the Mahanta, the Living ECK Master. He has the special ability to act as both the Inner and Outer Master for ECK students. He is the prophet of Eckankar, given respect but not worship. He teaches the sacred name of God, HU, which lifts you spiritually into the Light and Sound of God, the ECK (Holy Spirit). Purified by the practice of the Spiritual Exercises of ECK, you are then able to accept the full love of God in this lifetime.

Sri Harold Klemp is the Mahanta, the Living ECK Master. He has written many books, discourses, and articles about the spiritual life. Many of his public talks are available on audio- and videocassette. His teachings lift people and help them recognize and understand their own experiences in the Light and Sound of God.

How to Survive Spiritually in Our Times,
Mahanta Transcripts, Book 16, contains his talks
from 1996 to 1999. May they help you recognize
how you are in the grasp of divine love every moment
of every day.

PREFACE

*T*he challenge of this book is sweeping in scope. How to give spiritual help to people in need in every part of society, around the world, and at multiple levels of consciousness?

An awesome undertaking.

At the bottom of it, how to help you?

So this presentation is an honest attempt to cover all the bases for you, the *A* to *Z* of spiritual food. The format is in story form. Yes, it does require humility and sincerity to approach the altar of truth. The haughty, the learned may turn up their noses at these words, but it's OK. In time, life shall teach them better.

These words are for you.

The understanding of truth depends upon a willingness to learn something new. That, by implication, means the surrender of old, outworn ideas. A host of them.

Read the offerings that follow with an open mind. Above all, with an open and childlike heart.

With all goodwill I welcome you to my world and that of all the people whose chronicles are at the heart of these spiritual stories. Truth is a living thing. Is it a wonder, then, that it should reveal itself in the lives of average people too?

There is something in this book for you. If nothing more, it shows the workings of Divine Spirit and the high Masters at work in the daily affairs of a seeker.

Now, begin your journey into a fresh, exciting world of spiritual revelation.

Harold Klemp

Sri Harold Klemp, the Mahanta, the Living ECK Master gives tips on how to listen to the Voice of God, the Holy Spirit, for guidance and help in daily life.

1

HOW TO
SURVIVE SPIRITUALLY
IN OUR TIMES

*S*o often, when times are good, people don't have much use for God or for the master of their path.

Then times get hard, and there's a natural tendency for people to say, "I think it's time to call on God and let him know things aren't going so well." In their prayers or contemplations, they ask their spiritual master or God directly, "I wonder, are you listening?"

They've asked to be delivered from whatever it is they've gotten themselves into, and nothing seems to happen.

CAN YOU HEAR ME?

I heard an interesting story on *Paul Harvey News and Comment* about an elderly couple. The husband had a feeling his wife was losing her hearing, so he decides to test her. She's seated in an easy chair facing away from him. He comes up to the chair,

In their prayers or contemplations, they ask their spiritual master or God directly, "I wonder, are you listening?"

stands back several steps, and says, "Honey, can you hear me?" Nothing. He takes a couple of steps closer and says just a little louder, "Honey, can you hear me?" No reply.

Now he's concerned. He walks right up to her shoulder, bends over, and shouts in her ear, "Honey, can you hear me?" She jumps up. She turns around, furious, and says, "Yes, for the third time!"

That's a little the way it is when people say to God, "Can you hear me?"

Generally, help is provided for these people because they have opened themselves by asking for it. But they don't recognize the help. Why not? Because it's not the answer they were looking for.

So they ask again and again, and the answer comes several more times, until finally the person gets so disgusted and shouts, "God, can you hear me?" Of course.

The trick, then, is to learn how to listen to the Voice of God, the Holy Spirit. To know when the divine power is speaking to us. The answer may not be what we're looking for.

The trick, then, is to learn how to listen to the Voice of God, the Holy Spirit. To know when the divine power is speaking to us.

SURVIVAL SKILLS

People who are very set in their state of consciousness—they have their mind made up about a lot of things—are the least likely to hear when God speaks.

Tony from Nigeria wrote in a letter to me, "Survival as the drama of life is an ongoing battle. This battle is often overlooked because of the level of awareness of people." He sees Divine Spirit working around him all the time, and he has story after story about how the Holy Spirit has worked.

One day Tony went to visit a friend in town. Returning home, he stood by himself at the bus stop. It was on a very busy highway filled with vehicles of all kinds. A pickup truck loaded with bags of rice came along. Just as it passed, the truck hit this enormous bump. Some rice that had spilled into the truck bed flew up into the air and fell on the highway.

In the brush by the road were five birds. Two were just ordinary birds, but three were chickens, hens actually. Somehow these birds knew that some rice had fallen on the highway. Suddenly they were all out there, where traffic was speeding by, trying to eat the rice. The first cars that came past frightened them. With a cackle the hens all ran back into the brush, and the other birds flew away.

Only one hen came back.

She looked at the rice with one eye, and with the other eye she looked at the traffic coming down the road. She looked, she weighed her chances, and she ran right out into the road again.

The cars were coming fast. With one eye on the vehicles and the other eye on the grain, the hen ate a little bit here, a little bit there, dodging in and around all the vehicles. Finally, after fifty cars and trucks had missed her, she finished eating and ran back to the side of the road, very satisfied with herself. She cleaned her beak and went back into the brush where the others were still digging in the dirt for anything they could find. She had just had a feast.

"The battle for survival is adventuresome and not a game for weaklings," he said.

Tony looked at this. "The battle for survival is adventuresome and not a game for weaklings," he said. "To succeed one has to throw in all he or she has. Wit, skill, a daring spirit, and a heart full of love. The daring hen had it all." I guess she loved rice.

Getting Out of the Box

There are challenges at work—certainly you have them. I have them. These challenges go on day by day, week by week.

Most of us wonder, *Doesn't this ever stop? Is our whole life going to be spent trying to figure out how to get out of one box after another? Will we always have to fend off one antagonist or another—a competitor, a boss, other people we meet at work? Won't this ever end?*

A dream journal can be very important for helping with spiritual survival.

Victoria is an African woman who works as a nurse in one of the oil-producing countries in the Persian Gulf. She has learned the importance of keeping a dream journal. A dream journal can be very important for helping with spiritual survival. Dreams will often tell you what's coming, and at other times they will give you an understanding of what has happened in the past. Even though the trouble isn't removed, it helps to have an understanding of why this trouble haunts us.

Victoria saw the power of dreams to foretell the future. She wrote to me, "Before any self-directed change can occur outwardly, it must first arise within us. First the dream, then the reality."

So this is the role of dreams in her daily life. She said there are three things: Number one, dreams guide her directly in what to do. Second, they help her get insight or understanding of her daily activities. Third, they assure her of the protection of the Mahanta, the Living ECK Master—the Inner and Outer Master.

Victoria worked in the maternity ward of a large hospital. She was the fourth and newest African nurse there. Her supervisor was also an African woman.

Above her supervisor was someone called the regional matron, who was an Indian woman. The regional matron was constantly making trouble in this hospital, and the supervisor would do everything she could to balance things out and keep this person from causing too much of a morale problem among the nurses. But one day, the regional matron succeeded in getting rid of this African supervisor; the supervisor was fired and sent home. The regional matron replaced the supervisor with a man.

By this time Victoria was the only African left working in this hospital. She was a hard worker. She knew she did her job well, and the patients loved her because they could tell that she was someone who cared for them. But the regional matron hated her.

One day, the new supervisor called her in. He said, "I shouldn't be telling you this, but for some reason the matron hates you. To keep you out of her way so you can stay in the country, I can do two things. One is to post you to one of our health centers in the outer regions; the other is to put you on the night shift."

Victoria felt this wasn't fair. She went home and told her husband.

Her husband became very upset. Without telling Victoria what he was about to do, he went to the regional matron and laid it on the line. "Don't threaten to fire my wife," he said, "or I'm coming back." So the matron went to someone called the director general, the big boss. She said, "This man threatened me." She was trying to use this as an excuse to get Victoria fired and sent out of the country.

The director general called Victoria. "Monday morning, come into my office so that we can talk. And bring your husband with you."

She knew she did her job well, and the patients loved her because they could tell that she was someone who cared for them.

Victoria looked it all over and knew this was going to be her termination. But Monday morning before the meeting with the director general, she went into contemplation and asked the Mahanta, the Living ECK Master, "Please speak to the director general before our appointment." She visualized the director general in their appointment speaking kindly to her.

After contemplation, she and her husband went to the appointment. The director general invited them into the office, and he was very kind. "For some reason this has been brought to my attention, so I would like to hear your side of the story," he said. And her husband told his side of the story—what he had said and why.

The director general said that Victoria had always had a good job report, her patients liked her, and he was very happy to have her. As far as he was concerned, the case was closed.

This was a case of spiritual survival. Victoria was in a heap of trouble, but because she asked for help, the answer came.

This was a case of spiritual survival. Victoria was in a heap of trouble, but because she asked for help, the answer came.

Dream Help

About this time, she was writing some of her dreams in her dream journal. Before this she had never paid much attention to reading her dream journal. She would record the dreams, but she didn't review them.

But that day, the journal opened to an entry she'd made a couple of years earlier. She saw a dream that showed her very clearly that at some point she was going to be posted to one of the health centers in a remote region of that country.

Exactly a week later she had recorded another dream that said all four of the African nurses in this particular hospital were going to be fired, given a ticket, and sent home.

By looking through her dream journal, Victoria realized that this was how fate, or the line of destiny, had been arranged. This is what was to have been. The other three African nurses were all fired, given plane tickets, and sent home. But when she asked for help from her spiritual guide, her line of destiny was changed.

A True Spiritual Guide

Sometimes people don't understand the role or the place of a spiritual guide—whether it's Christ, the Mahanta, Buddha, or a church leader who has a very definite direct connection with the Holy Spirit.

Over all creation is the Creator, God. We know It as Sugmad. The Voice of God is the active force that goes out and is responsible for the actual creation of all the universes. This Voice of God is what is known as the Holy Spirit, the Spirit of God, the creative force. But it's a neutral force. It simply obeys, or does, the will of the Creator.

A true spiritual master is in tune with the Voice of God. As a human manifestation that people can see and understand, his will is that of Divine Spirit. And that's all.

In Eckankar this divine force works both in the Outer Master and through the Inner Master. That means the ECKists have the additional benefit of a Master who can come in the dream state and teach them, sometimes by Soul Travel, sometimes in contemplation. The Inner Master is working when the

The Voice of God is the active force that goes out and is responsible for the actual creation of all the universes.

individual sleeps, prays, meditates, or contemplates. The Outer Master is out here to provide the books and discourses and to give talks. They are not two separate things—they're just two different aspects of one being serving the Holy Spirit.

LINE OF DESTINY

After this was all over, Victoria still had her job. But she realizes, too, that life is a tenuous affair and everything changes.

From this experience, she learned three important things: First, never be too lazy to record your dreams; second, review past dreams from time to time; and third, do the spiritual exercises, and many of the bad things you dream about can be averted according to the wish or direction of the Mahanta, the Living ECK Master.

A person's line of destiny can be altered if the individual has grown spiritually.

One of the little-known benefits of a spiritual Master is that fate can be changed. A person's line of destiny can be altered if the individual has grown spiritually.

When an individual grows enough spiritually, then certain experiences of karma are no longer necessary. Often these can be worked out in the dream state. Sometimes people who are supposed to have a certain experience out here perhaps get it in a dream. They wake up the next morning saying, "What a vivid dream. Sure hope it doesn't happen here." It won't, because it has already happened. They've paid whatever they owed.

LIVING YOUR RELIGION

Some eight years ago doctors told Rebecca that she was barren—she never would have any children.

She's a member of Eckankar and has come to believe in her dreams. Despite this prognosis by the doctors, she still wanted to be a mother, to have her own children. So she opened herself to the ECK and said, "If there's any way for me to have my own children, please let it be so."

She determined at this time that she would begin living her religion. So as a member of Eckankar, she began to do her spiritual exercises every day. She read a lot of ECK books, and she practiced the ECK principles as best she could.

What was she doing? She was spiritualizing herself.

She was doing everything possible to put the most positive light on everything in her life so that it would uplift her, because she knew that then the power of God can get through more easily.

One time, Rebecca did a spiritual exercise which she felt would help. She used a visualization technique in contemplation. She was trying to imagine herself in a place of healing.

She awoke in a dream and found herself in a large hospital on a higher level of existence. A doctor examined her, took her into the operating room, and operated on her. After it was over and she was about to be discharged, the doctor handed her a prescription. He told her the name of the medicine, and she memorized it.

Just at the moment the doctor mentioned the medicine, she felt this movement in her lower abdomen. Something moved inside her. Then she awoke.

She wrote down the dream in her dream journal. On a separate piece of paper she wrote the name of the medicine. Then she went back to sleep.

Next morning she got up and began to call around

She was doing everything possible to put the most positive light on everything in her life so that it would uplift her, because she knew that then the power of God can get through more easily.

to all the pharmacies to try to find this particular drug. Everywhere she called, the answer was always the same. "Madam, this drug is very rare. You can only get it at the regional hospitals and some big private clinics." It was a new drug.

Rebecca looked at the situation and said, "I can't really go to a doctor and say, 'Here's my dream prescription. Would you fill it please?' " So she said, "I'll let this be." She'd wait for God's own time. She went about her life and practically forgot about the dream.

Then one morning she awoke with a terrible toothache. Her gums were swollen, and it felt as if her teeth were going to fall out. Rebecca got permission from her supervisor at work to go see a dentist at the dental clinic. When she got there, the dentist looked at her teeth. "You've got quite an infection," he said. "I'm going to give you a prescription." He mentioned the name of the medication, and it was exactly the same drug that the doctor in the dream state had prescribed—a very new, rare drug.

Rebecca went home with her prescription, and before the bottle was used up, she was pregnant. Her child is now a little over seven years old. For Rebecca this experience was proof that the Mahanta was listening, that the Mahanta is always with her.

The Spiritual Exercises of ECK build your faith in the Spirit of God and Its power to do miracles.

HEALING AND THE OPEN HEART

The Spiritual Exercises of ECK build your faith in the Spirit of God and Its power to do miracles.

There's a story of two blind men who came to Jesus, calling after him to heal them. Jesus asked, "Do you think I can do this thing?" They both said yes. Jesus touched their eyes and said, "According to your faith be it unto you." And their eyes were opened. Their great faith had opened them to the healing power of God.

Healing comes, as the Bible said, because their eyes were opened. But what actually happens is the heart opens. Some people get a healing, and some people don't. Some people can open their hearts, and others have no idea what that means.

The purpose of all these examples is to try to give you an inkling of where to go and what to do to open your heart so that you can have the guidance of the Holy Spirit to help you in your daily life.

KEEPING YOUR PROMISE

Linda is a member of Eckankar. For the past month, she hadn't been doing her spiritual exercises. One Sunday she called one of her friends and asked her if she'd like to get together later that day. Her friend said sure, but she was going to church and she'd call Linda back when she got home.

Linda waited and waited. It was a beautiful, sunny day. Linda's from the Minneapolis area, and when you get a sunny day in Minnesota, you take advantage of it. You don't let it go. Finally Linda said, "It looks like my friend isn't coming. I'm going to go out and enjoy this sunshine."

When she came back, she checked her answering machine, but her friend still hadn't called.

Linda got to thinking. Some of her other friends had done the same thing lately. They made promises; they'd say, "We'll call you." But Linda waited, and they didn't call. *What kind of friends are these?* she wondered. Suddenly there seemed to be a pattern.

She wondered, *Is there a message in this pattern?*

Then she started thinking. She remembered that a long time ago she'd said that she was going to do

Some people get a healing, and some people don't. Some people can open their hearts, and others have no idea what that means.

her spiritual exercises every morning. She hadn't been doing them. She realized this was a promise to the Mahanta, the Inner Master. She had promised to meet him in the temple of her heart, but she got too busy. She didn't take the time.

She realized she had been standing up the Inner Master all this time. He hadn't said a word, but he gave her this waking dream. A waking dream is an outer event in your life that comes to confirm some spiritual lesson in a way that fits only you.

Many times God brings you spiritual aid because you have first opened your heart to someone else.

Many times God brings you spiritual aid because you have first opened your heart to someone else. People who don't hear God have often not opened their heart. Even when God does answer, they usually don't recognize the help. Sometimes the help comes in such a different way than we were expecting. But it doesn't matter. The help comes, and we feel better.

Dog Messengers

Niki found two lost collies on her kitchen doorstep one day, and she took them in. She called the owner, and the owner came and got them.

Some time after this, Niki was again at home. She'd been having a very hard time. She was working a part-time, temporary job doing contract work, but the stress was awful. Some days it just was too much—plus raising her children—that she didn't know how she was going to make it from one end of the day to the other. And this particular day happened to be one of those dark days. She was so worried about her problems that she was having a hard time keeping her faith.

Suddenly, she heard something outside the kitchen door. She opened the door—and saw two more dogs. This time, they were two huge Irish setters. Very playful, but lost. So she looked at their collars and got a phone number and an address. Niki thought, *I'll leave a message with the owners, and they can come pick the dogs up.*

In the meantime, she went out in the yard with the dogs. Being Irish setters, the first thing they noticed was the frog pond next door. They both jumped in, paddled around for a bit, and came out shaking off the water, smelling like fish, and generally being as disagreeable as wet smelly dogs can be. Niki wondered what to do with two big wet Irish setters. She thought it over and decided this time not to sit and wait for the owner to come. So she said, "OK, everybody in the van." She and the dogs got in the van.

The address on the dogs' collars was quite a ways from Niki's home. When she pulled up, she saw that the fence was down. These dogs were so big, they had just flattened the fence.

Nobody answered the door, so Niki tried the garage door. It was open. She managed to push one of the big Irish setters into the garage, but when she looked around, the other one was gone—running down the street chasing two people on bicycles.

Niki got in the van, chased after them for a couple of blocks, and finally caught the dog. This wet dog that smelled like fish was very interested in where she was driving, so he leaned right up against her.

Back at the house Niki was able to stuff the second dog into the garage before the other one got out. Then she went home and took a shower.

As she was thinking about it, Niki said to herself: *What's going on here? Dogs. Two dogs the first time. Two dogs the second time. I know the Holy Spirit is*

Niki said to herself: What's going on here? Dogs. Two dogs the first time. Two dogs the second time.

trying to show me the need for service. I had to do something to get these dogs back home. Suddenly it came to her: She was feeling a lot better than she had felt before. She realized the Mahanta had sent the dogs to lift the stress that weighed her down so heavily.

The ECK, the Holy Spirit, had sent them to give her spiritual aid. She thought she was the one doing them a favor.

This is how the Holy Spirit works. If it hadn't been for her level of consciousness, she might have overlooked this, then tomorrow said, "Dear Lord, why aren't you taking some of the load off?"

THE DOG THAT CAME BACK

Veronika, a German woman, runs a real-estate business. Her office is in France. One time a German couple called her and said they would like her to help them sell their salvage company because they were planning to retire and move to Australia.

As they were talking on the phone, the elderly wife happened to mention that their dog Max had died.

They felt sad about it, but luckily another dog of the very same breed had shown up and they liked this dog. They had named the second dog Max too. And although they still missed the first dog, the second Max was starting to fill the void of love in their lives.

Veronika mentioned something she once read in an ECK book. The Mahanta, the Living ECK Master had said that dogs can give unconditional love, the same as some people can. She talked with the couple a little while. One thing led to another, and she gave them a few ECK books.

She realized the Mahanta had sent the dogs to lift the stress that weighed her down so heavily.

One day sometime later, Veronika got a nudge to call them during the work day. The phone rates were very high at this particular time, but she just had a feeling to call. The elderly woman answered. She said, "A very bad thing has happened. Our second dog Max has died."

They felt really sad. They didn't know what had happened.

Veronika listened, then she told a story she had read in the ECK teachings about a dog that had come back as a cat. The owner didn't realize that this cat was her beloved dog come back again. Finally the cat took the dog's old blanket in its mouth, as if saying, "See? I'm back. Can't you tell? Can't you tell!"

After Veronika told the Germans this story, the couple felt better. They said, "So it is possible for pets to come back in another body?"

Veronika said, "Yes. Rather than look at the past, it's better to look into the future and ask,'Where is the dog who needs our love? Where is he out in this world? Please, God, guide him to us.'"

The couple thought this was a good idea. After they had talked with Veronika, they looked in a dog magazine and visited a breeder. The breeder had puppies, but they wanted a full-grown dog. Then the breeder said, "I know a couple that has just the sort of dog you're looking for; they're going to have to get rid of it because the wife has become allergic to dog hair."

The German couple went to see these people. The owner of the dog said, "Well, I really don't want to get rid of this dog. Allergy or not, I may just keep the dog."

They went back and forth, and the owner could see that this couple really loved the dog. Finally she

Veronika listened, then she told a story she had read in the ECK teachings about a dog that had come back as a cat.

agreed. "This dog would have a very good home with you. You may have the dog." The German couple asked, "What is the dog's name?" The owner said, "We call him Max."

This Max was born right after the German couple's first dog had died. Actually they now had the first dog back in a new body.

When Veronika had told them about reincarnation, it helped the German couple. Now they knew that the eternal nature of Soul goes a long way toward helping people get along spiritually in life. The Law of Divine Love always brings loved ones together again. And this Law of Love also works for people and pets.

Step-by-step, your heart will open to the love of God.

I do everything I can to answer the spiritual needs that you bring. I think you'll find that the teachings will come to you, not just here, but during the time that you sleep and also during the times when you're at work, sort of daydreaming while you're doing a routine thing. Sometimes one of these stories will come to mind, and it will spiritualize you because it sets your mind on higher things. Step-by-step, your heart will open to the love of God.

DOORWAY TO A NEW WORLD

A certain ECKist felt she was about due for an initiation. This was just before the annual ECK Worldwide Seminar.

She had felt quite a surge in her spiritual life for a long time before this; she felt she had made progress. But the seminar came and went, and she didn't hear anything about an initiation. She wondered about this.

Initiation is both an outer and inner ritual that corresponds to the outer and inner teachings that correspond to the Outer and the Inner Master that corresponds to the Voice of God as It speaks outwardly and inwardly. It's all linked together. Many people don't know of the outer and inner Voice of God.

A new initiation shows the individual that a doorway has opened into a new world. When you go through the door, you're the new guy on the team. You start at the bottom of the pecking order, and you have to work your way up.

A new initiation shows the individual that a doorway has opened into a new world.

The way you do this is by getting experience in all aspects of life. At one initiation level you get experience on the emotional level. At another initiation level it'll be remembering the past, remembering and making connections between cause and effect. Other times the new experiences will be in the area of thought. Doorways will open, and you'll find new areas to explore. Then it's up to you to do it.

To move forward, you have to give up things that you have become used to in the past. It's necessary to give up certain of our dear ideas and pet notions.

The Green Door

This ECKist didn't get the initiation even though she felt she'd moved forward spiritually, so that night she tried to find the reasons in contemplation.

The first night, the ECK Master Lai Tsi came to her. He's an ECK Master still working on the inner planes. Thousands of years ago he served in China as the Mahanta, the Living ECK Master.

In the dream, Lai Tsi took her down a long hallway. He pointed to a light green door. He opened the door, and they went inside. Everything inside the room was green—a light, beautiful, effervescent green. Even the air was green. Lai Tsi said to her, "This is the purity of the earth. Below all the negativity that has been created by people, the earth is pure. The earth is OK. Don't worry about it."

This didn't mean that she wasn't to do anything to try to keep things clean. Because as more of us crowd onto this little piece of earth, there's more pollution, and it's self-responsibility to clean up after ourselves.

Here's the problem, though: The environment is used as an excuse by some people to get control over the lives of other people. And this is wrong. But people in this phase of consciousness are zealots, and there's no reasoning with zealots because they run on pure emotion, on blind emotion.

There is a way to clean up in the environment and make earth a better place for us and those to come, without turning everything upside down and taking away the freedom of the individual.

After Lai Tsi told her about the purity of the earth, she felt happy, because until then she had not wanted to live here. But now she realized that, despite outer appearances, there was a strength and vitality in the earth that was greater than the people who were trying to destroy it.

But what about her initiation? Lai Tsi hadn't mentioned anything about it, and she hadn't asked. So the second night she went back into contemplation.

But now she realized that, despite outer appearances, there was a strength and vitality in the earth that was greater than the people who were trying to destroy it.

RESOLVING THE PAST

This time another ECK Master came to her from the other planes: Fubbi Quantz. He too had served as the Mahanta, the Living ECK Master centuries ago. He met her in a cave and asked her, "What do you wish to know?"

She said she wanted to face the barriers between her and the next initiation. Fubbi asked her, "And what do you think they are?"

For eleven years this woman had lived with a man. About three years ago, the man had decided that he didn't want to live with her anymore, he wanted to live with someone else. So the relationship broke up, and she was bitter about the whole thing. She put practically all the responsibility for the failed relationship upon him. And she had carried this bitterness with her.

Fubbi Quantz said to her, "This is going to take seven nights, if you can come back in contemplation to this cave."

The next night she saw a previous life in which her former mate had been a child. The child had been deformed. In that life the woman had practiced smotherly love. She did everything for the child. He could do nothing for himself. In doing that, she had stopped his ability to grow spiritually. In this lifetime, she was now trying to do the same thing. This man was no longer her child as in the past. He was a grown person; he didn't want any part of it. She finally recognized her responsibility in this.

Over the next few nights she went back to the cave to meet the ECK Master Fubbi Quantz. She asked him, "How do I resolve this problem from the past?"

He said, "I'll let you go back and relive one day." So she went back and relived one day.

"How did you use your time?" he asked her.

During the day that she relived, she had let the boy do different things. She let him play a musical instrument and make his own decisions. When they played games, she let him win.

After that experience, the woman found that much of her anger had gone away.

Fubbi Quantz said to her, "This is going to take seven nights, if you can come back in contemplation to this cave."

Golden Qualities

On the seventh and last night, she met Fubbi Quantz in the cave again. This time she told the ECK Master about the anger she felt toward her father.

Fubbi Quantz said, "Let's sing HU and do a spiritual exercise."

While her eyes were still shut, Fubbi Quantz asked the woman to name two qualities about her father that she admired. She said, "That's easy. He's got a great sense of humor and a quick wit. And he has a great respect for hard work and a love for it which he passed on to me."

Fubbi Quantz wrote these two qualities on a big white board with a pen that wrote in gold ink. Then he asked her, "Which two qualities of his do you greatly dislike?"

This is easy, she thought. "Number one, he's cheap." She said she had spent four hundred dollars coming out to visit him. She had spent seven days there, helping him paint the house, clean the house, move furniture, wash the dishes, and do other little chores. At the end of that time, he took her out to a restaurant to eat. It was the cheapest restaurant in town. Dinner—$4.50. When she started to get up and get a second helping, her father said, "No, don't do that. It's too much money."

She couldn't believe it. She decided to have dessert. He said, "No, it costs too much." And to top it off, as they were leaving, her father said, "Do you mind leaving the tip?"

Besides being so cheap, she said he was also often rude and inconsiderate. Fubbi Quantz wrote these qualities on a second white board. But this time he wrote them in a light blue ink. Then he put this board behind the first one with the good qualities. He said to her, "These will someday be golden qualities, but they're not there yet."

Suddenly she understood. The anger that she'd felt toward her father vanished. She could now love her father for his good qualities. She knows that in time, as he unfolds spiritually, the rest will change too.

After these meetings of healing with the ECK Master Fubbi Quantz, the ECKist was surprised, less than a month later, to get notice from the Eckankar Spiritual Center that she was eligible for her next initiation.

Our Unfoldment

The greatest creative force you can use on your behalf is either contemplation or prayer.

Contemplation or prayer in the right way. Usually it's not to tell God, "God, I want this done in this particular way." Sometimes it's enough to say, "I'm having a hard time. Thy will be done."

We are in some very interesting times in human history. The unfoldment of the human race has come a long way in the last hundred years. As a result of this creativity, there is a whole new world of energy, a whole new world of possibilities to create things in a material way. But instead of learning how to work with the whole atom, we've split the atom. And we're bombarding ourselves and each other with electromagnetic waves up and down the frequency within a narrow range in the physical, which takes in anything you can see or hear on earth.

We have strength inside to accept the spiritual power that's here to help us come into accord with these strange new forces that are all around us.

But it's difficult. Many people will find they're going to want to make changes. Some of you will find

The greatest creative force you can use on your behalf is either contemplation or prayer.

that your diet will change because a different diet will make it easier to move into this new time of, shall we say, higher energy.

So many illnesses are popping up despite the efforts of science. Science has done so many things to cure strains of cancer. Tuberculosis and other illnesses were once thought to be under control. But the technology which has come from the expanded creation of the human mind has also created the ability to transport people in heavier-than-air machines above the globe, from one place to another.

So now people with tuberculosis can get on a plane and fly with you wherever you're going and you'd never know it. You're all breathing the same air. Germs and viruses that you never knew existed are now being transported from one country to another, and there's no way to stop them. This is the new world we live in. This sort of challenge is nothing new. The clash between the old and the new way of doing things has always existed.

In the past, it would be two people with swords fighting at the edge of someone's property to see who would prevail. Soon it was groups on either side with weapons, seeing who would prevail. Finally it's come to these people fighting with energies and electrical forces.

Traditional doctors are still very necessary, but people are also finding their way to alternative methods of healing.

Some of these electrical forces are not aimed at anyone. They're just roaming about, bumping into people and things, causing health problems. These health problems come up faster than science can find a cure for them.

So in these times, many people are looking to a variety of sources of healing. Traditional doctors are still very necessary, but people are also finding their way to alternative methods of healing. Why are they doing this? Because the level of consciousness is higher. People went to a certain doctor in the past to heal their troubles. But the troubles of the present and the future are going to take different kinds of doctors to address and heal them.

Remember that the main healing comes not from any outer source. Any true, humble doctor knows that healing does not come through pills, herbs, or anything else. It comes through the divine power—through the power of God getting through in some way to one individual to help bring about a healing.

Your Own Journey to God

You will learn that the path to God is not one of a group. You are on this path to God yourself.

You may be a member of a group that is very large or very small, or you may go all by yourself. But you are on this journey to God. The only important thing on this journey is you and God. Once you've established the correct relationship between yourself and God, then you're able to go back out into the world and serve all God's creatures. And you will serve with love, kindness, compassion, and understanding.

Because you've walked in those moccasins before, you can help others by listening. You've been there. And there are others who can help you because they've been where you are now.

All the help that comes to us is from the Holy Spirit, whether it comes in a dream or through the help of a friend or a doctor. The trick is the discrimination that you need: to tell what's good for you and what's not good for you. This comes by listening to your heart.

Remember that the main healing comes not from any outer source. Any true, humble doctor knows that healing does not come through pills, herbs, or anything else. It comes through the divine power.

So I would like to leave you with this thought: Open your heart to love because God loves you.

ECK Worldwide Seminar, Minneapolis, Minnesota, Saturday, October 25, 1997

"Daddy, this man's talking about God," she said.

2
TUNING IN

✦

This talk is about "Tuning In," as in tuning in the TV or radio. It's about tuning in to the Holy Spirit, learning how to do this in everyday life, to make your life better, more enjoyable.

I say "more enjoyable" with quotes around it, because sometimes it's not really more enjoyable. We meet life on its own terms, and the life we meet is the life that we have earned. Perfect justice, perfect truth, but also perfect love. Always perfect love.

God's love is always working to help Soul find Its way back home.

God's love is always working to help Soul find Its way back home.

BIG CHANGES

In the past week, the pope made an earthshaking announcement. He said that the theory of evolution was not in conflict with Christian doctrine. One of those real ecclesiastical problems for a lot of people in the Catholic Church. It may polarize the church more than anyone realizes today, but the pope is doing the right thing. He's recognizing the evidence. Anyone who is at all aware must recognize that there is something to it.

*Any person
who is at all
aware would
have to
recognize that
this universe
has so many
different worlds
which are
capable of
sustaining life.*

For the pope to make an announcement that there is validity to the theory of evolution is quite astounding. Evolution and Christianity have always been at odds with each other. Science hasn't been at odds with religion over this, because science just reports what it finds. But religion has always been at odds with science.

Within the last month, Reverend Billy Graham mentioned his belief that there is life on other planets. Any person who is at all aware would have to recognize that this universe has so many different worlds which are capable of sustaining life. It would be the height of vanity for the human race to say that the only life that can exist is here on earth.

BORDERS OF CONSCIOUSNESS

Very slowly, the borders of consciousness are moving back. Some leaders, especially in religion, are now recognizing that there is a greater universe and that there is more potential here than religion used to accept.

These monumental changes in doctrine are going to cause all kinds of problems in the Catholic Church. Some people are going to feel that the pope went too far. Others will support his statement entirely. It's a belief that's quite different from absolute creation, that God created everything as we see it today.

So we're seeing changes.

I was talking to a doctor from a remote area of China. He said that in the back-country areas, villagers have often seen a half-man, half-ape creature, a cross between a gorilla and a human being, like our Bigfoot.

Villagers had seen these creatures fairly often, he said. In this one case, a female came into a village and took big handfuls of corn underneath its armpits on each side, then walked out of the village. Like a shoplifter in a store. So you can't say that these beings have not been in contact with civilization.

These are some of the wonders that are happening in our society today. They're earthshaking.

And they're happening because some leaders and other people are beginning to tune in. They're tuning in to the greater truth that has been here all along, a truth that has been denied for centuries. Many people lost their lives because they spoke up about their beliefs; when these beliefs went against the church, they faced the Inquisition and suffered terribly for it, sometimes with their lives.

UPLIFTING ALL RELIGIONS

It's not just a coincidence that the teachings of ECK have come out during these times. Few people make a connection.

They ask, "Could there be a connection with the teachings of ECK being brought to the public in 1965 by Paul Twitchell? Have these teachings of the Light and Sound of God reached into private and public places to affect the consciousness of key people throughout the world?"

There are people from other religions who come to the Temple of ECK and watch how we do our worship services. They're taking those methods back to their churches and having a more informal worship service. Some churches in the local area are finding a great deal of success in using methods like this. They come to the Temple of ECK to see what's new, to see if there's anything they can adapt.

When some of the people at the Temple first

They're tuning in to the greater truth that has been here all along, a truth that has been denied for centuries.

became aware that the ministers in the local area were adapting our methods to fit their congregations, they wondered, *Why don't they stick with their own way of doing worship services instead of taking ours?*

But when the ECK teachings come into the world, they enliven and uplift all religions.

When I pointed this out to the people in ECK, they could see that this was natural. This is how the Holy Spirit will bring upliftment to the people around us.

People who give truth don't need or expect credit. This is one of the signposts of a person who's come far along on the path to God. You can see other people growing spiritually around such a person, but the person will never take credit for it. He'll never say, "Because of me, you are so much more intelligent and aware of the world around you. If it weren't for me, you would have the consciousness of a corncob." Some people who take credit for other people's unfoldment, progress, and gains will do it subtly. They'll say, "There was a time so and so wasn't getting along very well spiritually, and then . . . " They raise their eyebrows a little. Then they'll add, "I happened to have given him this brochure." You can tell that these people are not that far along spiritually.

People who give truth don't need or expect credit.

But don't worry about it. Everyone is at a different level. Some are higher than you, some are lower. Who cares? All you want to do is be a clear vehicle for God.

THE SOUND OF HU

Sometimes a letter comes to me from someone telling me how someone else found Eckankar. What's truly interesting to me is when it's a child who is the truth seeker.

An ECKist from Colorado told me a story about an ECK regional seminar she had helped with. The group had rented two-thirds of a hotel ballroom. The hotel used partitions to size the room for each organization that rented it. For their regional, the ECKists had two-thirds of this ballroom; one-third was being used by some other organization.

The ECK seminar began. The first thing on the agenda was a HU Chant. For this, the ECKists shut the doors to the hallway so they wouldn't disturb the other group. They began to sing HU, this love song to God. Suddenly the heavy door to the corridor started being pulled open. One of the ECKists went to the door. There was a little girl, about six years old. She had been out in the hallway. She had heard the sound of HU, and it drew her, it attracted her. She was trying to pull the door open so that she could hear a little better. The ECKist asked if they could help her, and she said, "What is that word?" The ECKist said, "It's HU, a love song to God."

Just about that time the HU Chant finished and a video of one of my talks began to play. The little girl's father came up to see what was going on. "Daddy, this man's talking about God," she said to him. The little girl asked him if she could stay and listen to the talk.

A six-year-old child wants to listen to the teachings of ECK. To me this is always a wonderful thing.

So with the father's permission, the ECKist led the girl to the front row. She sat there and watched the whole video. After it was over, the father came back and began asking questions about Eckankar. For thirty minutes he asked questions about Eckankar, because his daughter had heard the sound of HU and had recognized it.

For thirty minutes he asked questions about Eckankar, because his daughter had heard the sound of HU and had recognized it.

Accepting Reincarnation

Many people today still find it hard to accept the fact of reincarnation. Someday, probably many years from now, there will be another pope who announces to the public, "Reincarnation is a fact. There is no conflict between it and Christian doctrine." This could be twenty-five, fifty, or one hundred years. The pope has already jumped over centuries to finally admit in 1992 that the church had been wrong to censure Galileo for his theory about the earth not being at the center of the universe. It's taken centuries. Galileo's been dead a few years. This was quite an amazing pronouncement by the pope.

In time, the Christian doctrines will also be able to accept and incorporate some of the other facts of life, such as reincarnation. They already know about karma in different ways, but they are just not quite ready to accept reincarnation. It would upset their principle of creation, even though now they've almost come to accept creation and evolution as possible.

These are big times. Things happen, we hear it on the news, a sound bite here, a sound bite there. We just take it for granted. We say, "Isn't that how it should be?"

But these are monumental changes in the human consciousness.

In time, the Christian doctrines will also be able to accept and incorporate some of the other facts of life, such as reincarnation.

Dream Light

Last summer an ECKist was traveling to the ECK European Seminar in Germany. On the flight, her two seat companions happened to be young women in their midtwenties, dressed in black leather jackets.

They had rings through their noses. They were laughing and chatting and sipping on their wine. She was sitting by herself, thinking, *There's a generation gap here. I don't think I have a whole lot in common with these two young women.* So the ECKist mostly read or slept while the plane was en route.

Soon the flight attendants began serving a meal. The young woman next to the ECKist got a salad. By accident, the young woman bumped her salad, and pieces of lettuce, tomato, and cucumber went flying. A slice of tomato even landed on the ECKist's shoe. She looked down and began to laugh. The young woman started laughing too, as they were picking pieces of shredded produce off their clothes. Then they began to talk.

These two young women were not just close friends who hadn't seen each other in a long time; they happened to be twins. As they were talking to the ECKist, one of the young women said that some extraordinary things had happened in her life that were beyond explanation. Somehow, the conversation turned to Eckankar and dreams.

The young woman had a boyfriend, who in a previous relationship had had his heart broken. The pain was so great that one night, when he was ready to go to sleep, he asked God, "Please help me, take this pain away." During the night, a light suddenly appeared at the foot of his bed. This light was so bright that it lit up the whole room. The young man wasn't afraid of it but he wondered, *What is this light?*

As she heard this story, the ECKist knew immediately: This was the Light of God.

When the young man woke up in the morning, he was surprised to find that his pain was entirely gone. This light had come and healed him. And he wondered about it. He had no answers.

During the night, a light suddenly appeared at the foot of his bed. This light was so bright that it lit up the whole room.

This was one of the extraordinary things that these two young women had come across. It was no accident that the ECK had placed the ECKist in the seat beside them. Nor was it an accident that one of the young women tipped her salad all over herself and her ECKist seatmate, or that the conversation turned to Eckankar.

The ECKist said she had also gotten a lesson from this: don't prejudge people by how they look. Because of the black leather jackets, nose rings, and wine, at first she thought she'd have nothing in common with these young women. The ECKist was a few years older. It turned out that the two women were the sweetest people, most interesting, and also most interested.

How do you tune in in ECK? With the Spiritual Exercises of ECK.

Sometimes the ECK works this way, when people allow themselves to tune in to the Holy Spirit. ECK is the Holy Spirit, Divine Spirit.

Self-Discipline and God Consciousness

How do you tune in in ECK?

With the Spiritual Exercises of ECK. That's our form of prayer. It's a form of contemplation where we don't try to tell God what to do. We listen to hear what God's Voice is saying to us.

Another ECKist was grappling with the problem of self-discipline. She forgot to do her spiritual exercises, the thing that tunes you in to the Voice of God. One of the simple spiritual exercises she'd been working on was to give simple thanks before a meal. This was to be a spiritual exercise for a month.

She'd come into this life with a problem. She eats too much, too fast. She'd be halfway through her meal and realize she'd forgotten to do the spiritual exercise again; she'd forgotten to give thanks for the blessings of life in the form of food. She wondered what she could do to overcome this. And she realized that a person needs self-discipline if they ever expect to reach the heights of consciousness.

We call this God Consciousness. This doesn't mean we become God, as some religions teach. We become godlike, aware of our relationship with God and what our purpose in this life is.

God Consciousness means perfect attunement with the Holy Spirit. That's all it means. God Consciousness.

There are steps that lead to God Consciousness, like Self-Realization. This is the midway step. Other groups feel it's the highest step of consciousness. But we in ECK say that there's a stage even higher than God Consciousness. There are states like the Akshar state and higher. But for the immediate present, the goal in Eckankar is to become God-Realized, or God Conscious.

Even earlier than Self-Realization comes cosmic consciousness, which happens on the Mental Plane. This is where people feel life suddenly becomes superenlivened. Walt Whitman is an example of a person with cosmic consciousness. A person's awareness goes to the level where they can see through many of the illusions that hold most people.

Most people feel that the rat race is the race of life. This is what you've got to do; this is how it is. But there are a lot of people in the rat race today who have higher states of consciousness. These people aren't caught up by it. They just know that this is the pace of life today in their particular society. Somehow they can be at peace with themselves even with such a fast schedule.

God Consciousness means perfect attunement with the Holy Spirit. That's all it means.

There's a way to do it. And the way for ECKists is to tune in through the Spiritual Exercises of ECK.

So this woman was grappling with the problem of self-discipline, eating too much too fast, and forgetting the simple spiritual exercise to give thanks before a meal. She often wondered why she didn't have self-discipline.

Then it came to her: basically, she was spiritually lazy.

She often wondered why she didn't have self-discipline. Then it came to her: basically, she was spiritually lazy.

LITTLE LESSONS

One day, she went to a store to buy a curtain rod. As she was driving home afterward, she realized the salesclerk had overcharged her. She checked the receipt and saw she'd been overcharged by $4.62. She asked herself, "Is it really worth it to drive back, park the car, go all the way back in, get in line, and go through all this to get my $4.62?" In a lazy sort of a way she said, "My time's too valuable for that. I really should get home."

It was only a small amount of money. But then she realized this money was in her care, in her keeping to spend one way or another, but it was her responsibility. So she went back into the store and took care of it.

She realized that just the little act of getting this incorrect sale straightened out was a form of self-discipline. She'd been having trouble doing her spiritual exercises at night. She'd get home from work tired, the same as many of you. You come home tired, and you say, "I'm just too tired; I'll do my spiritual exercises after a few minutes." And then you go to sleep. The next morning you wake up and realize you forgot. Before you remembered, the night was over.

The woman realized she needed to do something different.

She changed the time of her spiritual exercise from just before bedtime, when she was exhausted, to the morning, when she woke up fresh. She began to wake up ten or fifteen minutes earlier. Soon she found that she was waking up even earlier, and her days became more fruitful. She said it made a big difference in the quality of her day to do the spiritual exercises in the morning when she was fresh.

She had learned this little thing. She realized that no matter how small the discipline might be, even as small as returning to correct an overcharge of $4.62, there was a reason to do it that was more important than the money.

LAW OF SILENCE

An ECKist from Accra, Ghana, learned a lesson about the Law of Silence through some cockroaches. Cockroaches are not a lot of fun. When they get in the home, they're a nuisance. They can also carry diseases.

The Law of Silence is one of the laws we're familiar with in ECK. It's simply this: if there's a certain truth that is very, very important for you spiritually, keep it to yourself.

This doesn't mean that you don't help people, that you don't talk to them about one thing or another. But if there is something that has come to you specially, a spiritual lesson that has come your way to teach you something about truth, as soon as you realize this, say nothing about it. Let the Holy Spirit play the scene out for you. Because then you'll get the benefit of the lesson. Otherwise, you waste it. It goes into the air just like empty words.

This young woman was living in a hostel with a

The Law of Silence is one of the laws we're familiar with in ECK. It's simply this: if there's a certain truth that is very, very important for you spiritually, keep it to yourself.

number of other young women. There were seven other women sharing the room with her. She had two friends, but they were in another room on the same floor.

One day the ECKist and her roommates got into an argument about who should have a certain bed. There were hard feelings; tempers flared. It went on for a time. The youngest woman in the room would listen to what the others said, and she would carry it back to the one who started the argument, the one who was the troublemaker. This made matters worse.

The ECKist said, "It'll be OK," and left it at that. She knew it'd work itself out.

One day, the ECKist forgot, and she talked about this argument to her two friends that lived in another room down the hall. Her friends were upset. They felt the ECKist had taken most of the insults that the troublemaker was hurling at everybody in the room. The two friends wanted to protect her. They would show up in her room, sit down, and make indirect insulting remarks about the troublemaker, and especially the young woman who had carried the tales.

One day, the ECKist forgot, and she talked about this argument to her two friends that lived in another room down the hall. Her friends were upset.

COCKROACHES

At first, the ECKist didn't see what was happening. Then she realized that her friends were getting into a game of anger. One side was trading angry, sharp barbs with the other side. Things were getting out of hand.

This ECKist was deathly afraid of cockroaches. She doesn't realize it's from a past life where she met her death by insects. This has stayed with her as an unconscious memory. She lumps all insects together. Whenever she sees a cockroach, she screams and jumps up; and that's the end of her peace and quiet.

The bed argument had been carrying on for a

couple of days when the woman began waking up at night. She'd feel a cockroach on her bed. She'd jump up and turn on the light, waking up everybody in the room. This didn't help the tension among the women to have the ECKist screaming, jumping out of bed, then standing there with the bright lights turned on, not wanting to go back to bed until all the cockroaches had run for the dark corners.

The two friends came to visit again. They were seated on the bed, rehashing the whole thing. The ECKist had some food on the bed. As they were talking, a very bold cockroach was watching the conversation from the edge of the room. And at one point, the ECKist forgot herself. She forgot the ECK principles: to let this be, not to get into it anymore, let the fire of this anger go out a little. And she got into the argument. As soon as she did, the cockroach came running up onto the bed and jumped on her food.

She forgot the ECK principles: to let this be, not to get into it anymore, let the fire of this anger go out a little.

She saw it, screamed, and made a big scene. She told her friends, "I don't want to talk about this argument anymore." But her friends kept trying to talk about it. When they saw she ignored them whenever they brought it up, they finally left. The woman went to bed.

Lying in bed, she asked the Inner Master, "What was this about? Why did the cockroach come up on my bed while we were sitting here?" The cockroach shouldn't have done that, according to the code of the cockroaches that lived in her hostel. Cockroaches have rules too.

She suddenly saw that the argument over the bed was spiritual food for her.

There was something in the argument for her spiritually. She had something to learn but didn't realize it until she asked and the Inner Master pointed out, "There's a lesson for you in this argument." Then she could see that her friends learned of the argument through what she herself had told them. Without knowing it, she had broken the Law of Silence. Until then she wasn't aware that the Mahanta was trying to give her a spiritual lesson.

STILL SMALL VOICE

This is an example of tuning in to the Holy Spirit. When something goes wrong in your life, there is usually a spiritual reason for it. Divine Spirit is trying to teach you something about truth.

Most of us have the reaction of, "I'm going to straighten this out right now." In fact, the woman had tried to straighten out the cockroach problem when it began in the hostel. They had a powerful insecticide. She sprayed it around the edges of the room, and it had always controlled the cockroaches before. But this time, it did nothing. In fact, when she began joining in the argument, there wasn't just the one cockroach. A whole bunch of cockroaches came running out on the floor. She quickly realized that something exceptional was going on.

So tune in. Tune in to the still small voice within you. If you're a Christian, it's the still small voice of the Holy Spirit speaking to you through Jesus. If you're from another religion, it speaks through the leader of that religion. In ECK, the Holy Spirit speaks through the Mahanta, the Living ECK Master.

LIGHT AND SOUND

Sometimes the Holy Spirit speaks very directly, and when It speaks in this very direct manner, it's through the Light and Sound of God Itself. The Light

When something goes wrong in your life, there is usually a spiritual reason for it. Divine Spirit is trying to teach you something about truth.

and Sound of God is divine love, the Voice of God. A number of different names have been given to these two pillars of the Holy Spirit, the Light and Sound. The Light and Sound of God are the pillars of the ECK teachings.

Everything we're talking about—Bigfoot, the pope recognizing that evolution and Christian doctrine are not in conflict—shows that behind the fabric of life is this Voice of God which we know as the Holy Spirit. And Its manifestations are the Light and Sound of God. This is one of the truths that most people have no awareness of. Many people know about the Light of God, but fewer know about the Sound. And there are many different ways that the Sound is heard.

The Light and Sound of God are the pillars of the ECK teachings.

I will briefly mention some of the forms of the Light and Sound of God that you may be aware of.

The Light of God can come as a violet, blue, pink, orange, yellow, white, or green light. The Light can look like a soft glow; It can look like a lantern; It can look like a pinpoint of light; It can look like a star off in the distance; It can look like the moon.

The Sound can be just about anything you've heard here on earth. It can be the sound of a waterfall, a jet plane flying over, a bee, birds singing in the morning. It can be like an orchestra playing. We're all surrounded by sounds, and we sometimes don't pay as much attention to sound as we should.

Some in our audience have a hard time hearing sound. Some are not able to hear sound at all. So we have people who use sign language to communicate with them. The words I am speaking to you through sound, they receive via sight. Any form of sight is a form of light, a variation of the Light of God. Any ability to see is a form of the Light.

The Sound can also come as the sound of the

ocean, the wind, the rain beating down on the pavement or grass. Sometimes it comes as the sigh of a loved one. A baby's cry. Just about any sound you can imagine. Some of these will come to you on the inner planes or during prayer, contemplation, or meditation. Sometimes you will hear a sound which is soothing and quiet, other times it may be as sharp as the crack of thunder. Sometimes it'll be rumbling like a tornado.

People have the idea that God's love is sweet, gentle, and kind. But sometimes God's love needs to shake the sleeping Soul and awaken It because this is the lifetime that Soul has chosen to awaken to truth.

God's Love

People have the idea that God's love is sweet, gentle, and kind. But sometimes God's love needs to shake the sleeping Soul and awaken It because this is the lifetime that Soul has chosen to awaken to truth. And Soul is often in a very deep sleep. It needs one spiritual jolt after another to finally become aware that there is more to life than what meets the eye.

Some people will have an astral experience; others will have a very vivid dream experience. Others will have a vision. Some will have the higher state of Soul Travel. Others will get a prophecy, perhaps through the dream state. All these experiences are in some way a miraculous healing.

These things are generally wake-up calls from the Mahanta. As an instrument of the Holy Spirit he is empowered to give these experiences to those Souls who are ready.

Wake-Up Calls

Gradually, over a number of years, people slowly wake from their spiritual sleep. As they do, they get a yearning. A yearning for something they can't quite put their finger on. They have a desire for knowledge first. Behind that they find there is a yearning for understanding, then a yearning for truth.

If they take it far enough, they'll realize that behind all their yearning is the yearning for God's love. They have been yearning for love all this time, and these other things were just bringing them closer and closer to God's love.

This is what we try to help people discover on their own through the teachings of ECK. I won't give someone a spiritual experience that he or she is not ready for. I can, but why? It's like giving a driver's license to a four-year-old child. You wouldn't tell a small child, "You're going to learn how to drive some-time, so here you go. Save you a couple years. Have a good time." Of course, you wouldn't do that.

A true Master will never give someone a passport to a higher state of consciousness until that person is ready for it. A Master won't do this, any more than a parent or a state government would give a driver's license to a four-year-old child. Because the child would do a lot of damage.

ARE YOU READY FOR MASTERSHIP?

As you unfold spiritually, you also unfold power—spiritual power—along with spiritual love. As this spiritual power comes to you, along with it comes the understanding of spiritual law that you cannot misuse this power at any time. Some people think, *I like Eckankar. Now maybe I can develop my healing powers and go out and heal people. I've always wanted to be a healer. I'll just go heal people.* But sometimes healing people when they haven't learned the spiritual lesson of their illness is interfering in their state of consciousness.

A true Master will never give someone a passport to a higher state of consciousness until that person is ready for it.

This is why my role, in this mission, this time, is not to do things for people that they should learn how to do for themselves.

I try to help people find their own way to a health practitioner to overcome an illness. I try to help people go into contemplation and find out about their future themselves, by studying the ECK-Vidya, which is the ancient science of prophecy. Do this for yourself.

My role is to help people who are ready for Mastership, not children who want to have things done for them. I help people who are striving to become self-sufficient and develop the very high spiritual state of being able to survive under any and all conditions. This includes such things as health and even wealth.

One of the most deadening lies of any society is that a government should take care of the people. The more the government takes care of the people, the more childish—not childlike—they become. They become slaves. They're putting their destiny into the hands of people who don't have a real interest in their lives.

Care about your spiritual state as much as you care about your money.

With investments, you can hire someone to manage your funds for you. And the longer you stay with a broker, the broker you get. He's managing your money away, away, and away, until he has most of it and you have very little of it. There's a saying: The person who is best qualified to manage your funds is you. Because who's got the most to gain by it? On the other hand, if they're managed poorly, who has the most to lose? Who would care the most? Obviously you. Nobody else cares. The broker doesn't care, your neighbor doesn't care.

Care about your spiritual state as much as you care about your money. And care about your money as much as you care about the food that goes on your table. In other words, take responsibility for what's on your table, for what's happening with your wealth, and for what's going on in your spiritual affairs. It's up to you.

My job is to find those people who want to become masters of the laws of life and help them reach this awareness, to one day become conscious of their Godhood. To know they are Souls made in the image of God—what this means and how it plays out in everyday life.

Love Each Other as Soul

Sometimes I feel so inadequate. I try to speak about the different truths, the biggest of which is: You are Soul, you exist because God loves you. And an interesting corollary of that is that everyone is Soul. God loves those of you over there because you are Soul, and God loves those of you over here because you are Soul. Souls exist because God loves them. God loves them; but do they love each other?

Very often the problems we have, come because the Souls God loves don't love each other.

They are not aware of the divinity of the other person. We can all recognize that God loves us, but we think, *Surely God cannot love that scoundrel over there, that crook, that criminal; therefore, I'm justified in my anger and my judgments.*

As the spiritual leader of Eckankar, I sometimes point out the behavior of people who are acting in an unspiritual way. This is not a reflection upon their state spiritually. When you see some people who seem to be the farthest down the spiritual ladder, it's hard to imagine that some day they, too, will become God-aware individuals. "When pigs can fly," you say. But

My job is to find those people who want to become masters of the laws of life and help them reach this awareness, to one day become conscious of their Godhood.

someday, pigs will fly. Someday all Souls who become aware of God's love for them will also realize that God's love is for other people too.

So for the first step in ECK, learn to love yourself as a creation of God. Then love those who are close to you. Because they are a special creation of God too. And once you've learned to love yourself and those who are close to you, then maybe you can love God.

1996 ECK Worldwide Seminar, Minneapolis, Minnesota, Friday, October 25, 1996

So, like a four-leaf clover, sometimes we say we're lucky to be in ECK. But it's not luck, it's the Holy Spirit, Divine Spirit, working things out for your spiritual unfoldment and for those people around you.

3
LIKE A
FOUR-LEAF CLOVER

⋇

A four-leaf clover is a rare plant. Most clovers have three leaves. Anywhere you go in the clover patch, you can find clovers with three leaves. But it's harder to find four, and that's why a four-leaf clover is rare. It's a special plant.

So the title of the talk, "Like a Four-Leaf Clover," can mean anything rare or special.

This spiritual year is A Year of Consecration. *Consecration* means "to make or declare sacred." We can't really declare or make ourselves sacred because we are each Soul, a creation of God that's already sacred.

What you can do is recognize that you are sacred and accept yourself as a child of God.

CHILD OF GOD

Try to remember that there is a sacred connection between you and God and that this connection makes the ground you walk upon holy. And, when you're on holy ground, you are in the presence of God.

The presence of God can be anywhere. It is everywhere, not just in church. Sometimes we get things

The presence of God can be anywhere.

49

backward: we feel that we have to go to a holy place and only there are we in the presence of God. Sometimes it's a holy mountain, or a holy building. But wherever you are is holy if you recognize at any given moment that you are in the presence of God.

This is the reason the ECK teachings have such spiritual power. They make you, the individual, the center of the universe.

Soul is the center of the universe, outside of God. God created you. God created me. We are of the essence of God, and therefore, no matter how imperfect our knowledge of God is, we are still holy. This imperfect knowledge of God is what makes for imperfect behavior among people, the so-called evil.

Whether you are out in the world or you're at home, you are simply an instrument of God's love in your own universe.

Whether you are out in the world or you're at home, you are simply an instrument of God's love in your own universe. This universe includes your family, the people who work with you, the people you meet in stores, and the people you meet during leisure.

This is your universe. It's your spiritual world.

LUCKY

An ECKist from the Detroit area got her driver's license. She's a new driver, and she just bought a used Toyota. She calls her little car Yoda.

One day she was out driving, listening to the radio, singing the word *Mahanta* to some golden oldies on the radio. Mahanta is the name of the highest state of consciousness on earth, and she was singing this word because it spiritualizes you. You can sing this word or say it in times of trouble or when you want spiritual upliftment to help you out of the blues or the blahs, to lift you to a higher, better place.

Traffic came to a construction zone and slowed

down. As the ECKist is sitting there, waiting, all of a sudden, she hears a thump! Somebody hit her car.

Before she got into ECK, she used to have quite a temper. Anger would get to her a lot. She wrote me, "Since I'm in ECK, anger isn't a problem any more." Then she wrote, "One more thing: I am very protective of anything I love." She loved Yoda, her car.

So when she was sitting there in the construction zone and the car behind her hit her car, she said, "Mahanta, this woman hit my Yoda."

In the old days before ECK those would have been fighting words. But now she was very calm. She wrote me, "In the Detroit area, if somebody runs into your car, you generally stay in your car because people do violent things here." That's how it is in the consciousness of some of the people there. But she decided to get out of her car and look at the bumper to see if there was any damage.

At this point, the driver in the car behind her rolled down the window, put her head out, and called, "Is there any damage?" The ECKist said, "No, there's no damage." The woman turned out to be a very nice person. And the ECKist was surprised and glad that she hadn't gone storming out of her car, making a big issue of this.

But maybe to get her last licks in, maybe from a faint memory of how she used to be before ECK, she added, "Drive more carefully." Just one last word.

As she sat in her car and looked over her past, she realized that if something like this had happened years ago, she wouldn't have just become angry. She would have jumped out, she would have cursed, she would have used all kinds of language. She would have made a point. But now she's like a four-leaf clover and lucky to be in ECK.

Before she got into ECK, she used to have quite a temper. Anger would get to her a lot. She wrote me, "Since I'm in ECK, anger isn't a problem any more."

Those of you who have come to the path of Eckankar, you know you're not here because of luck. You're here because you've earned it. You didn't earn it in the last year or the last month or the last ten years or the last twenty years.

Your introduction to the teachings of ECK was lifetimes in coming. The teachings of truth have been with mankind since the beginning.

Your introduction to the teachings of ECK was lifetimes in coming.

ECK Connection

A California ECKist was visiting her mother in Texas. Her return flight was via Minneapolis, with a four-hour layover. So she decided to visit the Temple of ECK. She called a car-rental agency from Texas and asked if they would accept a certain credit card. The agent said, "Sure."

Her flight had been delayed and she hadn't been eating right, so she had a headache and wasn't feeling well. She arrived late at the car-rental agency. The agent at the desk told her, "We won't accept that credit card," which meant no car for her to drive out to the Temple. All the careful plans she had made from Texas were going out the window. She argued with the desk clerk, and she got really upset. Finally she just set her bags down in the middle of the agency, wondering what she was going to do now.

She had first considered taking a cab, but then she found out the price. It was a lot of money, and she didn't want to spend so much. But now since the car-rental agency wouldn't let her have the car, she decided to take a taxi. What she didn't know was that the ECK had something lined up.

She had to fly all the way from Texas to California via Minneapolis just to introduce somebody to ECK. The man she was to introduce to Eckankar, the teachings of ECK, was from Africa.

At the cabstand, people were waiting in line ahead of her. And she waited and waited; time began to run out. The Temple tour was to be at 2:00 in the afternoon. She was supposed to have had a full four hours. But her flight was late by half an hour, so only three-and-a-half hours were left. Finally, the line thinned, and the ECKist caught the fourth cab. The driver was a Nigerian named Andrew, and she told him she wanted to go to the Temple of ECK.

"My brother in Nigeria is an ECKist," said the cabbie, "but he's never told me about ECK. What is it?" So as they drove out to Chanhassen, the woman told him.

She was struck by this: she was talking to a Nigerian whose brother in Africa is an ECKist, the Nigerian was working in Minneapolis, and she had to come from the southern part of the United States to the north just to tell this Nigerian about ECK because his brother wouldn't. And if the rental-car agency had accepted her credit card, she would never have met him.

The Holy Spirit was working things out for her, and also for him. Because after she left the office of the car-rental agency, she felt upset that she had let herself give way to anger with the agent. She said to herself, "I am in ECK; I should know better by now."

On Holy Ground

When they arrived at the Temple, she asked Andrew, the taxi driver, "Are you going to hang around town, or do you want to come in?"

Andrew had driven past the Temple of ECK before because he drove people around the entire area. He

"My brother in Nigeria is an ECKist," said the cabbie, "but he's never told me about ECK. What is it?"

said he wanted to come in. So they went inside. They got a special tour, and then after the tour they both sat in the sanctuary for a while just feeling the presence of the Temple.

The Temple is a very special place. You are on holy ground wherever you are, but I think you'll find that the Temple itself is on holy ground too.

There is a special feeling there that's hard to describe, a feeling of peace and love. It's something you'll have to go and find for yourself sometime. See if you can stay awhile and just soak up a little. You'll find it's an interesting place.

After they sat in the sanctuary for a while, it was time for Andrew to drive her back to the airport. They got back to the airport, she got on her plane, and she suddenly discovered she'd left her driver's license and credit cards in the cab. In any other city, you could just say good-bye to your things. There are people who like to buy driver's licenses and credit cards, and by the time she landed a dishonest person would have charged all the cards up to the limit.

But a couple of weeks later in the mail, there was her driver's license along with her credit cards and a nice note from Andrew.

A Vital Path

The path of ECK is probably one of the most vital paths you have ever been in.

So, like a four-leaf clover, sometimes we say we're lucky to be in ECK. But it's not luck, it's the Holy Spirit, Divine Spirit, working things out for your spiritual unfoldment and for those people around you.

The path of ECK is probably one of the most vital paths you have ever been in. The connection between God and yourself is very real—every day, every moment. Of course that depends on your state of awareness, as it does for anyone. But among ECKists we have former members of just about every religion that anyone could name from Pentecostals to Muslims, Hindus to Buddhists. Just about everyone is represented here.

If all of you as the group entity got together, you would say, "This is the most vital path we've ever been in association with." Because if other paths were as vital, you wouldn't be here. Case closed. Of course, the case is never closed.

SLIDING BACKWARD

People come into ECK, and people leave too. At some point they find that they've come a certain distance in their spiritual unfoldment, and they become uncomfortable. They want to go back to their original religion, or they want to go on to another faith. Others stay with ECK for years and years, just like any other organization. These are the people who are the mainstay of this path. Eckankar and the ECK teachings are alive for them.

But the ECK teachings are not able to lift everyone all the time, because upliftment depends upon the individual's state of consciousness.

Even people who are doing very well on the path to God sometimes forget. They forget the spiritual exercises. In other words, they forget their communion with God. They forget to consecrate themselves, to make themselves holy, either by prayer or meditation, or, in Eckankar, by contemplation. They forget, and they slide backward.

When they slide backward beyond a certain point, they say, "The teachings of ECK are not for me. I don't know how I could have been misled all these years." They'll go running out as fast as they can and say,

They forget the spiritual exercises. In other words, they forget their communion with God.

"I escaped!" Who are they running from? Themselves? Or life? That is what we run from whenever we're running from anything, whether we're in Eckankar or outside of Eckankar.

ECK is the Holy Spirit, and It pervades everything with Its presence. You cannot be outside of ECK. You may not agree with the terminology we use, but ECK is the Spirit of life. You cannot be outside the Spirit of life, or you would not be living.

You cannot be outside the Spirit of life, or you would not be living.

To Overcome Fear

A woman wrote me from California. English is her second language. She's not very comfortable with it, and yet she does very well in business. She writes very fluently. But she feels that when she speaks, she's choppy. She gets the English sentence structure backward, and sometimes she comes across as too abrupt. She's able to get along fine in her business and in the ECK community. But every Tuesday she's one of the leaders at a management group, and her language gets in the way. She also recognizes that her limited education handicaps her when she's trying to participate in this group.

She's come to dread Tuesdays. Sometimes she's able to pull it off, but other days she can't. She's simply reduced to tears afterward when she's going home. Since she's come into Eckankar, fear has gone away in many other departments of her life. But this one particular fear is still with her.

One day she was out for a walk. She was crying. "Mahanta, please help me overcome this problem that I have," she said. "Help me with this fear." In front of her there was a hill.

She heard a silent nudge—the silent voice from the Inner Master, the Mahanta—say to her, "Go to the top of the hill." So she walked up the hill, and she saw the clouds. They were blue and pink, very pretty and wispy. By the time she got to the top of the hill where the wind was blowing, much of the burden had lifted from her. She felt better, happier.

As she was standing up there feeling better, she looked down at her feet and saw an ant. This ant was pulling on a feather, a feather about thirty times larger than itself. It was trying to pull this feather into the wind. The woman looked at the ant and wondered, *Why does the ant bother? It's not food.*

The Weight of a Feather

The feather was a huge burden for the little ant. Why a feather? The ant struggled and struggled.

Where is the anthill? the woman wondered. Where would the ant possibly want to take this feather? You can imagine an ant coming home with this huge feather, and the mother ant saying, "You're not bringing that thing in the house!"

Finally, the ant figured it out. It let go of the feather, and the feather blew away. The ant then scurried off looking a lot freer and happier.

As the ECKist watched this, she realized her fear was just like that feather. If she could let go and let love enter into her life, love would displace the fear, and the fear would no longer have any power over her.

If she could let go and let love enter into her life, love would displace the fear, and the fear would no longer have any power over her.

What's a feather? It's a plume. Something to say, "Look what a dandy I am!" Like a peacock.

It's interesting that the image that Divine Spirit brought to her in this waking dream was a feather. It was a feather in the cap of the ant, so he thought, to come home with this beautiful thing. Wouldn't everyone envy him! But the feather was a burden, like her fear.

The woman found that if she could let go of fear the way the ant let go of the feather, her life would improve dramatically. It would be a more pleasant life. The way to do this would be to let divine love into her life. God's love had already come into her life to rid her of the other fears she had before, but this was a big fear.

LOVE OF ALL LIFE

Sometimes when we speak of love, we think of it being exclusive to the human race. People in their vanity, with their own peacock feathers, think they're a greater creation than animals. So this next story is about a Siamese cat, Misha. Misha is a cat who always wanted love more than food.

Misha belongs to Kristy. Misha's story is like a waking dream: an event of spiritual significance that happens in a person's life.

Kristy got a mate for Misha and called her Bani. Bani means Sound Current. And after a little while, Bani was going to have kittens. On the day that the kittens were to be born, Misha, the father, wanted to be in the room when the kittens were born. But Kristy said, "No, Misha, you stay out there." And so Misha had to stay outside of the room.

There were three Siamese kittens born that day, and afterward Kristy let Misha back in to be with them. Misha is so full of love that it's almost beyond belief, beyond comprehension.

Misha sat guard outside the box. He'd watch over the kittens, he'd lick them, he'd take good care of them. Whenever Bani wanted to move them around— mother cats have this instinct not to leave the kittens too long in one place because some predator might find them—Misha would help. He'd hold one of the

> The woman found that if she could let go of fear the way the ant let go of the feather, her life would improve dramatically.

kittens by the neck and very gently follow Bani.

One day Kristy needed to leave on a trip, and she asked her niece to come over and take care of the cats. She had mentioned her trip to the veterinarian, and the vet said, "If you're going to be gone any length of time, it might be a good idea not to have the father cat in the room with the kittens. Sometimes the male cats will kill the kittens out of jealousy." Kristy knew Misha and didn't think he'd do that, but she was going to be gone for a couple of days so she thought it might be a good idea anyway.

So Bani and the three little kittens were in one room, and out in the hallway behind the shut door was Misha. Misha wanted to come in, but he couldn't. So to show his love, he got some of the kitty toys and brought them to the door. Kristy's niece was sitting in the room with Bani and the kittens. She suddenly saw kitty toys being pushed under the door.

Misha was pushing the toys under the door, so Bani would have something to play with. The niece thought this was the most incredible expression of love she'd ever seen.

LOVE MAKES A DIFFERENCE

After a time, Kristy began wondering, "Are five Siamese cats too many?" She got a call from the vet one day and asked him. Not long after, the vet's secretary called her. A woman's mother's Siamese cat had died, and the mother was getting depressed. Did she have any kittens to sell? Kristi thought about it and decided it was time to give up a kitten.

When the woman met Misha, she said, "That cat has soul."

In ECK we don't say anyone has soul, like soul is something you can possess. We say, you are Soul.

In ECK we don't say anyone has soul, like soul is something you can possess. We say, you are Soul.

The woman was trying to say, "That cat is a highly developed Soul." She was impressed by the love that was coming out of Misha.

The woman chose a kitten and took it to her mother. This kitten turned out to be much more loving than her mother's original Siamese cat, and the mother was very happy. They were all astounded by the amount of love in this kitten. Pretty soon the woman called Kristy again. Was it possible to get one of the remaining kittens for her husband and herself? So they came out and saw Misha again. The woman looked at Kristy and said, "You have something very special with those cats of yours. There is so much love, and it's evident in your kittens."

Kristy kept one kitten. Just a little kitten, full of love, the same as its parents, especially Misha.

Like a four-leaf clover? No, much better. In this family, like in any family, there are hardships. There are hard times. But love makes a difference.

Love makes *the* difference. The richest people on earth are those who have love, God's love. If you have animals, you know that sometimes the animals are capable of giving more of God's love than humans of your acquaintance. I know we find this sometimes a little bit hard to believe, but it's so.

Love makes the difference. The richest people on earth are those who have love, God's love.

THE ANCIENT ONE

Kristy started a business, and she was on a business trip with a friend, a new ECKist. One evening, after a difficult day, they came back to the hotel room. They were recounting all the blessings that the Mahanta had given them during the day. They were talking about one blessing after another. They said good-night to each other, turned out the light.

Kristy, for her spiritual exercise, began thinking

of some of the different names for the Mahanta, and the one that came to mind was the Ancient One.

"The One who comes to wake us up," she said. This is the purpose of the Mahanta, the Living ECK Master: to awaken Soul. The Mahanta comes to let Soul know that Its true destiny is to come home again to God. This is Its purpose.

As Kristy was thinking about the Mahanta, the Ancient One, her friend, the new ECKist, was having her own contemplation. She was using an imagination technique, thinking of a boyfriend she had met and the possibility of their relationship developing. Both Kristy and the new ECKist, her friend, were thinking of love. Their hearts were filled with love as they were doing this contemplation.

THANKS FOR TUNING IN

Suddenly, in the dark of the room, for no reason whatsoever, the TV went on all by itself. They both sat straight up in bed and looked at it.

On the screen were the words "Thanks for tuning in."

They thought maybe somehow the remote control for the TV had gotten into bed and one of them had rolled over it, and this had turned on the TV. But the remote control was on the desk, far away from the bed.

The new ECKist began laughing. She wasn't afraid of this strange phenomenon. For her, it was assurance of the Mahanta's divine love for her, speaking to her through the spiritual channels, using whatever was available—the TV set. The message on the screen, "Thanks for tuning in," meant: thanks for doing your spiritual exercises, because that is Soul's link with God.

On the screen were the words "Thanks for tuning in."

Like a Four-Leaf Clover

Jim, an ECKist, was scheduled to lead an ECK Worship Service. It was Saturday. He was on the lawn, at home; his daughter, six years old, was with him. He was wondering what to do with the topic for the worship service tomorrow. The topic was, "The Spirit Is All Around You."

That really doesn't inspire any good ideas in me, he thought. *What am I going to do?* Time was running out. Tomorrow was coming quickly, and he had no ideas about how to approach his talk for the worship service.

He wondered, W*ould the ECK, Divine Spirit, give him any clues by morning?*

He wondered, Would the ECK, Divine Spirit, give him any clues by morning?

Jim was sitting in a patch of clover on the lawn, thinking about this, and his daughter was there with him. He said to her, "Sometimes the special things in life are hard to find." He was trying to think of what to do for his topic tomorrow. "For example, did you know that four-leaf clovers are very rare? Because of this, when someone finds one, it's considered good luck."

His daughter looked at him, looked around the clover patch, picked a clover, and said, "You mean like this?" She handed him a four-leaf clover.

"Yes, like this," he said. She ran off to play with her friends, completely unimpressed.

But Jim was impressed; he spent the next ten to fifteen minutes going through that clover patch trying to find another four-leaf clover. He never found one. Then he remembered from the Bible, Jesus saying that unless ye become as little children, ye shall not enter the kingdom of heaven.

Sometimes children pick up the teachings so quickly and so easily because they know that God's love is Light and Sound. That Light and Sound—which means anything that you can see, anything that you can hear in your world—is the expression of God's love for you.

The Light and Sound of God are the basis of the ECK teachings. This is why they are so powerful, why they are able to transform people, why they are able to make a difference in your life.

VAIRAGI BLESSING

I often end my talks with the ancient blessing of the Vairagi, which is an expression of God's love. The ECK Masters are the Vairagi, the Detached Ones, willing to be vehicles for God's love without caring about the outcome. They don't worry if they did it right or if they did wrong; they just simply do it in the name of Spirit. They don't worry if they could have done something better or worse. They just let it be.

The blessing of the Vairagi Masters is always with you. It is very simple: May the blessings be. God's love to you.

That Light and Sound—which means anything that you can see, anything that you can hear in your world—is the expression of God's love for you.

1996 ECK Worldwide Seminar, Minneapolis, Minnesota, October 26, 1996

In time of need, help comes if you know how to open yourself—sincerely, without any preconditions or any ideas that
God should act in this way and do this or that.

4
IN TIME OF NEED

n ECK, we recognize that whenever something comes up in our daily life, a problem that seems too difficult to solve, Divine Spirit has also given help and support to us.

In regard to my own health I found this very true.

HEALTH UPDATE

For the past few years, I've been battling a number of different health problems. At first it was sensitivity to electromagnetic radiation.

When you're used to working with computers or under fluorescent lights or enjoying television at break times, this technology becomes a way of life. You get used to the microwave oven because it's so quick: you just pop something in there; a few minutes later you come back and it's hot. You say, "Wow! This is some good technology."

Then suddenly you find out that all this technology, for some reason or another, is beginning to hurt your health. It's causing problems like numbness in the arms, your head feels like it's going to explode, and fever and chills.

In ECK, we recognize that whenever something comes up in our daily life, a problem that seems too difficult to solve, Divine Spirit has also given help and support to us.

From some of my travels, I got parasites. Many people have parasites, and the body's normal resistance is sometimes able to overcome them. But when the body is weak, these parasites can attack an organ or cause allergies and other problems that people would never associate with something like this.

Modern medicine is finding ways to help many of these problems. And where traditional medicine hasn't helped, there are the natural healing methods, which I have found very helpful.

I've gotten good help from a Chinese acupuncturist. This doctor practiced in China for thirty-five years as an orthopedic surgeon, then he came to the U.S. The license requirements here for orthopedic surgery were just too much for him to bother to pursue; he had served thirty-five years in China and he was getting along in years. Did he really want to go back to school? So he began an acupuncture practice.

He understands the physical body quite well. I don't enjoy acupuncture needles, but I find they don't hurt as much when I'm improving in health compared to when I was very, very ill. Back then, I'd jump when he put the needles in. It scared him. This good man was just trying to do his job, wondering why had he ever gotten into acupuncture. There must be gentler professions where patients don't jump and scare you. The needles don't hurt that much unless there is great stress on certain organs and the body really needs them.

HEALING WITH LOVE

I'm fortunate to have two excellent chiropractors helping along with the acupuncturist. A doctor of natural medicine has also proven very helpful. These people are in what I consider the healing class.

> Modern medicine is finding ways to help many of these problems. And where traditional medicine hasn't helped, there are the natural healing methods.

There are people who practice a profession simply because it's a job. It doesn't matter whether they're lawyers, farmers, or office workers. Some people only do it for the money. Others do it for love, because of devotion to whatever their specialty is.

If you can find someone who loves doing what they do, then you're much further ahead than if you are being seen by somebody who's just going through the motions.

I'm still very sensitive to electromagnetic radiation, and I keep away from it whenever possible. I also have a sensitivity to petrochemicals. A couple of times when I went to put gas in the car at the pump, the fumes got to me. Also, while a plane is still sitting on the ground, the fumes of the jet fuel come through the cabin and make me sick. So electromagnetic radiation and sensitivity to petrochemicals are changing my travel plans somewhat.

TAKE RESPONSIBILITY FOR YOUR LIFE

My job, my mission, is not to do things for other people in the line of healing or prophecies. But you who have come into ECK today are further along than any group has been in the past, at any time. Many of you are more ready and able to begin moving seriously on the path to God than you have ever been before.

This means that you learn to take responsibility for your own life, for your own health, for your own economics. You try to become self-sufficient.

It doesn't mean that you're never going to be short of money, that you're always going to have good health, or that you're always going to be feeling perfect and cheery every day. It doesn't mean that. It does mean that you recognize the responsibility for being where

Many of you are more ready and able to begin moving seriously on the path to God than you have ever been before. This means that you learn to take responsibility for your own life.

*The ways
you've been
looking at life
in the past are
what have
brought you the
problem today.*

you are, that it's somehow to do with your state of consciousness. That if you want to change any outer condition, the changes must first come within yourself. That somehow you have to look at life differently from the way you have in the past.

The ways you've been looking at life in the past are what have brought you the problem today. The past can be as recent as yesterday or as long ago as your birth or a previous life.

GODLIKE ELEMENT IN SOUL

In ECK, through the spiritual exercises and your experiences in the dream state and with Soul Travel, you can go back to find some of the reasons, the past life, that brought these problems to you today. Or if it's caused by a problem that came up in this lifetime, that happened maybe a week or a month ago, you can zero in on it too. You can find out what happened, what you did. Like a bad situation at work or in a personal relationship. Sometimes it's not something you're doing now. It's a reaction someone is having to something you've done to that individual in the past.

But at least you have something to work with. You have the creative power within you. This is the godlike element within each Soul.

The Holy Spirit is the creative power of Light and Sound. This is the Voice of God, and Soul was made from the Light and Sound. In other words, the creative power is in each human being. Therefore each human being has the inborn ability to take charge of his or her own life and not dwell in the victim consciousness that is so popular in some circles today.

I certainly would hope that the victim state wouldn't be popular in the higher circles of Eckankar. You can't be seriously on the path to God and constantly view yourself as a victim of life. It doesn't work. It means somewhere along the line you're lying to yourself.

You have to face yourself and realize that the problems you have today are of your own making. And then deal with it.

YOUR RELATIONSHIP WITH GOD

In Australia, a woman was to go to the hospital for one day for exploratory surgery. The night before, while packing, she wondered what she should take with her. She packed all her necessities, then for light reading decided to take a New Age magazine. She thought she'd also pack *The Slow Burning Love of God*. She had been reading and enjoying the book. Then she thought, W*hat if the medical staff thinks I'm weird because I'm reading something about the love of God?* This is the social consciousness that is common among us in the human state. She was wondering what will people think?

Any compassionate people on the hospital staff would recognize it's a very normal thing for patients to want some books of a spiritual nature with them. If people are going to become spiritual, it's likely to happen during a hospital stay. That's often when you're faced with your own mortality, when you want to understand your relationship with the great unknown.

Then she thought she'd also take John Gray's book, *Men Are from Mars, Women Are from Venus*, because it was popular. She was deciding between the two, and at the last minute she said, "No, I won't take *The Slow Burning Love of God*."

The next morning she got up, ready to go to the hospital, and literally as she's going out the door something changed her mind. She reached for the

You have to face yourself and realize that the problems you have today are of your own making. And then deal with it.

ECK book again, put it with her things, and took it to the hospital.

Beyond Death

As she arrived at the hospital and got checked in, a patient who was going up and down the hallway for exercise stopped at the door of her room. They got to talking, and it came out that this visitor had recently had two deaths in the family: Her father and her father-in-law had both passed away.

The ECKist said to her, quite out of the blue, "Did you get to see them in the dream state yet?"

This caught the visitor by surprise. "Well, yes," she said, "as a matter of fact, I did. My father came to me, and he came to see Mum too."

The ECKist had just been reading a section in *The Slow Burning Love of God* about an experience of someone who had died, or translated, and was now saying good-bye through the dream state. The person who had passed on was saying not to worry about him, he was in a place of love and perfectly happy. Happier now than he ever was on earth.

The visitor said, "Could I see the book for a moment?" She skimmed through it. She said, "This looks interesting. I would like to get it for myself." Then she handed it back.

In time of need, whether in our need or someone else's, Divine Spirit provides a way for help to come.

After that they talked about John Gray's book, which they both had an interest in. But the ECKist realized that the nudge to take this ECK book along was not coincidental; it was not an accident. Divine Spirit was trying to reach another Soul with the message of the Light and Sound, and that she was to be the vehicle for this.

In time of need, whether in our need or someone else's, Divine Spirit provides a way for help to come.

Karma Averted

A certain ECK couple in the northeastern part of the United States hired a health aide to come in and watch over the man's mother, who was needing care. This health aide had been coming for three months, five days a week, four hours a day. One day the couple had an appointment they had to get to, and the same day the health aide—who'd been coming to their home for three months, five times a week—got lost.

So the couple was waiting and waiting.

Finally the health aide arrived and they prepared to leave. But just at that moment, a neighbor in the apartment complex ran to their door. She asked if she could use the phone to call the American Automobile Association to have them come out and start her car. She had just gone out to the car and put her keys in, and the car wouldn't start.

The husband was getting a little bit nervous. He had an appointment to get to.

He went out to the parking lot to start his car and noticed that the neighbor had put her car in the wrong gear. This is why the car wouldn't start. So the man put it in park and turned the key; the car started. Problem solved.

Finally, the couple got in their own car and drove down the highway. There they saw a severe accident that had just happened. If they had left on time, they probably would have been right in the middle of it. They realized that Divine Spirit had come to help them out of trouble they didn't even realize they would be in the middle of.

This is Divine Spirit working through the Mahanta, helping people who no longer need to go through a certain kind of karma because they have worked it out through their spiritual exercises.

This is Divine Spirit working through the Mahanta, helping people who no longer need to go through a certain kind of karma because they have worked it out through their spiritual exercises.

On Hallowed Ground

These things happen all the time. Many of you have your own examples. Sometimes you are so kind as to share them with others. You write letters to me, and I'm able to share them with others.

This is how Divine Spirit works.

In time of need, help comes if you know how to open yourself—sincerely, without any preconditions or any ideas that God should act in this way and do this or that. If you just recognize that you're walking on hallowed ground, simply because you love God and you love life, this often is protection enough from many things.

Some people will say, "I got in trouble. Where was the ECK then?"

Maybe it was something they had to go through. When people get very argumentative about something like this, they probably need to get over their anger. They're going to go through problems until they finally work it out. Then they become much nicer people to be around, and they find it easier to live with themselves too.

In time of need, help comes if you know how to open yourself— sincerely, without any preconditions or any ideas that God should act in this way and do this or that.

Set Up on the Set

Sometimes the healing that takes place has almost a comical aspect to it, except for the fact that there's pain underneath.

A woman had left her husband. The marriage wasn't working out to her satisfaction. She had a feeling of sadness about the whole thing. She just asked the Mahanta one night in contemplation if she could have a healing from this sadness.

This woman worked part-time in offices, here, there, and wherever. But as a sideline, she was an extra in TV shows. One day her agent called and said,

"I have an opening for you." The studio people would send transportation for her, so she was soon in a car going to the location where she was to be an extra in this TV series.

When they got to the location, she went inside to the set. And who did she meet? The first person she ran into was her husband.

Her husband was in the acting business too. He worked with an entirely different agency, but he was an extra for this same TV series on this very same day. There they are, together. Just the night before, the woman had asked the Mahanta for a healing from this problem in their relationship.

Pretty soon the assistant director came up and put them at their proper places on the set. The assistant director was working up imaginary scenarios.

He said to the husband, "Now, you're going to be her ex-husband; sit right here beside her."

The husband and wife were looking at each other, thinking, *What's going on? This is crazy! This man couldn't have set this up better if he knew the truth.* The assistant director was just creating these scenarios in his mind, or so he thought. But Divine Spirit was at work.

On the set, the couple were healing something from the past.

So for the whole day, this couple was together on the set. Interestingly enough, the scene took place at an Alcoholics Anonymous meeting.

HEALING BEGINS

After the day of filming was over, the woman was talking to her friend about it. "You know, AA is about people who are trying to heal something in the past," the friend pointed out. On the set, the couple were healing something from the past. The assistant director was thinking he was creating these great fictional scenes, but he didn't know the real husband and wife were in front of him. You have to view these setups with a wry sense of humor.

Divine Spirit has a way of doing exactly what is right for everyone concerned at the moment. It's not always funny at the time, and it catches people off guard. But sometimes when we're caught off guard, our hearts open. Then the healing can begin.

It doesn't happen overnight, it may take months. But at least the seed of healing is planted.

Divine Spirit has a way of doing exactly what is right for everyone concerned at the moment.

The Blue Light

A man worked in a very high position with the largest commercial bank in Canada. After some time, he decided to quit his job. He was thirty-nine at the time. Ever since he was fourteen he had been searching for truth.

Four years earlier, the man had been driving at night from his aunt's home, going to his mother's, a distance of about three miles. He was very concerned about his aunt's health. She had been born in 1907, and her health was bad. So, as he drove these three miles between his aunt's place and his mother's, he asked God for spiritual guidance. He wanted to get some help because his aunt's failing health really upset him. This aunt had been like a mother to him.

In the last mile before he got to his mother's home, something happened that shook him to his roots. Suddenly, everything—all the lights in the night—turned blue.

Car headlights were blue, storefronts were blue, street lamps were blue, the lights on his dash were all blue. He pulled over. "Must be some kind of a neurological problem going on here," he said. He sat on the side of the road and looked around. Other cars were going by, and nobody seemed to notice these blue lights all around. It really startled him.

The man began looking for an answer, and he searched for the next four years. What had happened that night? What were those blue lights?

It turned out that his aunt, the one whose health he was so concerned about, was most interested in this blue light. Her ability to speak was much reduced as she was getting along in years, but by her simple actions she let him know that something important had happened to him that night as he was driving from her place to his mother's home.

This man looked throughout Christianity and then Tibetan Buddhism. He went to the highest lamas in that faith, and he asked, "What is the blue light?"

No one could tell him, but he kept looking and looking.

One day someone gave him *ECKANKAR— Ancient Wisdom for Today*, and in the book he found an explanation for the blue light. He realized that the Mahanta, the Living ECK Master had answered his call for spiritual assistance.

One day someone gave him ECKANKAR— Ancient Wisdom for Today, and in the book he found an explanation for the blue light.

In Time of Need

You may be wondering how a blue light would help him.

This is the wake-up call the Ancient One gives to Souls when they're ready to begin the journey back home to God. In one way or another, the Mahanta will approach the individual. The Mahanta has approached each of you, otherwise you wouldn't be reading this.

It doesn't mean that you're going to be an ECKist the rest of your life. Some people may say, "I have no more use for Eckankar." Or, "This is the strangest, most preposterous stuff I've ever heard. I'm going back home—to my church." They go back there for a while. But at some point, either in this lifetime or another lifetime, they're going to be in such a circumstance where they're going to need to search for truth again. They'll be in a time of need.

This is when the Master will approach and in some way try to awaken the individual. Again, that person has the right to either accept or reject the wake-up call.

Your Choice to Wake Up or Not

People accept or reject this wake-up call based upon their state of consciousness. But a state of consciousness is not fixed. It is anything but fixed. It fluctuates, it moves, it's like water.

Some creeks run muddy all the time. These are generally Souls that are in an early state of unfoldment. They're greedy; maybe they have this quest for power. The only thing that draws and attracts such people and makes them continue in their lifestyle is spiritual ignorance. Life hasn't yet come to the point of teaching them better.

Life will always teach you better.

Life will always teach you better. This is basis of the Law of Karma: what you sow, you reap. And in the reaping of what we've sown, we gain spiritual wisdom.

Eventually Soul cries out, "I want to go home, wherever that is."

Closing the Gap

Even atheists and agnostics cry out at some point. They don't say "home," they don't say "God," they don't say these words. But they realize that there is a separation inside themselves from something that they need, something as important as life itself.

What they don't realize is that it *is* life itself. People in the greatest need are those that have cut themselves off the most from life. Life means here Divine Spirit, the ECK, which through Its Light and Sound is responsible for every form that you can imagine in existence: humans, animals, birds, trees, minerals, and everything that's made from these. Everything that remains after the life-form Soul leaves whatever material form It was encased in for Its life period.

People in the greatest need are those that have cut themselves off the most from life.

Piano Lessons

An ECKist learned about the process of spiritual unfoldment that Soul goes through, and the lesson came about in a different way.

She and her husband were given an old upright piano, eighty years old or more. It took about a year before they could even get the piano moved to their home in another state. Finally they rented a trailer, got help putting the piano on the trailer, and hauled it home. They put it downstairs, and there it sat.

The woman made it her project to strip off the finish that had been slathered on it over the years and to try to get down to the Honduras mahogany that the piano was made of. Beautiful wood lay under the coats and coats of varnish. Over the years people had tried to make the piano look pretty, and in so doing they had also begun to deaden its sound.

This woman had often said she didn't like piano music. But she decided it wasn't the piano sounds she didn't like, it was what was played on the piano.

At that time, she was reading *The Living Word*, Book 2. One of the chapters had an unusual title: "Use What You Are." Not "Use What You Have," but

"Use What You Are." So she got to thinking about it, and she said, "There must be some way to use this principle of spiritual understanding with this piano."

LAYERS OF THE PAST

The piano had become a big monument in her life. There it stood, right in her home, dirty and needing a lot of work.

As she began stripping away the old layers of varnish, she suddenly realized that this is what the Mahanta does with Soul—a Soul that has many layers of karma plastered on It from past lives and this life. Very slowly and carefully the Mahanta takes off layer after layer after layer, finally revealing the beauty of Soul beneath.

The woman also realized there's a lot of work to finding the beauty underneath—a lot of work both on the Master's part and on the part of Soul.

This work involves things like the Spiritual Exercises of ECK. You've got to do them if you care about putting yourself on sacred ground, putting yourself in the position to be able to understand the phenomenon of God's Light and Sound. Understanding how these two aspects of God's love are absolutely essential for your existence and for your happiness.

Light and Sound, just like the rain and the wind, come to everyone equally and alike. But some people benefit more than others.

GIFTS OF CONSCIOUSNESS

Light and Sound, just like the rain and the wind, come to everyone equally and alike. But some people benefit more than others.

It's up to you in your state of consciousness.

And your state of consciousness depends upon whether or not you care enough to open yourself to this inner guidance of Divine Spirit so that you can have some of the experiences that are necessary to break through this hard human shell. Unless you do, you cannot rise into the higher states of awareness.

Sometimes we wonder, *Why would I want to go into a higher state of awareness?*

I say, "Would you like to be a baby again? In a crib, helpless, waiting for people to feed you? If you have the full knowingness that you do now, would you like to go backward and have the limitations of a baby's body? Totally dependent on the goodwill of those around you, and sometimes unfortunate enough not to have that goodwill?"

Maybe you can't stand the thought of going back to a helpless state, a precursor to where you are today. Let's say someday you reach Mastership, and you look back at today and also see it as the state of an adult trapped in a baby's body. It seems impossible to run the track of time forward and see what it would be like from a Master's state of consciousness, see what your life is like today.

A True Look at Yourself Today

If you're unhappy, open yourself to the possibility that there is something better. If you're an ECKist say, "Mahanta, please show me thy ways. Show me what may be there for me." If you're Christian or Jewish or of any other faith, look to the God of your faith. Look to your savior, look to your way of spirituality, and ask, "Show me truth, God."

If you're sincere, God's Voice, the Holy Spirit, will begin opening you to truth. You will be led to occasions and insights which will be subtle at first, but—sometimes through your dreams—you're going to have a glimpse of the future.

If you're unhappy, open yourself to the possibility that there is something better.

More important is to have a true look at yourself today: who and what you are here and now.

This is more important than a look at the past or a look at the future, even though we in ECK know that the past, present, and future are all one. They are a continuum. The past still exists now, the future is here and now, and as is the present. They're all mixed, back and forth, in and out.

Breaking Down the Walls

But with the logical mind, it's a linear way of thinking. We separate the continuum of life into three separate parts: past, present, and future. And we build walls between.

In building these walls, we sometimes limit ourselves, limit the potential of what can occur through the gifts of the Holy Spirit.

So sometime in contemplation or in prayer, maybe as a spiritual exercise, in your mind's eye just see a room with three distinct parts. A semicircular room where you are at the point of the room and the room curves out around you, divided into three parts. You can look into each one: past, present, and future. But there is a wall separating each of the three parts.

Life is love, God is love, and Soul exists because God loves It.

Dissolve those two walls between those three parts and see what happens.

Do that for a few nights before you go to sleep. Say, "I dissolve the walls that try to break life into parts." Because from the higher state of consciousness, you realize that life is not divided into parts. Life is all one.

Life is love, God is love, and Soul exists because God loves It. If you can get this overview that everything is a wholeness—that everything is right and in its proper place at this time—then you will have gained spiritually. You will have a viewpoint in life that is different from 99 percent of people.

HOW THE MAHANTA WORKS

For the members of ECK there are discourses to help you to another stage of understanding yourself spiritually. But the greatest unfoldment comes not through the books, discourses, or talks that happen on the outer side, in the physical world. The greatest unfoldment happens on the inner planes, in your dream worlds, through your intuition, through nudges, and sometimes more directly through visions and Soul Travel.

These are Divine Spirit's way of helping you. This is how the Mahanta works.

The Mahanta works to help you, to lift you, so you can understand why you're even in this life and why it pays to go on, because some days it seems almost impossible. You wonder, *Why bother?* Well, bother.

In my Russian class a long time ago, some of the students wondered why we had to learn Russian. We were in a military class at that time. The Russian instructors would just say, "You have to know," and that was it. The students would ask, "Why?" "You have to know," the instructors said again. It was one of those catch-22 things. You ask for an answer, you get it, and you still don't understand.

You have all the time in the world. There's no hurry, so go at your own pace. Go at a pace you're comfortable with.

I'm glad you are making the effort to learn more about the teachings of ECK and what they possibly can do to help you in your own search for God and

The Mahanta works to help you, to lift you, so you can understand why you're even in this life and why it pays to go on, because some days it seems almost impossible.

in your own journey home to the place of your creation. And so, as you journey homeward again, remember that I am always with you.

1996 ECK Worldwide Seminar, Minneapolis, Minnesota, October 27, 1996

As the Mahanta, Divine Spirit, or the ECK, is able to work
with you on a one-to-one basis, just like a tutor.

5

DISCOVER
THE MAHANTA

newcomer has been a member of
ECK for two months. Before this person came to the seminar, the Dream
Master, which is the Mahanta, the in-
ner side of myself, came to her and said, "I won't be
there, but I'll be there by satellite."

This individual really didn't know much about
the ECK teachings yet. And she wondered about this
message from the Inner Master.

At the seminar she learned that indeed this was
a historic day. It was the first time I wouldn't be there
in person but would give my talk in an exclusive live
remote telecast. The ECKist then knew that her
dream was real.

WHO IS THE MAHANTA?

The Mahanta, the Living ECK Master is a big
title. The Mahanta is the inner state, the Inner Master,
the one who comes as the Dream Master and works
with you in the dream state. The Living ECK Master
is the Outer Master.

*The Mahanta
is the inner
state, the Inner
Master, the one
who comes as
the Dream
Master and
works with
you in the
dream state.*

It sounds like there is a split here. You're at the seminar in Washington, D.C., and I'm someplace else in the physical body. But in the Soul body, we are together.

As the Mahanta, Divine Spirit, or the ECK, is able to work with you on a one-to-one basis. It can work with you with your strengths, it can work with you in your weaknesses, and it can help you just like a tutor. Sometimes standing behind your desk, sometimes working with you at the desk. Then sometimes just being with you. Being with you at work, on a walk, in rush-hour traffic. This is what the Mahanta, the Inner Master, can do and does.

In the inner self, I can be with all people in all places around the world. But only if they are in agreement with the principles of ECK. These are the principles of Divine Spirit that come through this state of consciousness, the Mahanta. If you're in agreement with them, there is a bond between us, a connection.

God has created all religions and all spiritual leaders to fit a certain place in the lives of certain people.

A TEACHER FOR EVERY STATE OF CONSCIOUSNESS

A person of another faith will likely have a bond with the spiritual leader of his own faith, and that is as it should be. God has created all religions and all spiritual leaders to fit a certain place in the lives of certain people. No spiritual leader is going to be right for everyone. I don't say I am.

Each person has to decide whether or not any other person is going to be their spiritual tutor. That is not something that any human law can decree. That doesn't work in the spiritual teachings.

God has given a teacher for every state of consciousness.

Sometimes this teacher is not in a religion. The teacher can be your boss at work. Or this individual may be your mate. Divine Spirit, the ECK, will bring the words of wisdom that you need for your spiritual unfoldment through someone very close to you. It can come through the words or the hug of a child. It can come through the cry of a baby. It can come through the love of your pet, your dog or your cat, as it comes up to you to greet you when you come home from work.

We in the human state of consciousness are sometimes too protective of what ways God can or cannot show love to Soul. We think well, God isn't going to show love through my dog, because my dog has fleas. Or not through my cat, because my cat has worms.

GOOD TEACHERS

A good teacher repeats. Repeats and repeats and repeats. And a teacher will use different approaches to the same truth.

In the New Testament, Christ constantly used parables, but basically he was saying, "God loves you. Don't you see? Don't you understand? Love your neighbor as yourself." He gave all these different examples. He pointed out that self-responsibility is one of the rules that a person who is on the spiritual path must accept and follow.

When you have self-responsibility, you are loving yourself as a divine creation of God.

It's just that simple. When you have self-responsibility, you are loving yourself as a divine creation of God. After you do that, maybe you have the capability to love your neighbor.

We in ECK say, "Soul exists because God loves It." Or more personally, "You exist because God loves you." It's the old, old teaching.

A teacher repeats and repeats, and a teacher tells stories. Sometimes they're humorous, sometimes they're very somber stories. They're the stories of other people, how they learned some principle that was trying to direct them closer to this underlying principle: God loves you.

It is that simple. Any true teacher in any religion will always bring out this very same message about divine love. People are so quick to forget their own beginnings and the paths of their own religions when they were very young. They look at other paths that are not very well established, and they'll say, "Oh, you mean human love." In other words, love cults. But that isn't a responsible way for people to live their lives.

Divine love means to love your neighbor as yourself. To do that, you have to love yourself.

What Is Divine Love?

Divine love means to love your neighbor as yourself. To do that, you have to love yourself.

Not the vain part of yourself, so that when you walk past the mirror you pat your hair and say, "Aren't I a good-looking one." Not that side. But the side that says, "I am a creation of God." This is the greatest gift that life could bring. And then, with the same voice, saying, "But so are you. You are Soul too. And if I am Soul and you are Soul, and we're both existing because of God's great love for us, then why can't we at least love each other as divine beings?"

Warm Love and Charity

This may not necessarily mean with warm love, because human beings don't have the capacity to love everyone with warm love. It's simply not within our power. It's not within us in the scope of human nature.

I'm not talking about people who rescue every cat from the gutter. Pretty soon they've got ninety cats in their home, and people who watch out for the welfare of animals come and take all the pets away because the place is filthy. The person had the mistaken belief that he was doing it out of pure love for all life. You might accept ninety cats, but could you accept ninety elephants?

What is the capacity for your love?

What is the capacity for your love?

Sometimes it's as much as your physical means are to take care of the things you have accepted in your life.

Warm love means basically that you have the means to serve those to whom you give this warm love. If you have the financial means to take care of a family of four which you are a part of, this might be the limit of your warm love. But you can give charity, or goodwill, to everyone else.

Charity is detached love. This is holding the door open for someone and giving them a smile. Why? Because they are Soul.

PROPHECY

In 1983, two years after I came into this position as the Mahanta, the Living ECK Master, the ECK-Vidya, the ancient science of prophecy, opened up to me. Divine Spirit, the ECK, showed me that I was going to go through a lot of hardships.

Frankly, I had already known about this, because a couple of years before 1981 when I actually took this role, the ECK-Vidya had also opened for me. I felt a lot of trepidation and downright fear when it showed me what was to be my lot if I chose to take this position. I trembled, shook in my boots, and wondered, *Am I strong enough?*

I said, "I think it'd be better if you pick someone else." Yet I felt as if I had been drawn along by the golden bond of love from Sugmad, the Supreme Creator. These cords of love, the golden threads that bind together all creation, pulled me on and on until 1981 when I came into the position. It was a time of fast learning. I also knew that the future would bring many, many brushes with walking at the very edge of the ledge.

By 1983, I had served a couple of years as the spiritual leader of Eckankar. I had learned to give talks in front of a lot of you, sometimes two to five thousand people. Then the ECK showed me the future again.

It said, "There will come a day when you're not going to be giving all the talks that you are now."

At that time I was going to three major seminars in the United States, another in Europe, and another in the South Pacific. Then I would go to the central Pacific area of Singapore, Hong Kong, or Malaysia. I'd stop at Hawaii to do another seminar there. And then I would go to Africa. At each of these seminars, I generally did three public talks, usually an hour each.

In 1983 when the ECK showed me the future again, I said, "How am I going to back off a schedule like this without the members of Eckankar getting up in arms?"

And Divine Spirit said, "There'll be a time. And at the right time, it'll all work out very nicely."

So seminar after seminar I gave the three public talks, met with the Higher Initiates, then with the Initiates, then with the local leaders, the RESAs, then with the youth. Plus I had a number of consultations and other private meetings. Sometimes before the seminar started we would do a board meeting all day Thursday. So I was all tired out on Thursday

I had learned to give talks in front of a lot of you, sometimes two to five thousand people. Then the ECK showed me the future again.

night. And then there came this incredibly heavy schedule.

I would go back home and hang on the ropes. I would say, "Well, I'm not down to the mat this round. I wonder if it'll be next round."

SCHEDULE CHANGES

Everything held off very nicely until we could build the Temple of ECK and open it in 1990.

Then in 1991, I had my car accident which was the beginning of cutting back on my outer duties. I took quite a bruising. This broke down and weakened my body. Over the next two years my body wasn't able to fight off the normal things that most people can fight off.

Then with all the travel I was still doing, my body was overwhelmed by parasites. That took a little while to figure out. The parasites weakened certain organs, making me very sensitive to electromagnetic radiation. It meant no more computers, no more TV. I even had to be very careful around electric fans. I expose myself to electromagnetic radiation as little as possible now.

After the car accident, I realized we might have to look into direct satellite transmission.

Back in 1991 the quality wasn't very good. There weren't that many satellites whirling around in space. And the cost was high. But the bottom line was this: I felt that the time wasn't right yet, that we couldn't provide you with the spiritual service that was necessary at the time to make this bridge between the Outer and the Inner Master, between the Living ECK Master and the Mahanta.

The two facets—the Inner and the Outer Master—have always been a part of the ECK teachings

The two facets—the Inner and the Outer Master—have always been a part of the ECK teachings.

ever since 1965 when Paul Twitchell brought out the teachings of Eckankar. But now we're seeing an emphasis on the Mahanta so you become very comfortable with the inner presence of the Holy Spirit as It's showing Itself in this particular way.

Maybe as direct satellite transmission moves out of its infancy, it'll be possible for my talks to be broadcast around the world.

So how many talks? For now, probably one major talk per seminar. In the future, it could be as few as one talk a year. We'll just have to watch how the development of technology goes.

LAW OF LOVE

For me, being here and serving you is a trust. I don't spend a lot of time saying, "Trust me." Because I've learned that when someone says "Trust me" too often, put your hand on your wallet and sit down.

Yes, there is trust in the Mahanta. But again, you always ask, "Is the Inner Master telling me to do something that is constructive and good?" If so, follow the advice.

The Law of Love alone should tell you, Do unto others as you would have them do unto you.

But if the advice tears down or is destructive to you or anyone else in any way, then it's not from the Mahanta. There can be all kinds of impostors that come with the face of the Master, of myself, on the inner. They'll say, "I'm the Master. Just do this." And they'll tell you to do something that is wrong, that is ethically against your own principles that you have been taught as a child and that you have learned as an adult. Don't do those things.

Because the Law of Love alone should tell you, Do unto others as you would have them do unto you.

It's the same message that Christ gave, that other teachers have given in one way or another. It's always the same old message. Why? Because God loves you. God loves you because God made you. And God made all other Souls too. So treat them fairly; treat them justly.

Treating someone justly applies in your daily life. For instance, if you find yourself on jury duty. Nowadays there is a very sick value system in place. It no longer works under God's laws, but under human laws. These laws can go absolutely strange, where people are not anymore acting under the Law of Love. They're acting under the Law of Greed, under the law of Take that if you will, which is basically an eye for an eye. That is the old law: eye for eye, tooth for tooth. The new law is: God is love.

MODERN ECK LEADER

In my first ten years in this position, I traveled a lot. And then, as I mentioned, my health began to go downhill. I realized that the ECK, the Holy Spirit, was using my health to bring about your upliftment and also to bring about the changes It had spoken of back in 1983.

Now some people may say, "I just don't like this emphasis on the Mahanta, the Inner Master, the Dream Master." But then, you have to remember that only recently has the Living ECK Master been able to travel as widely as I have.

Rebazar Tarzs was the Living ECK Master during the Middle Ages. He couldn't travel as freely as I have, yet there were followers of ECK all around the world. These people had a connection with the spiritual teachings through the Inner Master. Rebazar Tarzs came to them as the Mahanta. He came to the Native Americans. He came to the people in Central America, South America, Australia, China, and what

God loves you because God made you. And God made all other Souls too. So treat them fairly; treat them justly. Treating someone justly applies in your daily life.

is now Russia. He was with people all the way across Europe and Africa, because he could do this as the Mahanta, the Inner Master.

Since 1965, you've had an advantage you did not have in past lives. This is being able to see the Outer and the Inner Master together, at one time. And now the ECK has said that there will be fewer outer appearances. Why? Because those of you who have been in Eckankar for many years are now strong enough to help me reach others.

Reach others with what? With the spiritual aid to find a more direct way to the Holy Spirit if they're looking for it.

If a person has come to the end of their path or if they need help on their spiritual path, sometimes the help is as simple as telling them about the ancient name of God, HU.

HU, the Most Beautiful Sound

If a person has come to the end of their path or if they need help on their spiritual path, sometimes the help is as simple as telling them about the ancient name of God, HU. HU, this beautiful sound, this beautiful name of God.

You can tell people about HU whether or not they are in Eckankar. They can be Christians. It can be a mother who's going through labor pains. It can be a person grieving the loss of a loved one.

Sometimes it helps to sing this love song to God, HU.

So tell people about HU. And if the Holy Spirit chooses to reach the individual Soul and bring comfort and love in some way you could not imagine, that's between that Soul and the Holy Spirit.

God's Voice

The Holy Spirit, remember, is the Voice of God.

In the beginning was the Word. This is the Holy Spirit, the Word, the Voice of God. This is why we speak so often about the Holy Spirit, God's voice. God's voice speaks about love. We see this voice on the inner planes and out here as the Light. All different forms of light. We hear it as the Sound. All different forms of sound.

You mix light and sound, and you have the building blocks of creation, the building blocks of the entire material universe. It's all created out of the Light and Sound, because they create energy. The Light and Sound are the primordial forces.

DON'T TAKE LIFE FOR GRANTED

Many people took Paul Twitchell for granted when he was the Living ECK Master from 1965 to 1971. He was always at the seminars. One day I was so lucky as to see him come scooting out the hotel kitchen. I don't know what he was doing back there, probably using passageways where he could move with more freedom. Other times I saw him in crowds. I got to thinking, *Gee whiz, we always see Paul around.* He served his term and moved on, another ECK Master took over, then that ECK Master moved on. It's always in the hands of Divine Spirit.

The wave of life is like a flying carpet. It just flies along, and we go along with it. Sometimes we think our personal troubles are so overwhelming. We forget that there are other people who've gone before us, those who go with us, and those who will come after us. People are always experiencing life and learning more about God's love, whether very directly or indirectly.

It just depends upon the state of consciousness of the individual—how aware they are of what life means, as far as divine creation goes.

Anyone on earth who is living the true way of the

It just depends upon the state of consciousness of the individual—how aware they are of what life means, as far as divine creation goes.

Holy Spirit will always be working with the survival factor. You're going to do anything and everything to survive. Why? Because every moment of life here is precious.

Every moment of life here teaches you something more about God's love.

Earth is a very hard testing ground. There are some Souls that do not want to come back to earth. They put it off, they stall between lifetimes until finally the guardian angel that's working with them says, "OK, you stalled long enough. Time to go." Next thing you know there's another baby crying, and that Soul is now in another human body.

Memories of past lives, and even life between lives, are sometimes fresh in a child of two or younger. Just look in a baby's eyes. A baby will look directly at you, if it wants to. And if it doesn't want to, it won't. But if it wants to, it will look as directly as a Siamese cat. It's just another being studying you and trying to figure out what makes you work. Babies are wondering about their parents, and cats are wondering about their owners.

Memories of past lives, and even life between lives, are sometimes fresh in a child of two or younger.

Soul's Lessons on Love

Soul, at some point, has to come back, no matter how hard life's experiences are here. Because this is an excellent place to learn about God's love. Not just receiving it, but giving it. This is the whole point of any true spiritual teaching, and this is also true of Eckankar: to teach, to show each Soul a balance between giving and receiving love in this life.

That means giving and receiving love, first of all, to your own family. How can you do that?

You, yourself, must first receive the love of God in your own heart and give it back to God. Then, maybe you can love your family and your neighbor. And even your enemy.

Can the chain of events work the other way—can you first learn to love your neighbor or your enemy? No, it doesn't work that way. But sometimes people learn about love by giving to their close ones first, like their spouse. Through their spouse, through their mate, they learn about giving love. Gradually their heart opens to a greater understanding and realization of God's love. Then the love comes back down the other way. And you can even love your enemy.

Health Changes

Briefly I want to mention my health. I was doing very nicely until right before Christmas. I even caught myself going up the stairs two steps at a time. "Better slow down," I'd say. "Let's not have too much of this exuberance."

I had put some tape down in the basement, the kind that leaves this awful sticky mess behind if you try to peel it off. I had a petroleum distillate, which I had used before to remove tape residue. I'd always used it with gloves. But this time I had a life-threatening experience with it. After I used this product, I went into anaphylactic shock. The body just shut down.

My gloves were upstairs. I'd forgotten them, and that night I just said, "No, I don't want another trip up the stairs." So I didn't go get them. I just did the job, cleaned the goo off. Then I came upstairs.

After about twenty-five minutes, it was as if someone had hit me with a hammer. I almost went to my knees. My wife was making dinner. I won't go into the gory details, but for two hours, it was touch and go, trying to stay in the body. I couldn't breathe; my lungs began shutting down.

Through their spouse, through their mate, they learn about giving love. Gradually their heart opens to a greater understanding and realization of God's love.

This went on for two hours.

At the end of the first two hours, I thought maybe I would survive. When it was nearly over, I asked the ECK, "Is this all?" It's very concise. It said, "Nearly." I was very beat up, very weak. My heart and lungs weren't working the way they were supposed to. I still had a difficult time breathing.

I asked the ECK, "Will the second attack be as bad as the first?" It said, "Nearly." And it was.

It went on for half an hour. Slowly it passed, and I went to bed. Oddly enough I slept well that entire night. But my body's organs got weaker and weaker. For the last three months, I've been having a real hard time going up and down stairs again.

Building Strength Back

No matter how good your doctor is, the responsibility for your health is still in your own hands.

I'm having to work on restoring all my organs that were damaged. My heart is doing pretty well now, but the organs play leapfrog: when the heart is ahead, then the lungs are behind. Then the spleen, then the pancreas. It sounds like you're a parts factory.

Step-by-step I'm getting better.

But I will not rely on some of the chemical products I have in the past. I have a new respect, caution, and knowledge of what some of these things can do to the body over the long haul.

You may be able to learn from what I've learned about doctors and healing. No matter how good your doctor is, the responsibility for your health is still in your own hands. If the doctor gives you a prescription, says, "Take this," and you take it but you have a reaction, it is your responsibility to call the doctor and ask what is happening. Give the doctor a chance to change his or her mind. The responsibility is half yours.

SPIRITUAL CAT

Misha is a Siamese cat who belongs to Kristy down in Texas. One day Misha had an eye infection, so they went to the vet and came home with herbal eyedrops to use. Kristy tried to put the drops in Misha's eye, but the cat would fight and fight.

Kristy called the vet. "I think you'd better give me another kind of eye treatment; the cat does not like these drops." She brought Misha in again, and the vet said, "Yeah, the cat needs something else." He gave Kristy a cortisone eye cream. She tried to put it in the cat's eyes, and Misha fought worse than ever.

So Kristy put the cortisone cream away. When she went back later to get the tube and again try to put this eye treatment in the cat's eye, the tube was gone. Where did the tube of cortisone cream go? She looked all over, and she finally found it hidden in a corner with tooth marks all through it. The cat had punctured the entire tube.

Sometimes our animals and pets have a higher state of consciousness than some humans.

Kristy called the vet again. He said, "I think we better check this over one more time."When Kristy brought Misha in, the vet said, "Yes, I've got to change the prescription." Then he said, "This is the first time I've had one of my patients tell me in no uncertain terms to change the prescription."

Some people wonder, Is there a Soul in a cat? Sometimes our animals and pets have a higher state of consciousness than some humans.

MATURING SPIRITUALLY

When the news first came to the Washington, D.C., ECKists that I might not be at the seminar in person, an ECKist named Doug was in charge of telling the other ECKists and the media. He talked to each person, and they all said, "That's OK. Harold should take care of his health if he needs to. We can take care of things."

Doug wrote me about a realization, an understanding he had about the Inner Master that came to him from this experience.

He wrote: "Over the years, I remember reading in the ECK works that 90 percent of our spiritual experience is with the Inner Master, and 10 percent with the Outer Master. If the few ECKists I talked to are representative of the whole, then perhaps as a religion we have matured to where we now rely on the Inner Master and are not dependent on the Outer Master for our spiritual survival. This has always been a goal, and maybe now we are realizing this. I see it as a great step."

Learn to go inside yourself, because this is the source of all truth.

Most Sacred

He pointed out a very important principle: Learn to go inside yourself, because this is the source of all truth. There are a lot of holy temples out here, but the most sacred of all is the temple inside you, because this is where you meet with the Holy Spirit.

How do you meet with the Holy Spirit?

If you're in Christianity, you pray. You come to the holy temple, to the holy of holies, through prayer. You meet on holy ground with your God. If you're a member of any other religion, you have a means of going to that holy of holies, whether it's meditation or contemplation or prayer.

Go to the holy of holies. It's the temple inside you. This is the place where all truth comes from. Before there were words, before there was a written Bible or a printed Gutenberg Bible, before there was

Luther's translation, there was the Word in the heart of mankind.

This is the temple. Go there. The Spiritual Exercises of ECK can show you how.

This is the temple. Go there. The Spiritual Exercises of ECK can show you how.

DISCOURSE ON THE INNER PLANES

Robert, a retired minister from California, became a member of Eckankar about a year ago. Shortly after he began studying the *ECK Dream 1 Discourses*, he had an experience with the Mahanta, the Inner Master.

Before he went to bed at night, he read his discourse, shut his eyes, and didn't think anything more of it. He had to be up the next morning at four o'clock to go to work. But at one-thirty in the morning, he woke up and couldn't get back to sleep. Finally he dropped off to sleep and had a vivid dream.

In the dream a woman came to him, "I'm Harold Klemp's wife," she said. "I want to welcome you to Eckankar. My husband will help you anytime and in any way he can."

Then, as the Inner Master, Harold Klemp walked into the room. The woman said, "I want to introduce you to my husband." The Mahanta said, "Yes, I will help you in any way I can." But he also left Robert with the very strong impression: "I will help you only if you want the help. I will not intrude in your space in any way, because to do so would be to lose my own freedom."

Any person who is any distance along on the spiritual path will not try to hold another, either to his path or his belief. Because chains on another person are chains on yourself.

Then the Mahanta said to Robert, "I'm going to whisper your secret word to you."

This secret
word is a
personal word
that the
Mahanta will
give to
members of
Eckankar, to
give you a
closer link with
the Holy Spirit.

This secret word is a personal word that the Mahanta will give to members of Eckankar, to give you a closer link with the Holy Spirit. It attunes you to the Holy Spirit, at that state of consciousness which you are in.

Robert couldn't go back to sleep, and he was concerned. He had to be up at four o'clock in the morning. He needed the sleep. So he just shut his eyes. Suddenly there was the ECK Master Rebazar Tarzs, and he and Robert greeted each other like old friends. They hugged each other, and Rebazar said, "I've been working with you and with your wife." Robert couldn't believe it. "This sort of stuff happens to other people, not to me," he said. Rebazar Tarzs stayed for two hours until the ECKist had to get up at four o'clock in the morning and go to work.

For the next two weeks, Robert would think back to this meeting with Rebazar Tarzs in a waking state. He hadn't been asleep. He had been awake. Rebazar was there in the Soul body. And Robert would just laugh and say, "It's true. It's true what the ECK Masters and what the Mahanta, the Living ECK Master have said. It's true."

The Mahanta, the Living ECK Master and the other ECK Masters work with those of you who have an agreement with the Holy Spirit along the lines of the teachings of ECK.

Help in Everyday Life

A couple had just bought a new home; the movers were coming on Saturday. On Thursday, the wife called up the movers to confirm. "We're still on for Saturday?" she asked. The people said, "Yes, you're still on for Saturday. We'll bring the truck and two people to help you."

On Saturday, she confirmed again in the morning. The company said, "Yeah, the movers will be out there." So she and her husband sat in their home, surrounded by boxes, waiting. When it got to be twelve-thirty and nobody had come, the woman called the moving company again. The voice-mail recording said, "We close at noon on Saturday." They waited until 1:30. Nobody came.

She asked the Mahanta, "Is this all going to work out OK?" And the Mahanta said, "Trust. Everything will be OK."

She began to look around and finally found the Yellow Pages. She started calling around. It was Saturday at three o'clock in the afternoon, not a great time to be finding movers. The first two places she called didn't exactly laugh, but there was nobody to help her.

The third call was the charm. On the third ring, somebody picked up the phone and yelled to somebody else in the back room, "Hey, do you want to do another job?" The voice in the back said, "OK." Fifteen minutes later, two movers arrived with their truck. They moved everything very professionally, and they were cheerful. It was late Saturday afternoon, and they were cheerful.

How Guidance Works

When the other office opened, she talked with them, and they apologized. They even let the couple keep the moving boxes without a charge.

The woman realized that when her plans for Saturday went wrong, she could have become very upset at the first group of movers. But she would've shut down this love channel inside herself. She would have shut off this help from the Inner Master, the

The woman realized that when her plans for Saturday went wrong, she could have become very upset at the first group of movers. But she would've shut down this love channel inside herself.

Mahanta. So she kept it open. She didn't just trust to chance that somehow everything would take care of itself; she got the Yellow Pages and started calling. She didn't stop on the first or second call. She went on to the third.

That's how it works with the Inner Master. You ask for guidance and direction, but then you do what you have to do. Same as with your health care—it's 50 percent your responsibility. Fifty percent is with the Inner Master, and 50 percent is with you.

You ask for guidance and direction, but then you do what you have to do.

Why Go to an ECK Seminar?

Why go to an ECK seminar if the Living ECK Master isn't going to be there?

Duke Ellington, the jazz musician, and Billy Strayhorn, a young pianist-composer, made a wonderful team in the jazz world. There was an article in the *Economist*, the British publication, on them.

These two people worked together very easily through their whole life, without a contract. They always got along. Duke Ellington took care of the bills that Billy Strayhorn had. And Billy Strayhorn was an extremely talented pianist-composer. Together they formed something greater than themselves. Together they were able to inspire many jazz musicians who came after them.

I'm pointing out this connection because those of you who are longtime members of Eckankar are like Duke Ellington. You're the ones who've been here before. The people who are newly coming into Eckankar are like Billy Strayhorn. You're new. You have all this divine creativity inside yourself. But together, you will create something that is so much more than if you would just work at this yourself.

This is why I say to the long-term members of Eckankar: Meet the people who are new to Eckankar. Listen to them. See what they bring to the path of ECK. And to the new people: Gain from the experience of those who have been here before you.

The *Economist* article said, "The individuality of jazz musicians may yield its most magnificent rewards in likeminded and committed company." This is true in all creative fields, including the spiritual.

I hope, in some way, you will make a direct connection with the Mahanta—even as the new member of Eckankar did earlier when she was told in the dream state that I would not be here in the physical body, but that I would be here as the Mahanta. Maybe you will make a connection this stark and strong. But perhaps not. There are many of you who never have and never will, because you don't need that strong a connection.

I would like to leave you with the blessing of the Vairagi order: May the blessings be.

This is true in all creative fields, including the spiritual.

ECK Springtime Seminar, Washington, D.C., Saturday, March 29, 1997

The window of heaven is what all truth seekers are trying to open.

6

THE WINDOW OF HEAVEN—YOUR ECK INITIATION

he window of heaven is what all truth seekers are trying to open.

It's like a window in Minnesota. After a long, hard winter, it feels good to throw open that window and let the spring breeze and the sounds of the birds come in. It's a way of saying hello to a good time of the year and also good-bye to a hard time.

In *The Shariyat-Ki-Sugmad*, Book Two, Lai Tsi, the Chinese ECK Master, speaks about what people expect in this world. He says, "Man seeks too much the gold and silver of the world when he should be seeking the Window of Heaven through which, when opened, all the treasures that he believed were possible will now come pouring to him."

He lists the treasures of Soul, and he counts among them peace, contentment, and happiness which come with the opening of the Window of Heaven.

The window of heaven is what all truth seekers are trying to open.

Lai Tsi goes on to say, "The object of the ECKist, therefore, is peace and wisdom which come from seeking the highest through selflessness." Seeking the highest through selflessness. Very simply, it means that the first shall be last, and the last shall be first, which is from the Christian Bible and which is one of those truths that stands the test of time.

Making the Connection

How many years does it take some people to become members of ECK? Sometimes we are surrounded by family and friends who are members of ECK. Other times we find ourselves alone in a remote part of the world, and there is no one else who has ever heard about the ECK teachings. But whatever happens, somewhere there is a connection.

At some point, the word comes to us. Then we say, "OK, these are the teachings I would like to look into. This is what I'd like to explore."

The connection with ECK may come in any number of ways. It can come from a friend or a stranger who is traveling through. Often somebody gets a message in the dream state. One night somebody will say, "You need to find out about the teachings of ECK." Then the person looks for two more years, wondering, "What is ECK?"

Sometimes people are introduced to HU, this love song to God, and they wonder, *What is HU?*

They don't know the power of the name or the presence of ECK, the Holy Spirit. The Holy Spirit, the Holy Ghost, or Divine Spirit—it doesn't make any difference what people call It. We call It the ECK, which in ancient Sanskrit means *one*, the Source.

One woman who found ECK in her own way, was a member of a large family. Her sister and two broth-

The Holy Spirit, the Holy Ghost, or Divine Spirit—it doesn't make any difference what people call It. We call It the ECK.

ers were already members of ECK for a number of years, and everything was going along very well for her. She had her belief, they had theirs. Then suddenly life became very hard for her and her husband. They'd been married eighteen years. He lost a number of jobs, and there were personal problems in the family. But all this trouble brought the couple closer together.

The woman felt that changes were coming; life was good, she had a good job, her marital life had straightened out. Things had settled down, but she felt as though there was a turning point coming. So she went to visit her sister, who was an ECKist.

Just before she left she saw *The Wind of Change* in her sister's library. She asked if she could borrow it.

This woman had a great interest in dreams. For years she recorded her dreams, trying to understand the message that the Holy Spirit or some secret power was trying to send to her. In other words, she was trying to unravel her dreams.

For years she recorded her dreams, trying to understand the message that the Holy Spirit or some secret power was trying to send to her.

LET'S SING HU

She took *The Wind of Change* home, thinking it would give her an insight into some of the changes that had taken place in her life, her husband losing his jobs and everything else. Maybe she would get some sort of understanding.

The following Monday, she went back to work and asked around the office, "Hey, have you heard any news about job changes going on?" Nobody knew anything. But three days later, the personnel officer walked into her office, put a whole bunch of papers down on the desk in front of her, and said, "Do you understand these?" She saw they were her termination notice; that was the end of her employment. He asked her to sign the papers and then clean out her desk. Within fifteen minutes, she was out in the parking lot.

You'd think something like this would destroy a person, but she had a pretty firm foundation by this time. She believed that no matter what happened in her life, she was a very lucky woman because she had the support and love of her friends and family. So she went home.

For the next seven days the woman thought about all these changes that were now coming up in her life. The spiritual path had become much more a focus in her mind. She called up her sister, the ECKist, and said, "Can we get together sometime? I'd like to talk some things over." Her sister said, "Sure, I'll be over." Pretty soon they were talking, and her sister said, "All right, let's sing HU." And so they sang HU.

After her sister left, this woman sat down and sang the HU song again very softly because she wanted to see the Light of God. But nothing happened.

Soul Travel simply means being able to move into another state of consciousness.

That night she went to bed, and she had a dream. In the dream, this slim man with brown hair and glasses came to her, and he showed her how to Soul Travel. Soul Travel simply means being able to move into another state of consciousness. She was in a very awake dream.

Soul Travel Dream

The woman found herself in another world with this person. She saw structures, buildings, and people. She felt light and very happy. This is one of the marks of a spiritual experience: when it happens to you, you feel light and good and happy. If it's the wrong sort of experience—where it is based on power or control rather than love—you're going to come out of it feel-ing down. You're going to feel blue; you're going to feel bad.

The woman saw her daughter asleep on a bed. Being in the Soul body, the mother figured, *I'm going to go into her body. Why not? After all, I'm her mother. I carried her in my womb for nine months when she was a fetus; I have the right.*

There's a saying that an infinite number of Souls can dance on the head of a pin. It's true, because Soul does not occupy space. That's how she was able to move into the physical form of her daughter. But as soon as she moved in, she came bounding back out.

Somebody had kicked her out. I wonder who.

She came back to consciousness after landing hard on earth again. There at a table sat this man with the glasses and the brown hair, seated behind a large book. It was called the Book of Rules.

He pointed to the book and said to her, "Read this passage."

The woman grew up speaking French. It seemed to her that if anything was in writing on the inner planes in her dream state, it would be in French, wouldn't it? This book was in English, but she could read it, so she read the rule.

The rule said she could not invade anyone's body unless she had their *written* permission.

She suddenly felt bad; the light, happy feeling was gone. She had a feeling of disappointment in herself. She knew that her daughter was very angry with her. But she also knew that the man in the glasses would be there to work with her and teach her whatever she needed to know. She now had this desire to learn the spiritual laws, which lead each person to freedom.

She now had this desire to learn the spiritual laws, which lead each person to freedom.

SPIRITUAL LAWS

One of the rules of the spiritual world is that you cannot take away someone else's freedom and expect to have freedom for yourself.

Some people would call this a selfish motive; you want to give others freedom so that you can have it for yourself. Well, yes. That's how it is. Because the Book of Rules, or the spiritual law, is very exacting. The spiritual laws are based on the Law of Love. They do not punish for the mere pleasure of inflicting pain. They do it to teach people a spiritual lesson, which is part of their entire education. A little here, a little there; a little arithmetic, a little bit of language and geography. All the aspects of a spiritual nature. So that one day Soul can become a Co-worker with God.

This is the whole purpose of Soul studying the teachings of ECK: to become a Co-worker with God. To serve life out of love, because of gratitude for the gift of life.

This is the whole purpose of Soul studying the teachings of ECK: to become a Co-worker with God. To serve life out of love, because of gratitude for the gift of life.

This is hard to do. Often when people become independent, the last thing they want to do is serve anyone else. They're so busy serving themselves. If you'd mention this to them, they would become very upset. They can never see themselves.

But before someone comes to Eckankar, life usually becomes very hard. It teaches one humility.

GET THE BEST OUT OF LIFE

I was reading a book this week: *Make It Last* by Earl Proulx. He writes a column for *Yankee* magazine. *Make It Last* is very informative. I like how-to books—how to do something better around the home. He's got ways to make engines run longer, how to break in a car engine, how to plant your garden better. It's the sort of thing that makes some people go to sleep, but I love it. He had a good piece of advice for campers. He said, "Never try to light a stove inside a tent or any enclosed area."

He then explains that you're dealing with flammable gases and fluids, and if they explode, it could create a fireball many times bigger than the tent. As I read this, I was thinking, *There's a story behind this bit of advice.* But he doesn't say a word except, "Don't ask how we know."

Don't ask how we know. I think this is the case for many of you too. Before you come to ECK, and when you're in ECK, you get beat around so much by life because it's the purpose of this world to beat Soul around until It learns humility. Life takes away strength, it takes away youth, and it gives back frailty and old age. And if this doesn't make one humble, nothing will.

Life has ways to insure that people learn humility.

Life has ways to insure that people learn humility. Because how can you truly serve anyone—whether it's yourself, your family, your neighbor, or God—unless there is humility?

LIBERATION VIA INITIATION

In *The Shariyat-Ki-Sugmad,* Book Two, there is a comparison of the ECK initiations versus ordinary ways of liberation, including baptism.

Initiations existed long before John the Baptist baptized Jesus some two thousand years ago. The Essenes were one of the groups that John the Baptist was connected with, and they practiced baptism. They were also connected with the Far East and the rights of initiation. But whether it's baptism or initiation, the rite is a sacred one, to purify Soul.

Sometimes, as with baptism, there is no merit involved except to be born into a Christian family that believes in baptism. An infant is baptized right away to insure that they go to heaven in the event of a catastrophe. Other times, people come to church late in life and they get baptized as adults.

In ECK, too, we have people who receive the Second Initiation after several years of study of the ECK works, and the members of their family—infants and everyone else—may also receive the Second Initiation. So in that regard we're alike.

I would like to read from *The Shariyat-Ki-Sugmad*: "All the ways of liberation offered by the various orthodox religions generally must take Soul through the endless cycle of reincarnation until It becomes awakened to Its true self. But ECK [the path of ECK] gives the chela [the spiritual student] a concise way which is not known in any other path to God. Once the chela steps onto the path of Eckankar, his karma begins to resolve and his reincarnations become fewer. When he is initiated, it means that never again will he have to return to this physical and material world."

Your State of Consciousness

I would like to explain the term *state of consciousness*. In Eckankar we use it so freely that sometimes it becomes a buzzword, or jargon. We use terms like *ECK, Sugmad*, and so on. We're pretty much like lawyers talking legalese, and the client has no idea whatsoever what they're talking about. Lawyers have their own language, and people in a religion have their own language.

A state of consciousness is a state of acceptance.

A state of consciousness is a state of acceptance.

This means that someone who has a very open state of consciousness is able to accept more of what life has to offer—not just the hardships, but also the blessings and love that come to each individual.

Love is a very hard thing to deal with. Most people don't think so. They think that love just is one of those things, a buzzword just as much as *state of consciousness.*

To love truly means not just to give love, but also to accept it. Many people who are able—finally—to give love, cannot accept it. They're always giving people stuff. But as soon as people try to give something back, they refuse the gift. Other people are always accepting, and they do not have the capacity to give love.

Then there are the rare people who have the ability to do both—both to graciously receive love from those who love them and also to give it back in turn. For people who aren't used to it, this is much harder than it sounds.

To love truly means not just to give love, but also to accept it.

ACCEPTING HEALING

Most people have pain because they have unconsciously broken a spiritual law at some time in the past.

This completely wipes out the excuse of the victim consciousness. Just think, if this law were understood, it would change our society. It would end victim lawsuits and put a whole class of people out of work.

State of consciousness equals state of acceptance.

What does this mean in terms of health, for instance? Some person will go to a certain doctor. They'll swear by this person. They'll say, "This is the finest doctor on earth." Someone else will go to the same doctor and say, "This guy is straight out of the trees. I don't know where he learned his practice.

What's he doing to us?" Why do two different people have two opposite points of view about the same healer?

Simply because there are two different states of consciousness, two different states of acceptance. A healer cannot heal unless the power is given from somewhere else.

Drugs can do a lot and surgery can do a lot, but sometimes the health problem comes back. What does that mean? That five years is the success rate on surgery? Or when another healer does something and it doesn't work at all, is this a failure? Sometimes healers try to take too much credit for the healing that comes or the methods that they use for healing. They always count the wins and never the losses.

Another thing about the state of consciousness equaling the state of acceptance: Go to someone who's been through it. This is why the Living ECK Master goes through many of his health challenges. So that people can see he's been through the mud. If they have hard times, they know he understands, he's been there.

If you want to go to a marriage counselor, it would probably be a good idea to go to someone who's happily married. A young couple had gone to a counselor at a university where they had free counseling. The couple could go there at very low cost, which they thought was a good idea. The counselor sat in the room with them, asking questions, digging into their background, finding out how each had been a dog to the other and the other was a cat to the other, having a good time. Behind a mirror—and the couple knew this—other people in the field of psychology were studying them.

Later I asked them, "You let these people tinker

This is why the Living ECK Master goes through many of his health challenges.

with your marital life? Did you ask any questions?"

If you go to get financial advice, wouldn't you ask the adviser, "How's your own fund doing?" Would you just say, "He's a fund adviser, and I'm going to put my life savings in his fund"? Wouldn't you ask some questions?

I like to know where the doctor is coming from. I ask tough questions of my own doctors.

GETTING PAST THE PAST

Some people don't heal because they hang on to the past. We all know of people who have hung on to a failed relationship for half a century.

People who've hung on to an old problem for years and years would be the last to admit this: it has become an excuse for them. More than that, it's become a way to control other people. They say, "I'm a failure because of this unhappy event in my past. I'm a victim. If this hadn't happened to me all those years ago, things would be different."

This is somebody who is not facing reality.

The unhappy experience, whether it's losing a job or getting a divorce, happened a long time ago. Life goes on.

Life goes on, but the mind is a peculiar thing with its memory. The memory throws out anchors to that time in life. People hang on to that time, happy as can be in their pain and misery. And this is always used as a club over the heads of other people.

A mother will say, "I gave my life for you, my child, so that you could go to college." Or a father will say, "Be grateful, my child. I suffered for you. I walked all those many blocks in the hot July sun, changing the generator on my car over the July 4 weekend so

Some people don't heal because they hang on to the past.

that I could get to work next week so there would be money so that you would have food. You ungrateful thing."

We're very good at it. We've all got our buttons.

Self-Responsibility

An initiation into ECK is an opportunity to go to a higher plane or heaven in the next life, but also here. It's an opportunity, but it's not a guarantee.

Self-responsibility comes with the ECK initiations. An initiation into ECK is an opportunity to go to a higher plane or heaven in the next life, but also here. It's an opportunity, but it's not a guarantee. It depends upon how a person learns to apply this spiritual principle in this life.

If these lessons are not learned, it could mean a stay somewhere else in the physical or astral universes. An ECK initiation like the Second Initiation usually—but not always—means one will not have to return to earth in a later lifetime. But this is true only if certain spiritual lessons, such as love and compassion, are learned and the individual moves forward in his spiritual life.

Love and discipline are keys to spiritual success. This means that the ECK initiations can open people more to divine love.

On the news the other day a report said that love of pets can lower blood pressure. A study was done of some women who kept dogs because they were pet lovers. Others kept dogs for protection. Researchers found that people who kept dogs for love had lower blood pressure. If people kept a dog for protection, their blood pressure wasn't affected either way.

Do It for Love

A seven-year-old boy lives in our neighborhood. He shoots baskets with unfailing discipline. There are two baskets: the low one his dad put up for the little kids, and the high basket for the dad and for the kids who want to try to outreach their reach. What's a heaven for?

The boy is about two-and-a-half times taller than the basketball, maybe three times. One day he was out with his basketball. He'd make a shot and then back up. He was hitting 50 percent. He kept backing up until he was about fifteen feet from the hoop, which is a long, long ways. I couldn't understand how he could throw the ball that far, even to the post, much less through the basket ten feet off the ground. But he was doing it because he loved to.

This is how we need to learn to go about living: to do it for love or don't do it at all.

If you're doing something that is not for love, find out what's the matter—either within yourself or with what you're doing—and change it. But do it gradually; make smooth transitions, like shifting gears in a car. If you're driving along in first gear, you can put it into third gear and the engine will strain, but it will move. But if you're moving slowly in first gear and you jam that thing into reverse, you're going to find all kinds of shiny little bits of metal lying underneath your car, and the car won't run.

If you're doing something that is not for love, find out what's the matter— either within yourself or with what you're doing—and change it.

RULES OF DIVINE LOVE

In our society today, parents forget to discipline their children because they do not understand divine love. Divine love recognizes the rule that you do not invade another person's property without their permission.

On a ballfield there are rules and boundary lines. If you're playing a game of softball or baseball in a field where nothing is marked—the batter's box isn't marked, the pitcher's mound isn't marked, first base, second, third base isn't marked—you can still do OK. You can estimate the distance to first base and say, "We'll use that tree as a boundary." But you're still using a boundary.

If you follow the spiritual law, if you hit within bounds, you advance.

If the ball falls fair and nobody catches it, you have a chance to go to a base, to advance. The same thing happens spiritually. If you follow the spiritual law, if you hit within bounds, you advance.

But what if you hit a pop-up, a blooper, and someone catches it—meaning someone catches a blooper of yours at work? Maybe you have a bad reaction to it. Instead of saying, "Oh, thank you for showing me that; I'll try to do better," you carry a grudge. You say, "What right has that person to come in here and tell me that? They make mistakes too." Or what if you hit a ball completely out of bounds and then you try to run around the bases anyway? You're not going to be playing the game right, and nobody will play with you. You're going to find out that you're all by yourself. You're one of those loners in society.

A lot of parents try to teach their children how to grow up without putting boundary lines down on the ground.

Basketball courts have lines. Football fields have lines. Highways have lines. Everything has lines. But some people will not draw lines with their children. Then they wonder, *Why is the crime rate so high? Why are drugs rampant in our society?*

Some states are trying to enact laws that will let a government official come into the home whenever anyone reports that a child has been spanked in that home. It's true that there are abuses in homes, but many more abuses occur in government agencies that are taking care of veterans and other places.

And just because a child is spanked does not mean that this is some criminal act. Sometimes it's good to spank a child. All the generations that have made it up to my generation got spankings. I know I gave some. There's a way to do it correctly.

Some parents don't understand this; they're all full of gushy love, which they mistake for divine love. But it's without boundaries. Their children grow up not knowing boundaries, not knowing where other people's freedom starts, where other people's property begins. You don't go there unless you have their permission. That's how it works.

Many people today don't understand that, because they don't understand the spiritual law. You cannot go into another person's space without that person's permission.

You may say, "My space is the whole world."

Not so fast! Your freedom ends where another person's begins.

Your freedom ends where another person's begins.

This is hard to deal with. The more crowded earth becomes, the more crowded a country becomes, the more crowded a workplace becomes, or the more crowded a cabin becomes, the more likely it is that there will be hard feelings. Suddenly the freedom or space of one person gets dangerously close to the private space of another person.

THE LAW OF LOVE

People need people. We are here to work these things out. It's part of this world; it's part of the spiritual life. There is no victim. There's a lot of victim consciousness, but there is no victim.

Everyone earns what he gets. Like it or not, that is the Law of Love.

The Law of Love helps soften the hardened heart. Often there's no harder heart than that of a victim to some facet of life. It's hard like a walnut shell. And how do you get through? Divine Spirit will. It takes strength and youth and returns weakness and old age. It takes power and trades it for weakness. It takes freedom and gives back slavery.

How does love show up?

The Window of Heaven—the ECK initiation. Your initiation carries a great responsibility, but it also gives the ability to open your heart to life around you and to all of God's creatures.

Your initiation carries a great responsibility, but it also gives the ability to open your heart to life around you and to all of God's creatures.

THE BOY AND HIS FOUR CHICKENS

A mother wrote to me about her young son and his four pet chickens. Her seven-year-old son is a very gentle-hearted Soul. He has four chickens; he named them as they grew up, and he looks for ways to make them happy.

The name of one chicken is Smart Chicken. Another chicken is named First Flyer. And there's Brownie and Speckled Hen. The hens like this boy; they're very tolerant of his affection. So sometimes he will give them a treat. He takes his little tricycle, hooks his little wagon to the back of it, puts his little sister in the wagon with one chicken, and gives them a ride. Speckled Hen rides on the handlebars. That's her special place.

When the boy began school, the chickens missed him. They would go over to the tricycle, look up at the handlebars, and couldn't wait until he got home again so that he would give them a ride.

The same family also had a duck named Big Wig. It was a white duck with an iridescent purple and green head. But at the top of his head, cocked off to one side, was a white feather. Quite a dashing figure, this duck. And he knew it. He knew he was a handsome one. But one day he began to molt, to lose his feathers. They fell all over the yard. The duck got very upset.

Sparrows and swallows were taking his beautiful feathers to build their nests. This made Big Wig very angry. He ran back and forth across the yard, stretching out his neck and making an awful racket to drive away these thieves who were taking his feathers.

This duck was very much like us people. He was hanging on to something he could no longer use.

CHANGE IS OPPORTUNITY

There have been changes in the ECK program over the years, because the ECK, or Holy Spirit, is change. Everything is always changing. In the past you've been used to having me talk three times at the ECK seminars, and many of you saw me in private meetings. But for now, the ECK has changed the rules. The boundaries have changed.

It is putting more responsibility on your shoulders—you, the initiates of ECK. It's giving you an opportunity to help with serving God here on earth, serving your fellow creatures.

Unless you can love yourself first, you cannot love your neighbor.

And of course, this service must first begin by loving yourself and loving your family as you love God. Unless you can love yourself first, you cannot love your neighbor. That's why Christ said, "Love your neighbor as yourself." As yourself. In other words, get a better opinion of yourself. Not the ego, not what a great person you are with that white feather in your hat, but because you are Soul. And so is everyone else.

We're all creations of God, and for this reason, each Soul deserves the highest respect you can give.

We give the warm love to those who are close to us, to our family and close friends. We give goodwill, or what Paul the Apostle called charity, to other people. A human being simply does not have the capacity to give warm love to everyone. There is only so much warm love to go around. Reserve that for your family and loved ones.

OPEN THE WINDOW OF HEAVEN

Your ECK initiation can open the window of heaven. Your state of consciousness means nothing more than your state of acceptance.

The First Initiation comes in the dream state, privately, just to you when you're sound asleep. It opens your ability to accept God's love. The Second Initiation expands your state of acceptance more. Each initiation increases your ability to accept the blessings of life.

Each initiation increases your ability to accept the blessings of life. Love and discipline are keys to spiritual success.

Love and discipline are keys to spiritual success. Parents must teach their children the old precepts that are found in the Bible, that we teach in ECK, and that are taught in every major religious teaching. These different laws boil down to: Love God because God loves you. Love each other because God made you all. This is it.

If you truly love someone else, if you truly love yourself, and if you truly love God, you will treat all within this arena with respect. How could it be any different?

Each person will, in his own time, find the path that is right for him. And it may be many, many paths before he comes to the teachings of ECK. This is as it should be, as it must be, because God has made a path for every state of consciousness. There is a religion, a belief, or a lack of belief for every person on earth.

So as you journey home, remember that I am with you.

ECK Summer Festival, Anaheim, California,
Saturday, June 14, 1997

When people have a chance to tell their stories about how they find ECK, it gives them a chance to grow, but it also gives other people the same chance.

7

A New Face on Old Truths

After you've been in ECK—or on any path—for a length of time, the old truths get to be so familiar they're sometimes hard to remember. You've heard them, maybe you even memorized them. Yet it's hard to live them because they've become commonplace, like an old hat or tie or dress.

I've selected certain stories that each illustrate an ECK principle that is actually an old truth—an old truth that you've all known, you've all heard, and you've all gone to sleep over.

A new face on an old truth: Seek and you will find.

Seek and You Will Find

A new face on an old truth: Seek and you will find.

A young man in Africa was twenty-two, and he had all kinds of financial problems. He also had a serious health problem: his eyesight was failing. His relatives thought he was a handsome and a clever young man, but he was poor. His father was ill and his family didn't have much money either. The young man was very concerned about becoming a burden to other people. So he offered up a prayer to God.

He said, "God, please take me from this vale of tears. I have had as much as I can take of this physical world." He prayed that every night.

One night he was taken out of the body, perhaps in a similar way as Paul, the apostle, who said he was caught up even unto the third heaven. The young man fell asleep on his bed, and the next thing he knew, he was in another world. It was a very beautiful place. The temperature was just right, and there was an enormous amount of light. Everything had a clarity and a refreshing goodness about it that was filled with love and compassion. "I like this place," he said. "I would like to stay here."

There was a hut nearby, and two men stepped out of it. One of the men had a thick, black beard. Much later, after this experience, the young man would recognize this person as the ECK Master Rebazar Tarzs. But at the time he had no idea who this man was or where he was.

The man with the black beard said to him, "Why are you here?"

The young African said, "I'm here because I'm sick of earth and this is a nice place. I think I'd like to stay here with you." He explained his prayer to God. He said, "I've been praying to God to get me away from earth, and it looks as if it's worked. I think I'd like to stay."

As he looked around at the clear blue sky, he happened to notice a light coming from the little hut. It was a blue light, but it didn't seem to be coming from a single source. It seemed to be emanating from everywhere at once. He didn't know this was the Light of God, often known as the Blue Light of the Mahanta.

The man with the black beard said to him, "You can't stay. You have to go back."

One of the men had a thick, black beard. Much later, after this experience, the young man would recognize this person as the ECK Master Rebazar Tarzs.

The young man said, "No, I won't go back. I shall stay." He went through all his reasons again of why he wanted to stay in this place of love and beauty.

The ECK Master told him, "It's impossible because you haven't finished your mission on earth."

The young man said, "That may be, but I'm not going back."

The ECK Master came over to him very kindly and took hold of his hand, and the next thing the young man knew, he was back in his room waking up. He sat up in his bed, and he said, "What was that?"

He had become the seeker.

GOING TO HEAVEN

It's a curious thing: people who have an easy life, a good life with everything coming to them without much effort, trouble, or travail, really have very little need to look for God or truth.

Sometimes the blue light is connected with the Mental Plane. The Mental Plane is the equivalent of the third heaven. Heaven has different layers. But the only reference to this in the Bible is the statement by Paul about a third heaven. This presupposes heavens one and two; and who's to say not four and five?

This young African went to his priest and began asking questions. He wanted to know what this experience meant. Where was this place of love and beauty? While he was there in this other world, Rebazar Tarzs had asked him, "Do you know where you are?"

The young man did not have a clue. He simply said, "I don't care. It's a good place. I think I'll stay."

The priest had no answer as to where this place was or what it meant. But the experience gave the

The Mental Plane is the equivalent of the third heaven. Heaven has different layers.

young man hope. He no longer prayed to God to remove him from this physical world because of all his hardships. He didn't know what his mission was yet, but he did know that he hadn't completed it. So he began a search, and in time he came across some ECK books and began reading them.

In one of the ECK books he found a picture of the ECK Master Rebazar Tarzs. The young seeker recognized him immediately as the man who had met him outside the little hut in the other worlds.

*A new face on
an old truth:
Learn to listen,
listen to learn.*

LEARN TO LISTEN, LISTEN TO LEARN

A new face on an old truth: Learn to listen, listen to learn.

Some people are very good at listening, and others are not. I'd have to classify myself among the people who are not very good listeners. I would like to be, I'd like to pride myself on the fact that I am, and I can be a good listener at times. But my instinct, since youth, has been to talk.

One of the ECKists is working on the "Past Lives, Dreams, and Soul Travel" workshops, and she listens to the Inner Master, to the Mahanta.

She's helping to prepare these workshops so they will give the most benefit to people who come to them. So she listens very carefully. She takes the outline of the workshop and puts it under her pillow. Then she asks the Mahanta to help her during the dream state to distill all the information down to something better, something clearer, something that people can use for their own spiritual unfoldment.

One night in a dream, the Mahanta looked at her and said, "Well, what do you think I have to do?"

She had been thinking that it must be very easy for the Mahanta, the Living ECK Master to distill truth. But she realized that he also has to condense everything down very tightly. Giving one talk at a seminar instead of three means boiling the information as tightly as possible—to give the best possible help to anyone who's looking for spiritual help.

The woman went to an ECK book discussion class; two of her friends were conducting it. This ECKist sat very quietly and observed, listened, and watched.

Remember, the principle is to learn to listen, and listen to learn. So she listened, and she watched. She noticed that the two people who were in charge of this discussion class spoke very little. They would ask a few good questions, and then they would listen to the attendees. There was a remarkable amount of participation because the people had a chance to tell their own story about what the ECK, or the Holy Spirit, had done in their lives.

She realized that if you want to be a good teacher—a teacher of pupils anywhere—you need to learn to listen, and listen to learn. When people have a chance to tell their stories about how they find ECK, it gives them a chance to grow, but it also gives other people the same chance.

A new face on an old truth: To receive love, give love.

To Receive Love, Give Love

A new face on an old truth: To receive love, give love.

A certain woman had a hard time talking to others about the ECK teachings. One night she asked the Mahanta, "Please help me speak to people who appear to be ready for the teachings. Please let me talk to them in a natural and easy way."

She remembered how once she had been a seeker, looking for something that she couldn't put her finger on. Now that she had found it for herself, she felt a responsibility to give others the same chance. But she was uncomfortable doing it. So she asked for help.

At the ECK Worldwide Seminar in Minneapolis, she planned to go to a meeting of the ECK Writers Group, but a couple things got in her way. First, she was running late. Then she couldn't find her name tag to get into the seminar. And then, at the last minute, the babysitter who was going to watch her young daughter said, "I won't be able to watch your daughter." She couldn't really take her daughter to the workshop for adults because the young girl would have been bored. So she went to the parents room with the child, saying to herself, "I'm disappointed I couldn't get to the writers workshop, because it's a good one. But I'll just put in my time here in the parents room and play with my daughter."

In the parents room with her daughter, she began to play with some puppets. They started to have a good time, and even the woman began to enjoy herself. After a while the little girl said to her mother, "I want to go to the big room," the main hall where the main program was being held. The mother said, "Fine. Let's stop at the rest room first."

While they were in the rest room, they met two other women. One of the women says to the little girl, "What a pretty dress you have." And they began talking.

The younger woman looked at the mother and said, "Are you here for the health expo?" The health expo was being held at the same time as the Eckankar seminar in the convention center. The mother, who'd always had trouble speaking about the teachings of ECK to other people, didn't know what to say. She said, "No, I'm here with Eckankar." The younger

The mother, who'd always had trouble speaking about the teachings of ECK to other people, didn't know what to say. She said, "No, I'm here with Eckankar."

woman asked, "What's that?" The mother wondered how this was going to go. She said, "Eckankar is a spiritual teaching that shows people how to contact the Light and Sound of God." The Light and Sound of God together are the Holy Spirit, the Voice of God.

The older woman said, "Eckankar. I watch the Eckankar TV program that's on Channel 6 here in Minneapolis. I watch it every Friday night." She'd already heard about the teachings of ECK because the Mahanta had made a spiritual connection with her.

The ECKist had asked for help to talk easily and freely about the teachings of ECK to people who were ready. The chance came, and it was so natural. It came through the request of her little girl. One of the two women then said, after they talked back and forth for some time about the ECK teachings, "I was meant to be here today."

The ECKist found that to receive love, you must first give love. She'd missed the workshop; she was disappointed. There was little joy or love because fear, disappointment, and anger—and all the other negative traits that we have—shut out joy and divine love. But then she was able to tell these two women about the teachings of ECK. And she found that this brief meeting in a rest room had given her the joy and the love that she had been looking for. It came back.

A new face on an old truth: It is better to give than to receive.

BETTER TO GIVE THAN RECEIVE

A new face on an old truth: It is better to give than to receive.

In Switzerland there is a counselor. She understands the principle It is better to give than to receive. So she wanted to tell others about the teachings of ECK in an easy way. Whenever a person came to her for therapy, if the individual seemed ready or

open, the counselor would mention the teachings of
ECK and the Light and Sound of God, or the word
HU, which is a love song to God.

An eighty-five-year-old woman came to see her,
and they were talking about different things during
the session. This elderly woman said that she's always felt a close bond to God and the Holy Spirit.
This bond had been there her whole life. So her prayers
were never for help, but for wisdom.

And this woman had wisdom. Because the troubles
we have are to make us stronger. As we learn to
overcome the troubles or to work with them, we gain
in love, compassion, and wisdom.

This eighty-five-year-old woman told the counselor that her mother had taught her a long time ago
not to speak ill of others. So the therapist asked,
"Well, what do you do when people speak ill of you
or become angry with you?"

The woman said, "I start blessing them and go
my way."

*She found joy
in helping
others, in doing
things for other
people when
no one knew
about it.*

Lessons in Wisdom

This woman had learned several things that she
made the pillars of her life. They all show wisdom.
First, she learned it's better to give a blessing to
others than to receive or react to their negativity. A
second thing she learned was to give when nobody
knows about it. She found joy in helping others, in
doing things for other people when no one knew
about it.

Her comment was interesting. She said, "Otherwise, it's not real giving."

It's remarkable that people in government pride
themselves on being open-minded about helping
others when they are doing it with other peoples'

money. The real test of charity and giving—and a Christian life or an ECK life—is if the individual gives of his own, quietly, without anyone ever knowing it. Of course, if you did that in politics, you wouldn't get reelected, because you need to give other people's money to other people so that you can legally buy votes. But it's not a demonstration of superior humanity. It's a demonstration of selfishness and greed.

I always hesitate saying something like this because right away some very pompous people become angry with me. So, my apologies to anyone who is pompous and angry.

LIGHT BLESSINGS

Every day this woman does a third thing: She thanks God for all the blessings. She noticed that after she thanks God for these blessings, her room gets brighter as if a light is coming on.

She noticed that after she thanks God for these blessings, her room gets brighter as if a light is coming on.

She told the therapist, "Sometimes I see this blue light when I'm just resting or praying. What is that blue light? Is it responsible for my eyesight getting worse?"

The counselor began to laugh and said to her, "No, it's the Light of God showing you the way home."

The therapist then decided to tell this patient about the Mahanta, the Inner Master, the one who makes the connection for people in a human way with the Light and Sound of God.

The Mahanta's role is to put a face to the faceless, to the eternal, to the timeless, to the boundless, all of which we can call God or the Holy Spirit. God is God the Creator. The Holy Spirit is the voice that comes from God into all the worlds. It, Itself, is the creative action that comes from God the Creator.

TO LISTEN IS TO LOVE

A new face on an old truth: To listen is to love.

A new face on an old truth: To listen is to love.

A businesswoman felt spiritually stretched. At work, a coworker had a habit of picking on details, trying to unearth facts, and constantly go over strategies and procedures. He did this sometimes to no end; there was no point to it. The woman had to exercise all her patience as she explained, repeated, redefined, and used every example she could think of.

Her coworker always had a preconceived idea of what the problem was. And of course, he always had an idea what the solution should be—before he had the facts. But that didn't bother him one bit.

The woman spent her time trying to give him the facts, but it was as pointless as throwing ripe apples against a stone wall; that man's consciousness was a stone wall. He was always right; he always knew the answer before he asked the question. So it put other people around him against a stone wall, because he was the stone wall. Ideas, like apples, are thrown against the wall for no point. He even admitted sometimes, "I'm usually right." Which was funny, because he was usually wrong.

This is human nature. We have such an ability to protect ourselves from the truth of who and what we are. Mainly, we protect ourselves from what we are not.

If you find yourself in the same situation at work or anywhere else—where there is one person whose entire mission in life seems to make your life harder—look for the blessing.

The person who is causing us the most trouble is also giving us a chance to learn the most about ourselves spiritually.

This woman knew that. And she compensated by

treating other people the way she would like to be treated. Her coworker did not listen to her, so she went out of her way to listen to others. She was kind to them and showed compassion. In doing this—in listening—she was showing divine love. To listen is to love.

COMPASSION—THE WAY TO WISDOM

A new face on an old truth: Compassion is the way to wisdom.

The karma of a certain person is to suffer financial reverses in this lifetime. He's found this routine; it happens again and again. He makes some small gains, then he sees them all taken away—plus some. So he finds himself again standing on the edge of a financial ledge and wonders what caused this bad luck to follow him for so long.

Wondering about this, his mind flashed back years to when he was a young man. At that time he had heard someone say, "Don't give to panhandlers. It only slows up their spiritual unfoldment. It will take them longer to learn their spiritual lessons."

This person, being of a good heart, said, "All right, I'll do that." Soon after, he was standing on the street and a panhandler came up to him. The panhandler had clear blue eyes, and he was wearing a blue checkered shirt.

We often associate the color blue with a spiritual principle in ECK. So when he saw a beggar with clear blue eyes and with a blue checkered shirt, this young man thought, *I wonder if this guy is an ECK Master?* The panhandler asked, "You got thirty-five cents I can have?" The young man was reaching quickly into his pocket to get some change, when the thought came through: Don't give to beggars because it slows down their spiritual unfoldment.

A new face on an old truth: Compassion is the way to wisdom.

So he took his hand from his pocket. The beggar said to him, "You'd think I were asking for thirty-five dollars, not thirty-five cents."

The young man said, "You will have to earn this even as I do."

The panhandler looked at him and said, "Good luck," and began to walk across the street.

At this point the young man was suddenly taken out of the body. If anyone had been walking past on the street, they would have seen a young man standing as if he were in a daydream, with a quizzical and dumbfounded expression on his face. A second later, he looked across the intersection after the panhandler—but the man was gone.

He had vanished. The old disappearing beggar trick.

Spiritual Masters do this sometimes. They come to bring a blessing, but if people do not have the spiritual awareness or they need to learn something spiritually, then the Master will offer this gift to them. And the gift is asking them for a handout.

If someone gives them the money without reservations, the blessings of God are returned many times over.

For years he wondered, Was that an ECK Master? Had he made the right decision in saying no?

As the young man went through a life of financial setbacks, this particular experience haunted him. For years he wondered, *Was that an ECK Master?* Had he made the right decision in saying no? He did parrot the words of advice about giving to panhandlers. He wanted to do the right thing for them spiritually.

Years passed, and this same individual was facing new financial setbacks. He was walking along the street one day, and two panhandlers came up to him and asked him for money. They clearly did not want to work for it.

As far as he could tell, they were not ECK Masters. But it didn't matter to him. When they asked for money, he said, "No."

After the two had gone, he wondered if he had done the right thing this time. Or had he made another spiritual error? Would this come back to haunt him even as he suspected the first event had so many years ago? "Maybe I should change my behavior," he said. "Maybe I've been doing it the wrong way. Maybe I've been too much with the law of eye for eye and tooth for tooth. Maybe I should live the Law of Love."

Then he said, "But I think I'll need confirmation on this one."

Life had turned sour on him, and he said to himself and the Mahanta, "I feel like a target. I feel like the Kal or Satan has made me a target. How can I change my destiny? How can I change my luck?"

Soon after that he was driving along a freeway when ahead of him he saw a truck carrying a load of bags. The truck belonged to a delivery service. On each bag was a big red bull's-eye and the words "Target Concrete Company." Spirit was trying to say something about that attitude of eye for eye and tooth for tooth. In other words, a strict obedience to the Law of Karma. It's like a concrete wall.

Spirit was trying to say something about that attitude of eye for eye and tooth for tooth.

The man saw the bull's-eye and said, "So I *am* a target. What do I do about it?"

It looked like he would have to find a way to change his behavior, but how would he do it? A little while later, the driver of a car ahead of him opened and shut his door three times. "Apparently, the Holy Spirit is trying to tell me to shut out the past," the man decided. Shut the door to that experience.

Then he realized the ECK principle: first give if

you would receive. He also remembered what Christ had said some two thousand years ago: "Inasmuch as ye have done *it* unto one of the least of these my brethren, ye have done *it* unto me."

The man has now changed his behavior. He's determined in the future that he will give freely of what he has. If a panhandler comes up to him and he's able to help, he will help. He's not going to say, "You have to earn it." Because in doing that he's trying to tell the person how to live his own life. In ECK, we don't do that. We try to let other people be.

It's our decision whether or not we will give the money. That's our business. It doesn't matter whether we say yes or no. That isn't the point.

But when we preach at the person and say, "No, I won't give it to you because you have to earn it the way I do," right away we're imposing our spiritual values upon someone else. Maybe this is an intrusion upon that individual. And maybe this is where the wall of concrete is built in our own consciousness. At some point, one must give up the Law of Retribution, of Karma, for the Law of Love.

At some point, one must give up the Law of Retribution, of Karma, for the Law of Love.

Fifteen Times Exercise

Some of you are fans of the comic-strip character *Dilbert*. His creator is Scott Adams. Dilbert is a low-level employee in a corporate business, lost in a cubicle somewhere. He has no luck at all with women. He cannot get dates. He's not very successful. But he sits back and observes all the silly things that happen in a corporate office, and in this he is very good. A failure in everything else, observing the follies of his fellow workers—especially those above him—comes very easy to him.

Scott Adams spent seventeen years working in a

corporate environment, hidden away in a cubicle, doing the best he could to advance. He realized something after all that time: in order to advance in the company he was in, he not only had to be brilliant, come up with good ideas and good plans, but he also had to be tall and have a good head of hair.

But he was five foot eight, and his hair was thinning. He saw he was in a dead-end job and decided he would like to do something more creative.

As a young man, he had taken an art class in school. He got a B minus. He was not a very good cartoonist. But sitting in his cubicle in that corporate office, he was always thinking, *I would like to be a cartoonist.* He was making doodles all the time. When he figured out that he wasn't going to get real promotions because he didn't have the stature or the hair, he said, "I want to become a syndicated cartoonist." He told this story in the July 1997 issue of *Reader's Digest.*

He gave a technique there which you can easily adapt to a spiritual exercise. For him, this technique is an affirmation. But if you work with it along the spiritual lines, it becomes something more than merely a mental affirmation.

An affirmation is a discipline of the mind only. Whereas contemplation, which is a lighter way of going about opening doors for yourself spiritually, opens the door to the Holy Spirit to help you change your life according to Its will. So whenever you do a spiritual exercise of this sort as I will give in a minute, do it with the attitude Thy will be done. That lifts it from a simple mental affirmation into true contemplation.

Scott Adams said he thought it important to affirm his goal, to put it in writing. So every day he'd write

An affirmation is a discipline of the mind only. Whereas contemplation, which is a lighter way of going about opening doors for yourself spiritually, opens the door to the Holy Spirit to help you change your life according to Its will.

that goal fifteen times: I will become a syndicated cartoonist.

But he didn't just sit back and wait for the world to find him in his cubicle, buried away in some corporate office. He put together all his little cartoon characters in some cartoon strips of Dilbert, and he sent them out to a bunch of syndicates. He got back a lot of rejection slips, but a very big syndicate accepted his idea. And that was the beginning of *Dilbert*.

His technique was based upon the principle of focusing on a goal. He focused by writing that goal down very clearly, fifteen times every day.

How do you do this with a spiritual goal? I will give you an example. I've purposely chosen one with a broad reach. I don't want to put you into a tight little envelope. You know your goals. Fashion the spiritual exercise on them.

So the example I'll give you can be along these lines: "I am a healthy, happy, spiritual being." Or "I am a healthy, happy, spiritual person." Or you may use another goal, "I travel in my dreams." Or you can say, "I know the secret of divine love."

Scott Adams said the basic idea is that you just write down your goal fifteen times every day. Then observe things happening that will make that objective more likely to materialize.

His technique was based upon the principle of focusing on a goal. He focused by writing that goal down very clearly, fifteen times every day.

A New Face on Old Truths

A new face on old truths.

I've given several examples of people who wanted to tell others about the teachings of ECK and the Mahanta, yet they didn't feel qualified to do so. They felt uneasy. But it's very simple: If you appreciate the awareness you have gained about your life since coming to ECK, tell others your story—tell them about HU and the Mahanta.

Tell them your story, but only if they're ready. Let them experience the ECK for themselves. You don't have to push anything on them. All you have to do is tell them about HU and the Mahanta. And if the Inner Master has made a connection with these people, they're going to respond in their own way, at their own time. The ECK will either convince them or It won't, depending on their state of spiritual awareness.

Here's the important point: If you appreciate yourself, you will find it easy to tell your story to others. Some people are ashamed to talk about ECK. I would suspect it's because they're ashamed of themselves.

To overcome this shame, put your attention on divine love. Because where love exists, the lower things like anger, shame, and doubt cannot exist.

Count your blessings that these seminars are possible today. There may come a time in the future when the window will close on them. They are an opportunity for you to come together with others who are of like spiritual mind. Enjoy this time with each other. Listen and learn. And learn to listen.

If you appreciate the awareness you have gained about your life since coming to ECK, tell others your story—tell them about HU and the Mahanta.

ECK European Seminar, Lausanne, Switzerland, Saturday, August 2, 1997

When our hearts are open to God's love, then the divine power can use us as an instrument to pass divine love and blessings along to others.

8

YOU ARE A CUP FOR THE LIVING WATER

ometimes people feel that our approach to the spiritual life is too simple. They read some ECK books, and they say to themselves, "Is that all there is?" These people are looking for something really complicated, tough.

It's true that the workings of Divine Spirit can and do become intricate, down to the finest detail—in fact, intricate to the point where it boggles the human mind. I'm talking now about the playing out of cause and effect.

Often people look at society, and they ask, What has happened to the sensibility of people? Everything seems to have gone mad. The values of a few years ago are thrown out the window, and what seems right is wrong and what is wrong is said to be right. And people wonder, as they look perhaps at their leaders, *Where is justice?*

The problem with us as people is, number one, we should be minding our own business. Number two, the Law of God has long arms. And the justice of God has a long memory.

You can be assured that the complexity and fabric of life in which we live is regulated to the smallest degree—but not by the human mind. It's run by the Holy Spirit.

We call this Holy Spirit the ECK, which means simply *one,* because It's the Voice of God. It's the source—where it all comes from. When God created all the worlds it was done through means of this Voice—the Holy Word, the Holy Spirit. That's how God created the heavens and the earth. Today everything is maintained at this level by the Holy Spirit.

The point I want to make is about your relationship with the Holy Spirit, with the Voice of God. Because that is the means of talking with God.

The living water is the Holy Spirit, or the ECK. This water flows throughout life: your life, my life, your neighbor's life, your loved one's life.

A Cup for the Living Water

The title of this talk is "You Are a Cup for the Living Water." The living water is the Holy Spirit, or the ECK. This water flows throughout life: your life, my life, your neighbor's life, your loved one's life. It flows constantly. But you're a cup. And what sort of cup you are—whether of gold or of wood—will affect the gifts that then go back to the world. Is the cup leaking? Or is it a good cup?

You're trying to establish this relationship within yourself to become a clear channel for the Holy Spirit—a cup for the living water. I'll give some examples so you can see how this plays out in everyday life.

Opening to Divine Love

An ECK member, Niki, and her husband, John, live on the East Coast of the United States. Niki had been out of the workplace for twelve years—she'd been at home raising her family. But the kids were just about raised, and she thought, *It'd be nice to have a little bit more money, give the family a little more freedom.* So she got herself a job as a route sales-person for a cosmetics firm.

It was an unhappy situation almost from the beginning. She'd come home exhausted, and she'd cry. After she got home, she often faced two hours of paperwork. She wondered, *What's happening to me? I'm no longer in charge of my life.*

Even worse, she had begun to lose the sense of God's love for her. It used to be very strong, but even it had gone away. *Where is it?* she wondered. *Why am I so unhappy?*

On the surface the job looked as if it were not the place for her to be. But an interesting thing about life is that no matter what circumstances you find yourself in, be assured you belong there at that particular moment.

Why? Simply because you're there.

People will say that doesn't make any sense. But it makes all the sense in the universe. If you weren't meant to be in a certain situation, you wouldn't be there. And since you are, there's something there for you to learn. You will either learn it before you leave— or you'll miss the lesson and leave. But then you'll come back in a similar situation in the future to face the lesson again.

The lesson is always about yourself.

It is about how you can become a clearer, purer vehicle for the Holy Spirit. And the way this is done your heart opens to divine love. That's all there is to it.

What opens the heart to love? It certainly isn't flush times when everybody's walking around with their pockets filled with money. The most interest in spirituality comes when life is hard.

The lesson is always about yourself. It is about how you can become a clearer, purer vehicle for the Holy Spirit.

So Niki wanted more freedom, and instead she found more unhappiness. She worked on commission, and the company would give her a list of customers to call on. She'd go from place to place, and there was barely time between appointments to stop for food and water. But one particular day it was hot and sunny, so she stopped at a store for a bottle of water.

When she got to the door, there was a woman there with a small child hanging on to her leg. The woman was selling candy. The baby was crying, for some reason. Just crying and crying.

The crying of the child pulled at her heart. So she offered the bottle of water to the mother to give to the toddler.

Niki didn't know if the woman might use the money from this candy sale for drugs or alcohol. But Niki bought some candy from her, went inside the store, bought water, and came outside again. On her way to the car she stopped, turned around, went back to the mother and the crying child. The crying of the child pulled at her heart. So she offered the bottle of water to the mother to give to the toddler. The mother was very grateful, and as soon as the baby got the water, it stopped crying and drank, because it was hot too.

A Gift Returned

Niki went on with her life, and she forgot all about the incident until about a month later. She was out making sales calls—she had been running all day, and she needed to stop for food and water. She thought, *After my next stop at a salon I'll get some food and water.* But every time she'd look at the list of customers left to visit before the day was done, she just kept putting off taking a break, until she came to this one salon.

She went inside and sold some shampoo to the proprietor. He said, "Just a minute. I'll have to get you some change from in back." He went out back, brought her the change, and also brought her a bottle of cold water. "This is for you," he said to Niki. She was startled; she didn't know the man.

She asked, "Why did you give me this water? I'm a stranger." He said, "Because you looked like you needed it."

As she was going out to her car, it suddenly struck her that the store where she had given water to the mother and the child was right across the street. In fact, the man in the salon had given her the same brand of water that she had given to the woman.

She was surprised to realize that the working of the Law of Cause and Effect was so precise. Cause and effect for her happened within a month and right across the street, so she would recognize that the gift was returned to her. She had opened her heart, and the door was opened for her to receive the gift back when she needed it.

Niki was acting as a vessel for the living water.

She had opened her heart, and the door was opened for her to receive the gift back when she needed it.

Being an Instrument

Another time, Niki went to a restaurant with her mother. As they were talking, her mother began to tell her of an incident that had happened the last time the mother and her husband had been there, just a little while ago.

"We were having our meal," she said. "Your dad got up, walked over to the counter, and bought ten lottery tickets—instant scratch winners. He came back to the table, gave me half, and took half himself. We scratched them, and we didn't win anything. A few minutes later a little old man walked in the door. He went to the counter, and he bought the next ticket.

He scratched it and won three hundred dollars."

The mother paused in her story, and Niki's mind was racing ahead. She thought, *Aha! My parents learned the quick justice of Divine Spirit. You don't get something for nothing.*

Niki had just about settled on this as being one of those personal truths when her mother went on. She said, "It's very unlike your dad to buy ten tickets. He may buy one, but never ten. And he just got up. There seemed to be a flow. He just did what seemed to be right. When he bought those ten tickets it cleared the way for this little old man who needed the gift to win the money."

Her dad wasn't thinking to himself, *Gee, I've got this nudge and what am I going to do about it? I wonder what it means. Is it the Law of Cause and Effect pushing me? Is it the Holy Spirit making me want to go up to the counter? Is it greed? Why do I want to buy these tickets?* He didn't mentalize the situation. He just got up and did it. Then he came back to the table and finished his meal; and that was the end of it.

The mother said, "This was meant to be. It was simply meant to be. It's the way of the Holy Spirit."

Niki learned a profound lesson. When our hearts are open to God's love, then the divine power can use us as an instrument to pass divine love and blessings along to others.

When our hearts are open to God's love, then the divine power can use us as an instrument to pass divine love and blessings along to others.

This is an example of how someone was a cup for the living water. First, the father, and then the mother, as she explained the spiritual significance of this incident. Niki had taken it at face value. She had at first seen only the surface, but the workings of Divine Spirit were much deeper.

You are a cup for the living water.

Do All You Have Agreed to Do

Someone I'll call Dale is a young woman from Accra, Ghana. She was looking for a place to live. Through a real-estate agent, she found a nice single room in a quiet home. She thought this would be an ideal place for her because she wanted privacy and quiet and also a room she could afford.

But her landlady turned out to be a very spiteful woman. When Dale took the rent money over, the woman seemed very angry with her. And the landlady fell through in her promise to take care of some maintenance.

Dale had made a promise to herself when she came to this new place. She had said, "I will treat it the same as I treat my father's house." When she was at her father's house, she would clean it and keep it very tidy. She promised herself that she would do that here too.

But she got sidetracked because this landlady was so spiteful. The woman seemed to go out of her way to make things hard.

For instance, this house was in a compound with a wall around it and a gate. The landlady wouldn't let her have a key to the gate because she didn't trust Dale. Dale noticed that whenever she went out to work, the landlady would lock the gate. But when the landlady's son would leave, she would leave the gate unlocked so that he could come and go as he pleased.

Dale's friends said, "Go someplace else. The woman's no good." But Dale had a feeling from the Inner Master, her inner guide, the Mahanta, that she was supposed to stay there. Yet she didn't know why.

One morning, she woke up at dawn, and smoke was filling her lungs. Right outside Dale's window

Dale had made a promise to herself when she came to this new place. She had said, "I will treat it the same as I treat my father's house."

was a pile of leaves. The landlady had set fire to it and was burning the leaves. She kept putting damp leaves on top of the fire so they'd smoke really well. The smoke was pouring into Dale's bedroom window.

Dale didn't go outside and confront the landlady. Instead, she just sat down and began a spiritual exercise. She was determined to lift herself above the situation.

Apparently she did a pretty good job because she didn't notice the smoke for thirty minutes. When she opened her eyes, the woman had gone. In a few minutes, her bedroom was cleared of smoke. Then Dale asked the Mahanta in contemplation, "Why is this woman so mean to me?"

The Inner Master simply said, "Do all you have agreed to do."

The Inner Master simply said, "Do all you have agreed to do." She recognized the words as the first of Maybury's two laws.

Richard Maybury's book *Whatever Happened to Justice?* gives two laws to live by. Dale was learning about the first one. Law number one is: "Do all you have agreed to do." Number two: "Do not encroach on other persons or their property." If people in civilization would follow these two laws and all that they imply, this would be a better world.

Dale remembered her promise to herself to take care of this place as she would her father's house. So the next Saturday she got up at dawn. She went around the compound, raked up the patches of weeds, and disposed of them.

The second Saturday Dale trimmed the bushes and took care of the flowers. She swept, gathered up all the debris, and put it away. She worked at this a very long time. Then she noticed that the landlady was watching her. In her own language that she thought Dale didn't understand, the landlady said,

"My daughter is working very hard." Dale noticed the broad smile on the landlady's face. So Dale wasn't encroaching on the property of the landlady. She was helping to improve it.

Then through the inner communication link that ECKists have with the Inner Master, the Mahanta spoke to her and said, "You have opened the woman's heart."

This landlady did not like her neighbors. She would not speak to them. The feelings were mutual. But now, the landlady began to soften her attitude. One time she was going to be gone when Dale got back late from work. So the landlady wondered what to do with the key, because she wanted to let Dale in. Finally, she went to one of the neighbors and entrusted the key to this person with instructions to open the gate when Dale came back.

Later, the father of one of Dale's friends said to her that the entire neighborhood had changed since Dale had come. Her presence was changing so many things. Soon the landlady was even doing her part to keep her promise. She was doing the maintenance that had been part of the rental agreement.

Dale learned a few spiritual lessons from this: (1) Learn to do selfless acts. (2) Keep your promises no matter how small. (3) Always rely on your true inner voice. She was being a cup for the living water of life, for the Holy Spirit. She was being a Co-worker with the Voice of God.

PEOPLE ARE PEOPLE

I occasionally mention books by various authors who are not members of Eckankar when there is some element of truth in that particular work. Sometimes, unfortunately, when these authors are at a

Dale learned a few spiritual lessons from this: (1) Learn to do selfless acts. (2) Keep your promises no matter how small. (3) Always rely on your true inner voice.

public function, one of our members will go up to them and say, "We sold a thousand books for you." What's the author supposed to say? Someone actually came up to one of these authors and said, "We sold a million books for you." Of course, no such thing had happened. The author is a very polite man, and he's thinking, *If there had been a million sales of my book, I'd have a chalet in Switzerland, but I don't.*

But he was kind. He didn't say a word. He just listened very patiently.

I don't mention these titles to sell books for these people. In most cases I don't know the authors before I mention their books. After I mention the books, they may get in touch with me. I've even developed a correspondence with some of them. Generally, I make it a point not to mention books by people unless they're ECK books. But when I do, there is a spiritual point in that book that some of you may benefit from.

If you enjoyed the work of a writer and he's not a member of ECK, it would probably be more gracious if you simply tell the individual, "I very much enjoyed your book. It helped me greatly."

I can't be responsible for anyone else's behavior, even if it is a member of the group for which I am the spiritual leader. People are people. They do their own thing. This is true in every religion.

Spiritual Freedom

Every religion on earth has its range of personalities. There are people from every range of consciousness, from the very highest to the most elementary. I won't even pretend to be responsible for something I have no control over. Because I do not want to control you any more than I want you to control me. Where is spiritual freedom then?

I do not want to control you any more than I want you to control me. Where is spiritual freedom then?

I can suggest ideas. I can suggest ways to live a life that's more in keeping with the divine will. But I can't order you to do it.

If people go way outside the very loose boundaries that are established as to what's right and wrong as a member of Eckankar, I may ask them to please leave this path. Find a path where they're more compatible, a place they fit. But I very seldom do this.

LIVING THE LIFE OF ECK

The place of a spiritual teaching is to help people unfold into a greater state of awareness. That always presumes you start from a lower place, and you have the ideal and the realization of moving to a higher one.

The place of a spiritual teaching is to help people unfold into a greater state of awareness.

Living the life of ECK is a very responsible way of living.

Most of your neighbors may never know you're an ECKist. If you're living the life of ECK, they're going to know that you are generous, that you care about people and things around yourself. You won't necessarily get swept away by the emotions of the mob, with one sort of issue—political or community or another—simply because it's the thing to do.

They will know you as an individual who has independent thinking and independent thoughts. They will know you as a good citizen and a good neighbor.

You are a cup for the living water.

MYSTERIOUS HELPER

Laurie became a member of Eckankar in December 1996. As a child she'd heard about Eckankar. She knew about it. Her family were members. But Laurie kept telling her friends, as she went through grade school and into high school, "I believe in the principles of ECK, but I'm just not ready to follow the path. I have things to work out in my life. I need to straighten these things out first."

One morning she had an important job interview. Her old job was being closed out; the company was downsizing. That morning she had all sorts of last-minute things to do in and around the apartment. She ran outside to where her truck was parked, put the keys in the ignition, then jumped out to check one more thing.

And she slammed the door. "Uh, oh," she said. "Laurie did a bad thing."

She looked through the truck window, and there, securely in the ignition, were her keys. The door was locked. She quickly went around to the other side. That door was locked too. She'd heard that people use coat hangers to open car doors, so she ran inside, got a coat hanger, and tried that. But she didn't know how to make a coat hanger open doors.

About that time a man in a dark blue running suit came by. The hood of his running suit was pulled over his head. She thought, *That's odd. This is a hot day in California*. But she waved to him. The man looked around like, Are you waving at me?

She said, "Yeah. You!"

He said, "Me?"

"Yes, yes, yes, please," she said.

"So," he said, "you want me to come over?"

"Yes, yes."

So he came over. She said, "I'm locked out of my truck. I've got an important job interview."

The man asked, "Do you have a second key?" She said, "I don't think so." He looked at the truck and

About that time a man in a dark blue running suit came by. The hood of his running suit was pulled over his head. She thought, That's odd. This is a hot day in California.

tried the door but he couldn't get in. "You sure you don't have another key?"

She said, "I really don't think so." Then she said, "I can't believe I did this!"

And he said, "I can't believe you did it either."

Laurie had a strange sense the man knew her. But she said, "I'll go back inside and look." So she went back inside her apartment, looked around through her dresser and here, there, and everywhere. She couldn't find a spare key.

When she came back outside, the man was gone. So she went up to her truck and tried the door again; the door opened. She didn't know what to make of this. She figured that somehow the man had opened the door, but she had no idea how, in just the few moments she'd been inside. It seemed important that she not be there when he did it, whoever this man was.

She had a few minutes to spare before she had to start out for the appointment, so Laurie drove up and down the streets in the neighborhood, but she couldn't find any trace of this man.

Meeting Paul Twitchell

The interview went fine. When she came home that night, she had a nudge from the Inner Master, the Mahanta, to go to her dresser drawer, open the drawer, then shut it. It didn't seem to make any sense. But she had this intuitive hunch to do this.

So she opened up the dresser drawer, and there on top she found a book. It was *Paulji*, a book about the life of Paul Twitchell.

She had noticed that the man who helped her with her truck had deep blue eyes that seemed to go on forever. As she looked at this book, she saw these same eyes looking back at her. She realized that her

She had noticed that the man who helped her with her truck had deep blue eyes that seemed to go on forever. As she looked at this book, she saw these same eyes looking back at her.

mysterious helper had been Paul Twitchell, or Peddar Zaskq, his spiritual name. She also knew that he had died in 1971.

The ECK Masters—as do masters of other paths, like Christ—know that life goes on beyond death. Many of these ECK Masters are able to manifest a body even now, to help one of the students they have worked with in a past life.

Paul came on the scene at this particular moment because he knew she was going to need help. She recognized him unconsciously, but yet she didn't recognize him. When she said, "I can't believe I did this," he said, "I can't believe you did it either," as if he had known her from a long time ago. And indeed, he had.

The man who had opened the door was Paulji, Paul Twitchell. And he wanted nothing in return. He had come to act as a pure instrument for the Holy Spirit.

It opened her eyes to God's love.

Many of these ECK Masters are able to manifest a body even now, to help one of the students they have worked with in a past life.

SPECIAL SPIRITUAL EXERCISE

I would like to give you a spiritual exercise. This is the spiritual exercise I gave at the 1997 ECK European Seminar, with a few adjustments.

Sit down at a table or a desk and write a spiritual goal fifteen times. I'm not telling you what to write. But I'll give you an example of something that you may want to see or write so you can watch as Divine Spirit begins to bring these objects of your spiritual desire into your life. For instance, you may ask to be an instrument for God's love.

You could ask for money if you wanted to, but it's a waste of time. You may get money, but you may end up too old to enjoy it by the time you get it. Or you may ask for a particular person as your mate, end up with that mate, and rue the day you asked for this in writing.

So every day, fifteen times, all at one sitting—it doesn't take long—just write "I am _____." Use the present tense.

I would suggest something along this line: "I am healthy, happy, wise, and free." I think these are worthy spiritual desires. You may think of others that fit you more accurately. You may just say, "I am wise," or "I am healthy." "I am happy." Or put a whole bunch together.

Just remember, you're going to be writing this fifteen times a day for as long as you can stand to do it. So don't make it too long. Choose your words carefully.

As you write this, if you usually write in a very neat, tight handwriting, let yourself go. Scribble. Write very big. Use the back of shopping bags or a blackboard. Go first class, write on a piece of paper. Use both sides. Don't use any punctuation. If you ordinarily write in a certain size, write in a different size. Have fun. Because what you're doing is opening up the windows of your world.

BE A WORTHY VESSEL

As time goes on, watch how the Holy Spirit begins to make changes in your life. Little things will happen. For instance, if you're looking for happiness, events will start to shape themselves where you have new choices. It's up to you to make the right choice, but doors will begin to open for you.

Be aware. Watch the Voice of God, this Holy Spirit, the living water, pour into your cup. Be a worthy vessel.

So every day, fifteen times, all at one sitting . . . just write "I am _____."

Watch the Voice of God, this Holy Spirit, the living water, pour into your cup. Be a worthy vessel.

For those of you who may have need of this, I'll mention a book you may be interested in: *Your Body's Many Cries for Water.* I won't say more except to say that a healthy body is an aid to spiritual unfoldment.

You should be able to find this book at your bookstore or on the Web. It's written by Dr. Batmanghelidj, M.D. He did a lot of research in a prison in the Mideast where he was a political prisoner. He was fortunate to be released eventually. But while he was there, he made some interesting discoveries about the body and water and the relationship of water to disease. Now you may or may not find this helpful; you may or may not agree. The book, like any of the books I've mentioned, must always be used with good judgment.

If you have a health condition, work with your doctor. And even when you're working with a doctor, you are the final judge of what's right or wrong for you. If a good doctor is right 50 percent of the time and if he were playing on a major-league baseball team, he'd be batting .500. He'd be a superstar. If you can get advice from anyone that fits you half the time, you're doing very well.

So I'd like to leave you with this. I know that those of you who made the trip to San Francisco to this ECK Springtime Seminar will receive spiritual blessings many times over. It was worth the trip for you. Keep your eyes open, whether or not you write the statement fifteen times for the spiritual exercise.

Be aware of how your life is changing from day to day. The water of life is everywhere. It flows for thee.

Be aware of how your life is changing from day to day. The water of life is everywhere. It flows for thee.

ECK Springtime Seminar, San Francisco, California, Saturday, April 11, 1998

Each and every little thing in my life, each little secret that comes to make my life easier is a gift of love from the Holy Spirit.

9

A GIFT OF LOVE

ome visitors to our home were passing through the kitchen as Joan was making our lunch. She was going to bake some winter squash. Winter squash has a very hard rind, and there's always a risk of injury when you try to cut through it. What Joan was doing caught them by surprise. They laughed and laughed.

Instead of using a knife to cut the hard rind of this winter squash, so she could clean out the seeds inside and bake the squash in the oven, she was using a hacksaw. She said, "Harold showed me."

After our visitors left, I said to her, "It was very kind to give me the credit; but it was actually the ECK, or the Holy Spirit, that had given me the idea. I'm not smart enough for those ideas myself." And so it is. You have dozens of ideas like that all the time too. Little secrets that other people would laugh at, but they make your life easier.

Where do these gifts come from? You could say, "I just thought it up. It came from the brilliance of my mind." Or "I saw it on TV." Or "I read it in a book."

GIFTS FROM SPIRIT

But there is more than just hearing and seeing. It's the awareness to recognize that whatever your

You have dozens of ideas like that all the time too. Little secrets that other people would laugh at, but they make your life easier.

little secret is, it is exactly the right thing for you. Ten thousand other people may be watching the same TV program and hear the same secret, but maybe only seven think it's worth the discipline and the trouble to try it out. To put it in your own little toolbox of life.

We're speaking about a gift of love. A gift of love from the Holy Spirit.

My wife got me a new suit for this seminar. Each and every article of clothing, each and every little thing in my life, each little secret that comes to make my life easier is a gift of love. And I recognize them to be gifts from the Holy Spirit.

Sometimes I say to my wife, "That's too much. Don't spend that on me." She says, "My money is a gift from the Holy Spirit, from the ECK." She works at the Eckankar Spiritual Center, and she works extremely hard. She turns out a mountain of work.

We're doing the best we can at the ECK Spiritual Center, and we rely on your suggestions and help. We recognize each of your suggestions and each of your ideas as a gift of love. Each of these is a gift from the Holy Spirit. It's the Holy Spirit, the ECK, that is responsible for our very being, for our thoughts and our feelings. If we keep them in a spiritual or a positive light, we are walking the path to God.

> Each of these is a gift from the Holy Spirit. It's the Holy Spirit, the ECK, that is responsible for our very being, for our thoughts and our feelings.

Your Own Path to God

This is what the path of ECK is all about—walking the path to God. Even more, it's about walking your path to God. Because your path is not my path, and my path is not yours. God made you a unique being. You are Soul.

You are Soul; that's the identity behind your name, behind your physical form, behind the comeliness of your face. You are made in God's image. It's an image of divine love. But remember: if you are made in God's image, so is your neighbor and so am I. Imagine the respect that you would give to the one you most love; and when I say "the one you most love," it can be person, animal, place, or thing—whomever you give the most love to. If you can have that same love for yourself, then you are recognizing yourself as this holy divine light of God that you are.

That's what the path of ECK is about.

A gift of love takes the awareness to see it, to recognize it. These gifts of the Holy Spirit are around you every day. In fact, you're sitting in the middle of thousands of gifts of love at this moment.

You are a gift to the others you meet, but only if you act in the spirit of light and truth. Act in the highest interest. Keep your business interests at home rather than use an ECK seminar as an opportunity to sell your products. The ECK seminar is for a spiritual reason. And if you keep it at that high level and your intention with your profession is to serve others, you will do very well.

You are a gift to the others you meet, but only if you act in the spirit of light and truth.

AWARENESS

The ECK staff is a hardworking group, and they like to have a good time too, in the sense of openhearted fun. One afternoon at four, Susan was working with the schedule for all this work that you finally see as an ECK book or an ECK discourse. One of the computer department men came up to her and said, "Do you notice something unusual about my shirt?"

She said, "Nice shirt."

"No, no, no," he said. "It's something special."

The shirt seemed to be stitched all right, seemed to be clean and pressed. Susan wasn't overly impressed.

It was an hour before closing, and she had a lot to do.

The man pointed to someone else in the computer department. "Look at his shirt." Susan noticed it was burgundy just like the first person's. Burgundy, a reddish purple, is the color robe that the ECK Masters often wear when they're working here, there, and everywhere, when they're not in ordinary suits or in sport clothes as they are many times when they meet you.

Vairagi means "detached." Not cut off and separated from life, but in balance and understanding the interplay of life.

Maroon red, or burgundy, is sort of an official color of the ECK Masters, the Order of Vairagi Adepts. *Vairagi* means "detached." Not cut off and separated from life, but in balance and understanding the interplay of life. Understanding the good things and the bad things that happen.

The computer department had decided to wear burgundy in recognition of that, and also to see whether the women in the office were as aware of color and style as they would like to think.

"Look over there in the computer room," the man said to Susan. "What color is he wearing?"

By now, Susan is noticing. She says, "Burgundy!"

She began looking around the whole office. All the men were wearing the color burgundy.

One of the men confessed to her, "We were just having a little fun to see whether the women have as much awareness as they often think they have." It was four in the afternoon before the first woman noticed. Even then the man had to tug on her sleeve and say, "Notice anything unusual about my shirt?"

The lesson was this: That what they had done was actually a gift of love. It meant that they cared enough about those who worked with them to do something just a little bit different, to say, "Hey! It's a fast day, but don't let it be so fast. We're here too, all of us. We're in this together serving the Holy Spirit, the ECK."

Susan wondered later what the lesson was. It was only a lesson in awareness.

Helping God's Creatures

Paul Harvey has one of the most widely listened-to radio news programs in America. It's on for fifteen minutes every day, around noon. Yesterday morning on Paul Harvey's News and Comment a news brief caught my attention. Somebody had mentioned to Paul Harvey that birds were eating the figs off the tree in his yard. What could he do about it? How could he stop the birds?

One of the suggestions came in from a woman. She said, "If you hang little tinkling bells on the fruit tree, the birds won't eat the figs."

Paul Harvey said, "Sorry," because someone had tried that and it didn't work.

Someone else said, "If you spray grape Kool-Aid over the trees, it'll keep the birds away. They won't eat your figs." Someone had tried the grape Kool-Aid. The birds love grape Kool-Aid.

Most of you gardeners would have immediately said, "Just go down to the gardening store and buy yourself some tree netting. Throw it over the tree. That'll take care of most of the birds, and you'll have most of your fruit." This was an idea that works.

The man who offered Paul Harvey this suggestion said that years ago, when he was young—long before such tree netting was available—his dad used to put cheesecloth on the tree to protect the fruit. This worked very well. One day, his mother was working at the kitchen window, and a hummingbird flew up to the window. It flew from the kitchen window to the cheesecloth-covered tree, back to the kitchen window.

His mother was very aware. She said, "Something's wrong."

She went out to the tree, and she found that a young hummingbird had been caught and couldn't get out. It was caught underneath one of the folds of the cheesecloth. She lifted it; the young bird flew out and joined the mother hummingbird, and the two birds fluttered there for a minute, hovering in midair as if to say, "Thank you for this gift of love." Then they flew off, very grateful for her act of kindness.

The mother also had a gift of love from the Holy Spirit. It was knowing in her heart that she had done something to help another of God's creatures.

The mother also had a gift of love from the Holy Spirit. It was knowing in her heart that she had done something to help another of God's creatures.

A Runner's Gift

Kristy is a member of ECK who would go out running every day. She did this for health reasons. One day she decided to run in a marathon, and an ECK friend volunteered to help.

Every five miles her friend would meet her to give her water to drink. This good-hearted ECKist ran the last six and a half miles with Kristy. The friend had a water pack strapped on her back and also another pack with nutritional fluids, so that Kristy could have nutrition and strength as she finished the marathon.

I found it hard to imagine anyone running with that much weight on their back for six and a half miles. I thought that was quite a feat in itself. But it was given as a gift of love, and Kristy accepted it in the very same way.

Lighten Up

One day, after her daily run for exercise, Kristy came inside all worn out. But then her cat Misha gave her a gift of love.

Kristy had her own nutrition business, which was very challenging. All her cares about it weighed upon her. And this particular day she was worried. Should she keep her business, or should she accept a job that a nutrition company had offered her which paid very well? The downside was it meant a lot of travel. She wondered what to do.

She was sitting there wondering about what to do, tired out from her run, and even more tired from the worries of her business and a decision of what to do with her future. Then Misha, her Siamese cat, nudged her.

He had his favorite toy in his mouth and he was saying, "Hey, it's time to play. Lighten up. This is my gift of love to you."

This made all the difference in the world to Kristy. It was a gift from one of God's creatures. Another Soul. Yes, animals are Soul too. You'll notice I'm very careful not to say animals have a soul.

You are Soul. You cannot possess Soul. Soul is free.

You are Soul. You cannot possess Soul. Soul is free.

The Gift of Life

Sometimes we mistake our human body for us. That's not us. This body will someday cease to exist, return to the ground, and decompose. It will become fertilizer so that other body forms may grow. And these body forms—whether of people, or animals, or plants—are expressions of Soul.

My wife, Joan, brought up a good point in this regard. She said, "It wasn't so long ago that some

African tribes had so little regard for each other they'd sell people from other tribes into slavery. And the white people had so little regard for their black brothers that they bought them." This was the basis of the slave trade. Back in ancient Egypt, the Egyptians looked down on the Orientals because they were a fearsome enemy.

You treat each other with the respect that you should give yourself because you and your neighbor are both children of God.

Today there is a recognition that has been painful in coming—that we all are equal in the sight of God.

To be sure, this awareness is not an awareness of the majority. But many of you have this awareness. You treat each other with the respect that you should give yourself because you and your neighbor are both children of God. Your pets too, and your birds.

This world is a dog-eat-dog world. This is a world of parasites. Parasites are in our bodies. These little organisms are inside you, living off you. They're part of your family. When they get out of balance, they can do much harm. But we all have these microorganisms working in us.

If the truth be known and accepted, people are parasites too.

Some people eat animals to live, even as some animals eat other animals. Some animals eat plants, but plants are alive too. People who eat plants often look down on people who eat meat. Is this sort of pride much different from the same pride that once sold brothers into slavery? Basically it says, "I am better than you are. Either because I look different, or you look different, or we behave differently."

Is it so different? We all have to eat something to survive. It's not important whether you are a meat eater or a vegetarian, whether you exist on water or fruit juice or air.

The Native Americans had a very nice approach.

They ate the buffalo, and they ate the deer, but whenever they had to sacrifice one of these beings so that they might live, they would always give thanks. To the buffalo and the deer they'd say, "Thank you for this gift that I may live."

They thanked the Great Spirit, the ECK, the Holy Spirit. They lived with a heart full of gratitude, a heart that recognized a gift of love from the most high.

FREELY GIVEN

They lived with a heart full of gratitude, a heart that recognized a gift of love from the most high.

One day Kristy was taking a shower. She opened the bathroom door, and Misha, her Siamese cat, did something that he'd never done before. He jumped to the top of the bathroom door and perched up there, like a hawk.

Kristy wondered, *Why is Misha acting so strange?*

Kristy recognizes Misha as Soul. She knows that animals often work in images, so she made herself still inside and tried to put herself in Misha's little booties. She got a picture of Misha's daughter Isabella perched on a high fence separating their yard from a neighbor's. If Isabella had toppled over the other side, it would have been very hard for Kristy to get a ladder and get Isabella out of there.

Kristy caught the image, got dressed, went outside, and, sure enough, there was Isabella perched on this fence, wobbling back and forth trying to keep her balance. Kristy picked her off the fence, and Misha and Isabella were both very grateful for her help. They knew it was a gift of love.

In this way the gift of love that Misha earlier gave to Kristy came back. Neither animal had said, "I'm giving you a gift of love today, so I'll be looking for yours." Love doesn't work like that.

A gift of love must come freely from your heart without any expectation of reward. A gift is a gift.

Some things called gifts actually have strings attached. Usually you can tell very quickly. The string goes like this: "I will give you this *if . . .*" You look at the word *if* and listen to what follows. "If you will do as I say." Or "if you behave." Or "if you sell that to me at a discount." Or "if you will give me that heirloom." Here's a gift of love *if*, always an *if*. Then it's not a gift of love.

> A gift of love must come freely from your heart without any expectation of reward.

A Humble Gift

At the ECK Springtime Seminar in San Francisco, we had a dance with a swing band. The bandleader was an ECKist, but none of the semiprofessional musicians who played were ECKists. So they all needed to be paid. Russ, the bandleader, paid their costs out of his own pocket. It cost him a thousand dollars. It was his gift of love.

Many people came up to Russ after the dance to say thank you. Someone gave him an envelope. Since he was very busy at the time, he slipped it into his pocket to look at later.

In the meantime, he had to pack up all the equipment. This took him until almost one in the morning. But a gift of love came to him as he was looking around for some way to haul all the equipment downstairs. Some of the ECK youth were nearby, and they offered their help. When they got the equipment downstairs, they offered to watch it while he brought his car around.

Russ got in his car and drove to the exit of the parking garage. The booth attendant said, "That'll be five dollars."

Russ had just paid out a thousand dollars, and

all he had left in his wallet was four dollars. He didn't know what to do. He reached in his pocket and felt the envelope. He opened it.

Inside was two dollars.

With his four dollar bills and this gift of love, he was able to get out of the parking lot. He realized it was a humble gift, but it was a gift from the Holy Spirit. Because the Holy Spirit knew he would need this.

Back at his hotel, a bellhop came to help him unload the equipment. All Russ had was one dollar. But he gave it to the bellhop to say thanks.

Russ realized that he had given out a thousand dollars, but it was a gift of love. The gift in the envelope was only two dollars, but it too was a gift of love. Both givers knew that the gifts they were giving were needed by others. The lesson here is that there are times that a monetary gift is all right. Because, after all, like my wife said about her paycheck, it's a gift from the Holy Spirit.

He realized it was a humble gift, but it was a gift from the Holy Spirit.

MIRACLE GIFT

Sometimes a gift of love comes in a totally different way. A woman from Canada wrote to me about an experience that happened to her when she was two or three years old, a good forty years ago. Her family lived on the third floor of an apartment building, and that particular day the little girl was wondering whether her friend was going to come over to play.

At the end of the hallway was an iron grill to keep anyone from falling to the concrete steps below. But she was only two or three years old, so her head fit between the bars very easily.

As the girl leaned out between these bars to see

whether her friend was coming up the stairs to play, she fell. She fell twenty-five feet. Below her were concrete steps. She was going down head first. She remembered being out of her body; she remembered very clearly being away from the body of this little child that was falling. Just before the child hit the concrete steps twenty-five feet below, something turned her body around so that she landed completely flat, and her head gently went back against the concrete. Otherwise the fall would have killed her.

A neighbor carried her back upstairs to her home on the third floor. It was too expensive to get a doctor, and the parents looked at their little girl. She seemed to be all right. She could move. So they didn't take her to a doctor.

But this little girl had a serious injury to her spine, and over time her spine fused at the area where the pancreatic nerves join the spinal column. At the age of fourteen she was diagnosed as a diabetic.

One day the Mahanta, the Living ECK Master, the spiritual leader of Eckankar, opened her vision.

One day the Mahanta, the Living ECK Master, the spiritual leader of Eckankar, opened her vision. He opened her awareness so that she saw and remembered the experience as it happened when she was three years old.

The little girl had said to her mother, "Mommy, the doctor came."

Both parents told her, "No, dear, the doctor didn't come."

But the girl said, "Oh, yes, he did. He put me on the kitchen table, and he looked at me. My legs were all striped pink and white. And he fixed me."

Beside this man she mistook for their family doctor was a man dressed in black. This was the Kal Niranjan, the negative force. In Christianity this force has been personified as Satan. The Kal Niranjan, or Satan, wanted to take her. But the doctor was not the family doctor. He was a very special person. Their family doctor bore a very close resemblance to Paul Twitchell.

Paul Twitchell brought out the ECK teachings in 1965. He was the Mahanta, the Living ECK Master at the time. When he died in 1971, he passed many of his responsibilities on to his successor. His successor left the position in 1981 and passed the duties of the Mahanta, the Living ECK Master on to me.

But way back then, Paul Twitchell was the Living ECK Master. He was the man she had mistaken for the family doctor. She had seen the inner bodies of these two beings. One, a being of light—Paul Twitchell, the Living ECK Master. The other, the being of darkness, Satan. The ECK Masters can have the last word over this agent of karma and reincarnation.

Kal said, "She's mine."

Paul said, "I think not. It'll be enough for her spiritual lessons in this lifetime that she ends up with a fused spine. She will be a diabetic. But she will be able to get around and not be immobilized in a wheelchair."

As an adult, this woman had been struggling with being a diabetic until she got this insight, the remembrance of what had happened way back then. She could now accept her condition with an open heart. She knew that it was a gift of love from the Holy Spirit to her.

How many people who have diabetes could say that about their condition? How many people who suffer poverty will say that of their condition? Everybody's always pointing fingers saying, "If only

She could now accept her condition with an open heart. She knew that it was a gift of love from the Holy Spirit to her.

I were someone else. If only I had better health, more money. Then I'd be the most charitable, giving person you ever saw."

Of course, in the meantime, they aren't putting to use the gifts God has given them, to be what they say they could be.

GOOD READING

I'd like to mention some books. Each of these books is a gift of love.

Over the past seven years I've been very, very ill. I am slowly regaining my health. I am thinner than I've ever been. But every moment of life is a gift of the Holy Spirit.

Many of you have sent books and information about healing. Some of these ideas were useful; many were not. I try to pass along the ideas that you've given in the form of books to those who can use them. Something may not work for me, but it may be the very thing that someone else is looking for. We all have our own state of awareness.

If you have benefited from the ECK teachings in your life, then you will want to let others have the same gift.

So I pass along your gift to someone else, even as you pass the gift of the ECK teachings along to others. If you have benefited from the ECK teachings in your life, then you will want to let others have the same gift.

I mentioned one of the books at the last seminar. It's *Your Body's Many Cries for Water* by Dr. Batmanghelidj, M.D. He speaks about the importance of drinking enough water. He tells how many diseases today are really part of your body's many cries for water. Doctors who don't understand this or recognize a certain disease as a cry for water will treat you. The treatment may help. But remember, one treatment or many treatments will often bring you back to a doctor, because a treatment is not the same as a cure.

Some of you may find that something so essential as water is sometimes a health remedy—one of the gifts of love that has been around you your whole life. It only needed your awareness to recognize its value.

The second book I'd like to mention is a very good one—*A Cosmic Sea of Words: The ECKANKAR Lexicon.* Basically, it is an expanded ECKANKAR dictionary. You may ask, what's so great about a lexicon? It's what you do with a gift that makes it special.

One of our friends in ECK told how she uses the book in her spiritual exercises. Whenever she's looking for a new word to use as a love song to God, as an alternative to HU, she opens the lexicon at random. She takes a word from the book that has a very high spiritual connotation. It must mean something special.

She will sing this word to herself quietly in contemplation. Then she lets the Holy Spirit do what It will. She may have a vivid inner dream, a vision, or maybe nothing. It may be an insight into something at work tomorrow. Or it could be something more dramatic, like a Soul Travel experience. It doesn't matter. Whatever the experience, it's a gift of love from the Holy Spirit. And the way she keys in to the Holy Spirit is by singing one of the words chosen from this ECK book.

Lately, she said she's been looking for more words under "C." Now she's going to have a lot of words to choose from. She'll open the lexicon to the listing for "C" and choose the word that seems to strike her right at the moment. She will use this word as a song of love to God.

You can sing this word quietly to yourself, or you

Whenever she's looking for a new word to use as a love song to God, as an alternative to HU, she opens the lexicon at random.

may sing it out loud. Sing it once or twice, for five or ten minutes, or for half an hour; then just go to sleep. Don't worry about it. If something happens, great. If nothing happens, it's OK, because your attitude as a child of God is always: not my will but Thine be done. It's a very easy way to live.

God Consciousness Is the Goal

I'd like to mention two more books. Those of you who are in ECK know that good health is important for anyone who seeks a higher state of consciousness. This state of consciousness may be the cosmic consciousness; Soul consciousness, which we call Self-Realization; or even God Consciousness, which is the granddaddy of them all.

God Consciousness is the goal—or will be in time. When you're ready, it will be your goal. And until you're ready, seek another goal.

God Consciousness is the goal—or will be in time. When you're ready, it will be your goal.

For those of you who are very, very ill, there is an excellent book out called *The Body Ecology Diet* by Donna Gates. I think those of you who are having very serious health problems will find some ideas in this book that may help you.

The fourth book is for those of you who like to read for enjoyment. Back in the 1930s, a woman by the name of Joan Grant wrote *Winged Pharaoh*. This is one of seven of her "far memory" books. *Winged Pharaoh* is a memory of a lifetime she spent in Egypt about 5500 B.C.

At the time, some people couldn't believe *Winged Pharaoh* became a bestseller. They dismissed it as historical fiction. Archaeologists disagreed with some of her facts. But she said that all she knows is this was life as she lived it at the time. In the meantime, archaeology had been making new discoveries and found that many of the things she spoke about are indeed true. They still have a few other things to learn.

She puts flesh and human love and emotions into a time far past. But the reason I mention this book is because it has so many beautiful spiritual insights. It could be an ECK book; the only thing missing is the word *ECK*.

Winged Pharaoh is the first of four books on her Egyptian lives. The other three are *Eyes of Horus*, *Lord of the Horizon,* and *So Moses Was Born.* Several of her books are available in bookstores. Once you get one, you can look in the back and order the rest from the publisher.

Joan Grant was very, very good. I think you'll enjoy reading these books. The first book, *Winged Pharaoh,* is about fighting for freedom and independence. The second book speaks of continuing that fight and finally gaining this freedom and independence.

The third book speaks of how the people almost lost it because of their leader, the pharaoh. When the pharaoh finally came to his senses and realized what happened, he asked for help from the holy ones, called the Watchers. Then the pharaoh put himself into agreement again with the ancient laws and the ancient principles. And those ancient principles were very much like those in the American Declaration of Independence.

A GIFT OF LOVE

So this is an important time. It's an important place. You are there. You are here. You are in this very

So this is an important time. It's an important place. You are there. You are here. You are in this very moment in the center of God's love.

moment in the center of God's love.

A gift of love.

To all who love God, to all of you who are my friends, this is my gift to you—even as you have given your gift of love to me and to each other. So I would like to end this with my gift of love to you: May the blessings be.

*ECK Summer Festival, Philadelphia, Pennsylvania,
Saturday, June 27, 1998*

On a hunch, she decided to stand way back. From the distance, the picture was almost as clear as if it had been painted by someone in the realism  school of art.

10

STAND BACK
FOR A BETTER LOOK

*E*ckankar, Religion of the Light and Sound of God, teaches that God speaks to all of us through Its voice, the Holy Spirit. Another way of referring to this Holy Spirit is the Sound and the Light. These are two of Its aspects. God sometimes talks to people through the voice of one of the messengers of God, but other times it can be through just a sound or even a light.

Claude Monet was a French painter who loved light. Unfortunately, he also developed cataracts, which may account for why he used certain garish reds and yellows.

Claude Monet removed blacks or grays from his color palette. He saw colors as from a prism. A prism takes white light, which is a composite of all colors, and breaks it down into the different colors. In a sense, this is what he saw, and he put together his palette based on the full spectrum of color broken down to the individual parts.

A MONET EXHIBIT

An ECKist named Carol decided to visit a Monet exhibit in Minneapolis. The exhibit was showing

Eckankar, Religion of the Light and Sound of God, teaches that God speaks to all of us through Its voice, the Holy Spirit.

Monet's paintings from a certain period, and she didn't much care for them. There were a lot of people at the museum for this show, and she heard similar comments.

The Holy Spirit, which we call the ECK, always brings us to situations, events, and places, or lets us meet people, because there's something to learn spiritually.

But Carol decided to stay and look at the whole exhibit anyway. Maybe she would carry away some reason for having even bothered to come. The Holy Spirit, which we call the ECK, always brings us to situations, events, and places, or lets us meet people, because there's something to learn spiritually.

Then Carol remembered she had been to a Monet exhibit in Chicago some time ago. One painting there was almost abstract, and she couldn't see anything in it. On a hunch, she decided to stand way back. From that distance she was able to see a beautiful plant. The picture was almost as clear as if it had been painted by someone in the realism school of art.

So at the exhibit in Minneapolis, she went way back. The crowd was so heavy in front of the painting she was trying to look at that she found it very difficult. She was trying to look at *The Japanese Bridge*. All she could get was an occasional glimpse of one little piece of the painting here and there from that distance.

But the picture she kept getting of this painting was very clear. It was just as she had observed in Chicago. From that distance, she saw a very clear picture.

I've often thought that painters who do these strange portraits and strange pictures probably are painting exactly what they see. Some were near-sighted, some had cataracts. Some could see auras, and they would have strange lines coming out of their artwork. But people can't understand that today, because whenever we can't see well, we go to the optometrist and he fixes us up. We come away wearing contact lenses or glasses, then everything is in focus again. It's hard to think back to a time when people didn't have the eye care they have today.

The lesson that Carol learned was this: We need to stand back to see the workings of the Holy Spirit, the ECK. We need to stand back. Stand back for a better look.

CAT WHO CAME BACK

Stories are a good way to give the message of ECK. Sometimes it's easier to listen to a story than a lot of spiritual philosophy. Stories can make us think about life from a different angle, so at least it's worth a listen.

Laura Lee, from Canada, had a cat named Crabby. Guess why. The cat was mean; she showed no consideration to anyone but Laura Lee. In fact, she loved Laura Lee so much, she'd get under her feet so that Laura Lee would trip. Laura Lee used to think that she was Crabby's owner. Cats know humans have it backward, but cats are very generous. They allow humans their little vanities. If people want to think they're the owners, that's all right. Just bring the food at the usual time, and they'll let it go.

After nine and a half years, Crabby passed on. Within a year, Laura Lee got a call from her son.

"Our cat has been in labor for three days and is having a very hard time," he said. "It doesn't look as if she's going to make it, nor any of the kittens either. Could you come over and see what you can do?"

Laura Lee was a registered nurse, but she wasn't sure how she'd be able to help a cat deliver her kittens. When she got there, she found that the first kitten was sideways in the birth canal, blocking it so that

We need to stand back to see the workings of the Holy Spirit, the ECK.

none of the kittens could be born. The mother cat was so tired that she simply couldn't fight anymore, and it looked almost as though she were going to give up.

Laura Lee got the kitten straightened out and pretty soon the kittens were being born, one by one. When kitten number three was born, the three humans in the room felt a presence immediately.

They looked at the third little kitten and said, "It's Crabby. Crabby the cat's come back!"

One of the basic beliefs in Eckankar is reincarnation. You and I are Soul, but animals are Soul too.

Animals Are Soul Too

One of the basic beliefs in Eckankar is reincarnation. You and I are Soul. And this will be news for some people, but animals are Soul too. Cats, dogs, and birds carry bodies the same as humans do.

We wear a body like a suit. When it gets old and worn out, we get rid of it. Soul then goes to one of the heavens. St. Paul spoke of the third heaven, meaning there are more than two. Soul goes to one of these heavens; it has experiences there in a body that fits that heaven, that's of the same vibration and matter. This is important, because otherwise people in that heaven couldn't see each other.

People on earth couldn't see each other if their bodies were composed of something other than physical substance. That's where ghosts come in. They're not of a physical substance.

A Strong Bond of Love

The mother cat recognized that Crabby II was Laura Lee's cat from the last lifetime. And so, on the next visit, the mother cat brought the little kitten to her. Crabby II had exactly the same mannerisms as she did in her old body as Crabby I. But instead of being mean, she was kind and gentle and sweet to everyone.

She still had the same habit of getting underfoot and tripping her pet, the human. Cats that love you very emotionally will be underfoot all the time, so you never know if you're going to make it from one room to another. Cat's tails always cause a meow of pain and indignation like, Why did you step on me again? The human pets can't always look down there through bifocals to see what's going on. A cat doesn't know this, and a cat doesn't care.

After about a year, Crabby II became a mother herself. Crabby II lost her milk, but she remembered how things should be done.

She came to Laura Lee, and she said, "Here take care of my kittens," because Laura Lee had also raised Crabby II. Every hour and a half around the clock, from the time the kittens were three days old until they were weaned, guess who had to get up and feed them? Laura Lee. Sometimes she didn't want to wake up, but Crabby II would nibble on her ear until she would have to get up and do it. You can guess who was very happy once the kittens were weaned.

Then Crabby II remembered the next thing: "Hey, this registered nurse litter-trained me. I think she can litter-train my kittens too." So she turned the kittens over to Laura Lee for litter training.

Laura Lee had had a very good relationship with Crabby I. They had their own private language. They could speak to each other, communicate by images. Cats are very good at that. It's a form of mental telepathy. Those of you who are cat owners know that. Crabby II had that ability and more.

They had their own private language. They could speak to each other, communicate by images.

GOD'S LOVE IS EVERYWHERE

They named one of the kittens Bear. He thought he was a human being. He would sit on the floor the way a child does, flat on his bottom with his legs spread out in front of him. When Bear laid down to sleep, he slept flat on his back.

Bear loved to play with the grandchildren when they came over, and he even knew how to play with toys and make them work. He developed a way of communicating with Laura Lee. He liked to say hello, good morning, good-bye, please, thank you, and I'm sorry. He also liked to give kisses and little bear hugs. When Laura Lee was angry at one of the other animals in her home, Bear, the son of Crabby II, would become very angry too. He would swat the other animal on the behind.

One day Laura Lee's stepmother came to visit. The woman was feeling very sad because she was far away from her own family and missed them. So she began to cry. Bear looked at her with the saddest eyes you can imagine.

God's love comes through all beings who have a golden heart, an open heart.

As the tears came down the woman's face, Bear reached up a paw and wiped the tears from her cheek.

Everyone else in the room was laughing, because Bear thought he was human. He showed sympathy; he gave the woman a hug and wiped away her tears. Even the stepmother had to laugh; she realized that God's love is everywhere.

God's love comes through all beings who have a golden heart, an open heart. That means people who love others more than they love themselves.

This does not mean that you think little of yourself. How could you? As Soul, as a creation of God, you should have the very highest regard for yourself. You should love yourself in the highest, purest way, not in the low ways that many of you would normally associate with love—meaning pride and vanity.

Love yourself as you would love God. And love

others as you would love yourself, because then you
are truly loving all as God loves you.

The lesson that Laura Lee got was this: Some
animals, like people, have a high state of consciousness because they are Soul too.

So stand back for a better look.

LIFE, LOVE, AND ATTENTION

Linda worked in an office. In the reception area
was a plant. One day as she walked by, Linda had
this feeling that the plant was calling to her for help.

For the first time she took a good look at the plant.
There were no windows in this office; the plant had
survived a long time in artificial light. But now some
of its leaves had turned brown and dropped off. Other
leaves were drooping. Someone had been pouring Coke
and coffee grounds into this plant's pot. Its roots were
exposed. That's why the plant was dying.

Linda asked around the office to find out who
cared for the plant. No one cared for it. So she gave
it some water.

The next day when she came back to work, she
brought all the little things necessary to make this
plant well. She put soil over the exposed roots, then
she gave it more water. When she came back the
second day, she found someone had put eggshells on
the soil as a fertilizer. Someone else cared about the
plant too. But when she asked around, no one admitted taking responsibility for the plant.

So Linda put up a note on the wall behind the
plant asking people to stop putting coffee grounds
and Coke in the pot. And the next time she came in,
she brought a saucer to put under the pot, because
the one that was there was cracked and didn't hold
much water.

Love yourself as you would love God. And love others as you would love yourself, because then you are truly loving all as God loves you.

Pretty soon the plant was back on the road to health. And once a week Linda would give it water. She asked that no one else do that, because as a gardener she realized that too much water is as bad as too little.

A short time later, Linda found out that she had been appointed to the clergy in Eckankar. She realized that the love and attention the plant needed is the same sort of love and attention people need. Linda needed this lesson brought home to her. The Holy Spirit did that through the sick plant at work.

The lesson she learned was that our love and attention can make things in our lives better.

The lesson she learned was that our love and attention can make things in our lives better.

Stand back for a better look.

RED SILK TULIPS

Joyce lives in St. Louis, Missouri. One cold January, a heavy snow had fallen. She went out to shop, and she noticed that the store sold bunches of silk tulips. *Anything that promises spring might bring a ray of sunshine to my children,* she thought. So she bought six or seven bunches of these tulips.

When Joyce got home and arranged them, she had one bunch left over. She didn't know what to do with it.

Looking outside at the cold and the snow around her mailbox, she thought it would be a good idea to leave the extra flowers for the mail carrier. And she did. Then she pretty much forgot about the gift she had given.

Ten years passed. Joyce's husband passed on, or translated, as we say in Eckankar. One day his daughter was at a gathering where she met the wife of the mailman. The mail carrier's wife expressed sympathy for the passing of her father and said, "I'll never forget the woman your father was married to."

Ten years earlier this mail carrier's wife had been very sick, facing a serious operation. She asked God, "Please give me a sign." She said to God, "If I'm supposed to survive this operation, bring me some flowers."

The chance of getting flowers in January put the odds very much against her. But that's what the mail carrier's wife asked of God. It happened to be the same day that Joyce bought an extra bunch of red silk tulips and gave them to the mail carrier. When the mailman walked in the door with the red tulips, the sick woman knew that God had answered her prayer. The operation would be a success. And it was a success. The woman had since lived a healthy life.

The Holy Spirit, the ECK, works through us to bring love and assurance to people we may never meet.

The lesson for Joyce: The Holy Spirit, the ECK, works through us to bring love and assurance to people we may never meet.

Stand back for a better look.

CYCLE CHANGES

A woman I'll call Ellen had a problem with a neighbor. She learned a spiritual lesson from this that was painful, but Soul-cleansing at the same time. And it took seven years.

Ellen felt she was at a spiritual standstill. She had come to the end of a twelve-year cycle. In Eckankar we know that a twelve-year cycle is one of those major cycles of new spiritual growth. Big changes often happen at twelve-year cycles. But Ellen was also at the end of a seven-year cycle, a minor cycle, but also very important. The seven-year cycle was with her neighbor.

When they moved in seven years ago, Ellen's son and her neighbor's son were the same age. The neighbor was a strongly outspoken Christian. This was no problem for the ECKist. They got along fine for a while, then suddenly their friendship began to turn cool.

Ellen's husband said, "It's the phone you're using. They're listening in on your calls."

This is the age of cordless and cellular phones, and these are really radio broadcasting stations. If there's anything private you want to say, don't do it on a cordless or cellular phone. A lot of people can overhear you, because the electronics industry has thoughtfully provided scanners which eavesdrop on conversations over the air. So one or two of her neighbors had been listening in on her phone calls to the ECK center.

Pretty soon the neighbor's son began to make fun of Ellen's son. The neighbor's son called her son "Buddha man." Then her son came home and said, "Mom, am I saved?" The children's play had suddenly turned into something that was not very friendly. There was no freedom involved, no respect for another person's religion or beliefs.

Ellen's son always allowed the neighbor's son freedom to be a Christian.

Ellen's son always allowed the neighbor's son freedom to be a Christian. But the Christian family began to speak badly about the ECKists.

Years passed, and the neighbor had more children. These younger siblings would hide at the fence that separated their backyards. They'd tell their friends who came over to play, "Look over there. The devil's house." It's a terrible thing what people do to each other. The ECKist mother was very hurt by this. If you ever want to know what your neighbors think about you, listen to what their children say.

The Christian husband was a good man. He came over and apologized for his children. But the ECK mother and the Christian mother had an old enmity from previous lifetimes.

They wouldn't allow each other to have their beliefs. Now Ellen, the ECKist, began to be a snob. When she'd meet the other mother in a store, she would ignore her. And when the other mother was outside and waved to her, Ellen ignored her. Their sons were in the Boy Scouts together, and the fathers would usually make sure that the sons got to these meetings. But whenever there was a gathering where both fathers and mothers came, Ellen would ignore the Christian woman.

Ellen realized she had hit a spiritual wall.

But now, after seven years, Ellen realized she had hit a spiritual wall. Not only that, she and her family were soon going to move away. This was old karma, and she recognized that. She didn't want it to hang over. She didn't want to leave the situation like it was.

She got the feeling that she should go to the neighbor with some flowers and apologize for her rudeness. But she found it hard. One day she finally got up the courage, bought the flowers, went to the door. The husband opened the door. He was kind and gracious, but he said, "My wife's been in bed all day with a headache."

Ellen said, "I came to apologize for my rude behavior over these past seven years." Ellen thought, *I'll give him the flowers, turn around, and leave.*

But the husband knew a good thing when he saw it. He said, "Wait here. Let me go check and see if she'll see you."

Change of Heart

Why did Ellen have this change of heart?

The Holy Spirit worked it out like this: A few weeks earlier, Ellen's sister had brought over a baby monitor. Baby monitors are basically radios. They work through the wiring of the house, sending radio waves just like a radio station, just like cellular and cordless telephones. Ellen plugged the baby monitor in, and she was surprised to hear her neighbor's voice.

> In Eckankar, we allow total freedom to other people. That includes not eavesdropping on them.

Here's Ellen's test. In Eckankar, we allow total freedom to other people. That includes not eavesdropping on them. It's not our business.

Ellen realized this must have been what happened earlier—the neighbor had actually overheard her. Ellen's husband had tried to tell her, "They're listening in on you because of the phone you are using." Ellen wouldn't believe it. Her husband had also told her the reason the Christian lady looked down on her and turned her children against her is because of religious bias against their religion.

Yet every time Ellen would then see the Christian lady, the lady was all smiles—false smiles. That's what hurt Ellen, and that's why she became a snob.

Ellen said, "I'm an ECKist. I cannot listen in on my neighbor's conversation on this baby monitor." She turned it off and put it away.

But one day she said, "I want to listen one more time." The ECK, the Holy Spirit, had given her the nudge to listen one more time. She overheard a phone conversation between her neighbor and one of the neighbor's friends. The neighbor said, "The public doesn't know who I am. I always wear a mask in public." She told of her heartaches, her pain, her insecurities, so that by the time Ellen finished listening to her neighbor's conversation, she was crying.

That's when she decided to buy the flowers, go next door, and make things right.

MENDING FENCES

The neighbor came out without her makeup on, something she never did in public. Her makeup was part of her public mask. She accepted Ellen's flowers and gave her a very warm hug. For the next two hours they sat there talking things out. They ended up laughing. Ellen even joked, "You know, when I showed up today, I thought you'd kick me right off your doorstep."

Later they met in stores and in public, and they were able to say, "Hi, how are you? How are you doing?" They never became close friends in the short time that Ellen was still there, but they became friends.

Ellen's lesson: She realized that everyone has something to work on or they wouldn't be here. That means you, your neighbor, everyone. To move ahead spiritually, we must let go of the past. To love others despite any ill treatment they may give you.

Stand back for a better look to see the workings of God.

She realized that everyone has something to work on or they wouldn't be here. That means you, your neighbor, everyone.

VIRTUAL LIFE

People learn spiritual lessons better when times are hard. The United States of America has been enjoying an unprecedented boom—some call it a bubble—for many years, with one dip in the early nineties. So people lose their ability to listen to the Voice of God.

Things are so good. People can buy so many things—like bigger TV sets. And computers. It's possible to go into the virtual world of a computer and get totally absorbed in an unreal world, so that it no longer matters whether the sun shines or the rain falls. Computers at work, computers at home, computers early, computers late. And when it's not computers, it's TV or movies.

We're virtually alive. Or another way of saying it is, We're virtually dead spiritually.

Baby Chicks

This story is from Nigeria. There has been much political turmoil in that country, and members of Eckankar gain from the spiritual lessons that occur during times of hardship.

A Nigerian man learned a spiritual lesson through some baby chicks. One night in November, a very heavy rain fell. Sometime during the night, a woman came to him and said she'd found three little chicks. They were separated from their mother. The woman said, "I know you have chicks like that. Are these yours?"

The man looked at them and said, "No. I wish they were, but they're not."

The woman said, "Would you please take care of them?"

The chicks were about three days old. They were peeping; they were cold and hungry. It looked as if they weren't going to make it through the night. So this good man poured out his heart to these three little chicks. He gave them food and medicine and vitamins. He warmed the room for them. All he had was a kerosene lamp for warmth. Kerosene was very expensive, but he kept the lantern lit all night.

When morning came he looked around for the mother hen and for the owner. But he didn't look very

A Nigerian man learned a spiritual lesson through some baby chicks.

hard, because he thought of keeping the chicks for himself if they made it.

A week later, his landlady came by.

His landlady was an ECKist too. She said, "Oh, I'm so glad you found them. My hen had six chicks and lost all of them in the rainstorm. But you found three. Would you take care of them until they grow up?"

The man suddenly lost interest in the chicks, because they could not be his. He told the landlady, "No, I won't take care of them." But then he noticed she didn't feed them, so he began feeding them grudgingly.

A week passed. The next day was Sunday. The ECKist went to the worship service at the local ECK center. After the talk, the group sang HU, a love song to God. During the HU Song, as the ECKist sat there with his eyes shut, the Mahanta, the Inner Master, spoke to him. The Mahanta said, "What kind of love do you think you're giving to the chicks? You gave love when you thought them yours. When you found out they weren't yours, you withdrew this so-called love. And yet you're always asking the Master to show you how to give divine love, to serve life. Now you waste a chance. Later you'll again ask for ways to serve God."

After the ECK Worship Service was over, he said to the ECK woman, "I'd be happy to take care of the chicks for you."

The woman said, "If any survive, you can have one of them."

One chick. What good's that? he thought. It's what made him angry in the first place. He had saved the three chicks. Look at all the money he'd spent, all the time he'd invested. And now his landlady says, "Oh, if they survive, you can have *one*"?

During the HU Song, as the ECKist sat there with his eyes shut, the Mahanta, the Inner Master, spoke to him.

He was hurt, so he closed his heart. It's when our feelings are hurt that we close our heart. And then the Mahanta, the Living ECK Master, spoke to him again through the inner communication.

The Master said, "What kind of love is that?"

The lesson that this Nigerian ECKist learned was that true love has no strings attached to it. True service to God is always an adventure in learning spiritual things.

> True service to God is always an adventure in learning spiritual things.

Showing True Love

Good parents discipline their children so the children grow up in their society as good citizens. Poor parents let their children do whatever they want, in the mistaken belief that this is love. It's not love. It's almost the reverse. Not hatred maybe, but guilt. The parent says, "I've had it so good. How can I make it even better for my children?" Perhaps the parent's parents had come through the depression, they knew hardship. So when their children came along, they gave them things—material things—as much as they could.

Now the generation that grew up with so many material things asks, "What can I do for my children to show them love?"

Illusion comes onstage and says, Give them the freedom that adults have earned. So children in these misguided homes are given freedoms they haven't earned. And people wonder why there is so much crime. Look in the home. Look at how the parents raise their children.

It hurts to look at ourselves in the light of truth. We don't like to hear the truth. People become very angry. Even good ECKists say, "That is not true. We are giving our children spiritual freedom."

Actually, the parents are shirking their spiritual

responsibility to their children. But it takes a mature Soul to know that.

Stand back for a better look.

Stand Back for a Better Look

Carol learned at the Monet exhibit to stand back to see the picture clearly. This is what you must do as a truth seeker.

If you want truth, you must step back. Learn to see more than other people do. You do this by putting your attention on God. In ECK, we do it through the spiritual exercises. In other religions people do it through meditation or prayer.

Whatever you can do to create a closer link with God, do it. It's very important. You're here, as well as your neighbor, to learn something—or you wouldn't be here.

If you want truth, you must step back. Learn to see more than other people do.

ECK European Seminar, July 25, 1998,
The Hague, The Netherlands

Only Soul Travel, which is in the care and teaching of the ECK Masters, can take you to the Soul Plane.

11
God Is Love

*E*verybody knows that God is love. It's very easy to say. But if people who say they believe this principle would hold to it and practice it in their everyday lives, this would be a better world.

This is the main divine law of all laws: simply, God is love.

The second of the two great laws is: Soul exists because God loves It. And that's it.

This is the main divine law of all laws: simply, God is love. The second is: Soul exists because God loves It.

Opening to New Ideas

The information age has opened up so many subjects that used to be taboo. Not so many years ago, dreams were held in very low regard. But now people are starting to accept dreams. Television has broadcast so many shows about near-death experiences that people are getting quite accustomed to hearing about light, beings of light, and modern manifestations of angels. They don't need to rely on someone's account of a saint who lived three centuries ago or more.

People today are experiencing the sort of miracles that the church would not acknowledge just a few short years ago. People even claim to be out of their bodies—can you imagine! Doctors, social philosophers, and religionists are now studying the question: Were they really out of their body, or was this some sort of mind trip?

Someday people will even get used to the fact of Soul Travel. This goes beyond astral travel and mind travel, the common teachings of psychic groups. Generally, astral travel takes the individual to the next plane closest to the earth, the Astral Plane, which is the plane of emotion—the area where emotions originate. Some of the more spiritually advanced people can go on to the mental areas with mind travel. This sort of travel can take them to the lower Mental Plane, which is the Causal Plane; then to the true Mental Plane; and finally to the high area of the Mental Plane, which is the Etheric Plane.

Only Soul Travel, which is in the care and teaching of the ECK Masters, can take you to the Soul Plane.

But only Soul Travel, which is in the care and teaching of the ECK Masters, can take you to the Soul Plane.

Many Heavens

If you want to understand it in everyday terms, a plane is simply a level of heaven.

At one point Paul the Apostle said that he knew a man who was caught up even unto the third heaven. Not just heaven, but the third heaven. That presumes heavens one and two. The third heaven often equates to the main Mental Plane. It is the home base, or the foundation, of Christianity. This doesn't at all mean that all of its followers go there. Most of them go to a heaven on the Astral Plane. But the saints of Christianity, those who are of the highest spiritual level, go to the Mental Plane and perhaps the Etheric Plane.

How We Realize Spiritual Truths

One morning I was up at four o'clock, and the host on one of the local radio stations told about a dream experience he had had just a short time before. He called it a profound dream.

He'd been having financial difficulties, and he didn't know quite how to resolve them. So he went on a camping trip with a friend, because when he got to the great outdoors, he felt he was in God's garden. It gave him a chance to get away from the hustle and bustle of everyday living and look at himself, reexamine his values, and see who and what he really was.

One night while out camping, he had a dream with his departed grandmother. He woke up in the dream, and she was in the kitchen.

One night while out camping, he had a dream with his departed grandmother. He woke up in the dream, and she was in the kitchen. She handed him a catalog. She pointed to it, saying, "It can solve your financial problems."

When he woke up he told his friend about this dream, then forgot all about it. But his financial worries were still troubling him. All he needed was about two thousand dollars to resolve them. Then he remembered the catalog that his grandmother had shown him in the dream. There was a circle around the picture of an Italian motorbike, a Lambretta. It was just like the old one he had in the garage. But it didn't make any sense.

Two months later, the man was talking to someone, and he happened to mention that he had this old motorbike sitting in the garage. He hadn't used it for years, but it was in good condition. The friend asked him what kind it was. "A Lambretta," he said. "What year?" When the man told him, his friend said, "That thing's worth about two thousand dollars."

All of a sudden the man said, "Two thousand—the magic number." And just that quickly his dream came back to him.

This is how the spiritual truths are making their way out into today's society. Why did his grandmother help him? Because she loved him. We come back to the principle: God is love. And the second one: Soul exists because God loves It. Because God loves Soul, Souls should love each other. Or as Christ said, "Love thy neighbour as thyself."

He didn't say to hate yourself, wear a hair shirt, and treat your neighbor better than yourself. No, he was speaking about Soul to Souls. He was telling them, "You are God's creation. But so is your neighbor."

This is a point that has been missed in so many religious teachings in churches today. Love yourself because God loved you, and love your neighbor as yourself. It's very simple.

The toughest job of the Mahanta, the Living ECK Master has to do with changing the incentives of a truth seeker.

Go Outside the Box

The toughest job of the Mahanta, the Living ECK Master has to do with changing the incentives of a truth seeker. People are born into the world of material goods. This world has certain values. Pay homage to these values, and everything goes along better than not. But if you want to find truth, sometimes you find the tide is going against you.

The inclination is to follow the path of pleasure and avoid the one of pain. It stands to reason. If people have a choice of walking barefoot on a gravel road or on a grassy lawn, most would pick the grassy lawn. I would.

Yet when it comes to the search for truth, you've got to go outside the box. You've got to go outside the area that other people are afraid to go beyond. This doesn't mean you have to talk about your inner life to others. It means everyone owes it to himself to try new things spiritually.

If something is boring you, if you've become tired in your teaching, if it's become nothing more than a comfortable routine, it could be a sign of spiritual stagnation.

So the Master's got to give the truth seeker a new incentive.

Everyone owes it to himself to try new things spiritually.

INCENTIVES

Two cowboys were riding in the desert. They got into an argument. Each said he had the slower horse, and they bet ten dollars on it. They said their goal would be the next water hole. An hour later they were still there in the desert. Neither had moved his horse one step. Each was afraid to lose the ten-dollar bet.

Along rode an old cowboy. He came up, stopped, dismounted, and said, "Hello, there. What are you two doing sitting up there?" The two cowboys got off their horses and explained the problem to him. They told him about the bet.

The old cowboy thought for a moment. Then he whispered two words to each of them. They immediately jumped on the horses and took off for the water hole.

And what did the old cowboy whisper? "Switch horses."

The old cowboy changed their incentive. And that's my job—in some way to help you change your spiritual incentive. Actually, it's to change your incentive from a material to a spiritual one. I wish it were as easy as just saying, "Switch horses." It's not quite as focused as that—but nearly.

The way to change your spiritual incentive is through the Spiritual Exercises of ECK.

You can use any method, from whatever religion you're in, to go to the quiet place within your heart. Go there and be still. Just be still. Don't go there and numb God's ears with a list of requests and demands. God knows what's good for you without your little point of view, with your materialism, and deciding what's better or worse.

Just go to that quiet place and listen. Listen to the divine Voice of God. The Voice of God is the Holy Spirit. That's the answer to the great mystery of what the Holy Spirit is. It's simply the Voice of God. It's so simple—as simple as *God is love.*

Listen to the divine Voice of God. The Voice of God is the Holy Spirit.

Making It Right

Janet and her sister take their mother to a big picnic in a nearby state every August. The mother likes to go there because it's a place that offers games where people can win homemade quilts, cakes, and other prizes. Other good things are available besides—like boxes of peaches. And vendors sell fresh fish sandwiches made right on the spot. So Janet and her sister enjoy taking their mother there, even though it involves a little travel, because they all have such a good time.

Janet likes to play bingo. So at the picnic, Janet sat down at the bingo table. Janet's mother and sister wanted to go to some other games, but they stayed with Janet because her game was starting first.

Janet wanted to play two bingo cards, and each card cost a dollar. Janet only had a twenty-dollar bill. She really didn't want to give the bingo vendor such a big bill for just a two-dollar charge, but she had no choice. The vendor gave her change and walked away. The bingo game started. Janet had her cards down in front of her, and she looked at her change. The man gave her four dollars too much. She said to her mother and sister, "He gave me too much."

They said, "Just keep it. You'll spend it anyway."

But it didn't feel right to Janet. So she waved her arm to get the bingo-card seller back. The people around her are wondering, Why doesn't she just keep the four dollars and buy four more cards with it later?

The man came back. Janet said, "You gave me four dollars too much. It's best always to make something right as soon as possible." The man couldn't believe it. He thought she was a special woman. He was grateful, and he walked back through the crowd selling more cards for the next game.

And so the game goes along. Two games later the card seller happened to be standing right behind Janet. He said, "You're going to win." He could see she almost had her card filled. Janet won a home-made quilt.

A little bit later she won twenty-five dollars— that was the same amount she'd spent that day. Plus a basket full of kitchen supplies. People began to look at Janet and wonder.

Now Janet's getting a little bit cocky. She tells her mom, "I'm going to win the cake for you." And she did.

But it was the sort of cake that her mother couldn't eat. "Could I trade it for an angel food cake?" Janet asked. Since there were a lot of cakes on hand to give away or sell, she got the angel food cake, and, like an angel, Janet gave it to her mother.

Her mother looked at the cake, and she began to wonder too. She said, "I always feel guilty when someone gives me the wrong change. But the difference is that I never make it right."

Janet said, "You gave me four dollars too much. It's best always to make something right as soon as possible."

Her mother may have given Janet and her sister the right training, yet her practice in everyday life was to fudge on the corners just a little bit with little white lies—things that wouldn't really hurt anyone very much. Yet Janet came out of that household, and through Eckankar she learned that you've got to make things right.

> You've got to make things right. Do it now, or do it later. It's cheaper now.

Do it now, or do it later. It's cheaper now.

Back at home the next day, Janet got a call from the parish. She had won a raffle. The prize was a basket full of Beanie Babies. Janet gave the Beanie Babies to her daughter, who was thrilled.

A short time later, there was a radio contest. The prize was a case of tomato juice. Janet doesn't really care for tomato juice, but she entered the contest anyway. She thought about how nice it would be to win a prize and surprise her husband. They had moved into a new home, there was a lot of landscaping to do, and there wasn't time to put in a full garden. But her husband had found time in his busy schedule to build three wooden planters and put plants in them for her.

She got a call from the radio station, telling her she had won. So she drove to the station to pick up her case of tomato juice.

Before she got there, the lobby was full of bickering people. One of the other winners had complained on the air about having been cheated out of the right prize. Another person felt she should have had that other person's prize. They were arguing and back and forth, each grabbing for the prize they wanted. The prize that was left was a case of tomato sauce. The receptionist decided to store it under the counter so nobody could see it. She didn't want to hassle with those people anymore.

When Janet arrived, the case of tomato juice was gone. But the receptionist handed her the case of tomato sauce. Much more useful to Janet. She gave this prize to her husband as a thank-you gift.

All these prizes weren't important to Janet. She said the spiritual qualities that were strengthened in her were of more value. The real prize was meeting so many people and sharing love with them.

WHAT ARE VIBRATIONS?

Joyce has been in Eckankar for thirty years, and through the many years one of the principles she could never understand was the idea of spiritual vibrations. What impact could they have upon this world, anyhow? It didn't make any sense. To her, vibrations were flighty, fluffy things that went twittering and flying out there in the ethers somewhere. They certainly had no connection to this gross material plane. Vibrations were simply too far out. She found this very difficult to resolve in her mind.

As a volunteer, Joyce was driving cloistered nuns from the Catholic church to their medical and dental appointments. They all looked forward to it. Joyce enjoyed these trips, and the nuns did too.

Cloistered nuns have no contact with the outside world except on a very limited basis. Even when friends or family come to visit them, they talk through a grill, just like in a prison. You might wonder, *Are these people more spiritual? Or are they just out of it?* There have been people throughout history who have felt a special need to devote an entire lifetime to listening to God. That's what these nuns do. They have their duties, their worship service, but there's also time to be alone. There is time to be still. There is time to listen to the Voice of God, the Holy Spirit.

There have been people throughout history who have felt a special need to devote an entire lifetime to listening to God.

Most of you have lived a cloistered life in a past lifetime. If anything would define an ECKist who is walking the talk, it would be compassion. I feel that anyone who has advanced to any degree on the spiritual path will have a lot of compassion.

If anything would define an ECKist who is walking the talk, it would be compassion.

COMPASSION AND SYMPATHY

There's a difference between compassion and sympathy. A lot of people have sympathy for others, but sympathy is feeling sorry for someone lesser than you.

What does this automatically do? Puts you above them. That's sympathy. You'll find a lot of sympathy in the social welfare programs that abound in society today. You will find this misguided sympathy is the basis for the government programs and the taxes that support them.

A lot of emotion goes into these issues. Save the children, save the poor, the planet is going to warm too much and people in the South Sea islands are going to wake up knee-deep in water. That happened thousands of years ago. Suddenly, for no reason at all—certainly it wasn't from human pollution—earth's temperature just went above normal. Many scientists who study earth changes believe that the cycles of warming and cooling are actually caused by solar bursts from the sun. There have been many studies done. People who support the idea of global warming usually bring up some study backed by scientists, but it's often a broad body of scientists that includes dentists, doctors, psychiatrists, and a lot of other people who have no special knowledge about earth temperatures. And often their words are twisted to be something other than what they originally said.

This is sympathy. It's people taking the viewpoint that they are of a higher sort of an elite, and they know what's best for their inferiors.

ECKists have compassion. Compassion is different. Compassion means that I've walked in your moccasins, but I won't tell you of the pebbles I felt in my journey. Instead I will listen as you tell me about the pebbles in your moccasins. Compassionate people listen and understand what the other person is going through. They really understand the pain. It's not just an easy phrase that's thrown out: "I feel your pain." Most people who say this don't feel the pain. If they did they couldn't talk about it, because the pain hurts too much.

When you see someone else walking the road you have just come, you may put your arm around the person and say, "I love you." Then be still and listen, the way God is still and speaks to us in the silence with the voice of silence. The voice of silence is the Holy Spirit, the ECK.

The voice of silence is the Holy Spirit, the ECK.

SEAT-BELT WARNING

So Joyce and the nuns loved this drive to and from their medical and dental appointments because it gave them a chance to talk about spiritual things. They'd laugh, they'd talk, they'd joke, and they'd just have a good time.

The nuns knew Joyce was an ECKist, but they felt she had so much love to give to others. Of course, they did too. That's why they got along so well.

One day Joyce took the Mother Superior on one of these appointments, and they got talking. They became so excited talking about spiritual subjects. Suddenly the seat-belt warning bell started going off, saying, Fasten your seat belts. They checked their seat belts, but they were already fastened. They fiddled with the belt attachments, but the warning buzzer wouldn't stop. So they just sat there quietly, trying to figure out what to do next.

As soon as they were quiet, the seat belt warning would stop. It took a few trips with this happening, but pretty soon Joyce and the nuns began to make a connection. They began to notice that when they got excited talking about spiritual things, their vibrations went very high. They were getting out of control. They were out of balance.

The ECK, the Holy Spirit, would send a reminder to them through this seat-belt warning. It got so they'd joke about it. Whenever the buzzer would go off, they'd just say, "Oh, our vibrations are too high again."

From this, Joyce learned the connection that vibrations have between spiritual and material things. She had wondered, *How could a spiritual vibration have any effect upon the material world?* She realized that these things do happen. It had happened right in her car. And if positive thoughts have an effect, then wouldn't negative thoughts have an effect too? She realized how destructive negative words and thoughts can be to us in this world.

Many people who are poor, but not by conscious choice, have made themselves poor because of negative thoughts or deeds.

Many people who are poor, but not by conscious choice, have made themselves poor because of negative thoughts or deeds. It may have been in a past lifetime. It may have been in their current lifetime. Sometimes just having an inferiority complex is the reason some people are poor. They think they're not worth anything. When they go to a job interview, they have no idea of their worth. They don't know their worth to themselves, so how can they know their worth to a prospective employer? They usually settle for too little.

There's a fair price for any job. Sometimes, especially for the staff at the ECK Spiritual Center, you get the pay in other ways too. Sometimes there are spiritual gifts. Sometimes what you learn through service to others repays you many times over.

LEARNING THE SECRET OF LIFE

Remember, if you're in this audience tonight, you probably came into this lifetime with a particular goal. And that goal was to learn the secret of life.

I've just told it to you: God is love.

But you knew that before you came into this hall tonight. So what's keeping you from truth? It's the realization, not the knowledge. Knowledge is just a mental thing. But it's the realization that you are Soul. That you are worth something. Because God loved you first.

Once this becomes a realization in you, you will find yourself helping others. Not because you feel you are of the nobility helping the trash down there, even though you veil it in nice words: the *poor*, the *children*, using all those nice words which are based on emotional values. But when you have the realization, the true realization, of what *God is love* means, then you're just willing to serve others because you love them. You love them because God first loved you.

You exist because of God's love. So does your neighbor. And if your neighbor needs help and you can give it, you help yourself.

LEARNING TO SERVE OTHERS

A friend of mine was trying to make the jump to serving others. So he wrote to me. He wanted some help and some insight. I wrote a note back to him,

Sometimes what you learn through service to others repays you many times over.

suggesting that whenever he's in a situation where he doesn't know what to do, to ask himself, What would love do now?

Then he asked me about discrimination. Who do you give to? Some people don't deserve it, and you've got only so much time, energy, and money to give. This is earth. Everything has limitations. In this time and age where everything is against discrimination, he was trying to figure out how to discriminate between right giving and wrong giving.

One morning this businessman was cutting across a parking lot on his way to work. He noticed two teenagers approaching him. One called out, "Hey, Mister, you got any spare change?" Without thinking, the man quipped back, "You're too young to beg."

"No, I'm not."

"You look healthy, you can earn your own money."

The teen snapped back, "What are you afraid of? Are you holding it for retirement?"

Just at that moment, a disheveled man in his late thirties approached them. He had the eyes and complexion of an alcoholic. He asked if he could have some change for breakfast. Without even a second thought, the businessman reached in his pocket, pulled out a dollar, and gave it to the panhandler.

The panhandler was surprised. Usually he got just a few nickels or dimes, or was told to be on his way. A whole dollar!

The two teens looked at this man, who a moment before wouldn't give them spare change. And even while they're still talking, he reaches in his pocket and gives money to a panhandler—more than the panhandler expected.

The lesson the businessman learned is that he can help those who approach him. The teens, how-

> *Who do you give to? Some people don't deserve it, and you've got only so much time, energy, and money to give.*

ever, got something other than coins. He said in his letter that the experience was a lot of fun. He's finding that when he opens his heart to God's love and just lets the Holy Spirit, this Voice of God, tell him what to do and when to do it, he's happy. It's the sort of regard that no one else could fully understand, unless it's a person who's been beat up by life himself and has learned compassion.

LIVING THE PRINCIPLE OF LOVE

The two supreme laws again are: God is love, and Soul exists because God loves It. Very simple.

But how do you make this work out in everyday life?

Whenever you're in doubt about any action, ask yourself: Is it true? Is it necessary? Is it kind? You can also ask, as I suggested in my note to the businessman, What would love do now?

Another person has broken this down a little bit more. I've mentioned Richard Maybury before. He's an author, educator, and economist who's written a book called *Whatever Happened to Justice?* In it he gives the two laws he condensed which are common to all good religions in the world today.

For those of you who haven't heard of Richard Maybury's two laws, the first is: Do all you have agreed to do. This is the basis of contract law. The second law is: Do not encroach on other persons or their property. This is the basis of tort law and some criminal law.

Maybury's two laws spell out in very concrete terms how to apply the great supreme laws in everyday living.

If people truly live the principle God is love, they will do all they have agreed to do. There would be

Whenever you're in doubt about any action, ask yourself: Is it true? Is it necessary? Is it kind? You can also ask, What would love do now?

none of these legal disputes, or very few of them. And people who actually live the principle God is love will not encroach on other persons or their property. They wouldn't steal from them or use lawsuits to try to get something for nothing. They would take responsibility for their own actions and their own behavior.

With that I'll say, God is love. So enjoy God's love as it comes through you and as it comes through your neighbor. May the blessings be.

ECK Worldwide Seminar, Minneapolis, Minnesota,
Saturday, October 24, 1998

God's love is a wonderful thing. It shows up in people we love, in the animals, birds, and other pets we have that we love.

12
God's Love Is a Wonderful Thing

A newspaper article in the Minneapolis *Star Tribune* was titled "Sit up and listen. It's good for your heart." Kim Ode, the writer, mentioned that when people hear an old-timer in the family begin to reminisce, sometimes they say, "Oh, no. Not again." But two professors and a student did some research on this. They found that listening as well as reminiscing are essential to mental and physical health.

We feel better when someone is really listening to us. The physical benefit for the listener is that listening lowers a listener's heart rate.

One of the professors gave advice to a friend who was soon to visit his crabby old grandmother; the friend dreaded the visit. The professor said, "Let her go on for a bit, then find the least bad thing she said and ask her about that. Then find the least bad thing she said about that, and keep going."

The friend later said not only was it a nice visit, but Grandma kept in a good mood for days.

> We feel better when someone is really listening to us.

It's Good to Be Alive

Those of you who have gone through hard times with your physical health find you have more compassion for those in a similar situation. When you get well from something that's been really tough on you, you say, "It's good to be alive." It's a way to check how difficult an experience was.

Other people may wonder how such a person even manages to get along from day to day. Still the person says, "It's good to be alive." They're recognizing the blessing of the spiritual life.

Grace under Pressure

After a while, he said to the receptionist, "Every time I come here, you people are so happy. How do you keep this good attitude?"

A print vendor came to the ECK Spiritual Center. He was a few minutes early for an appointment with someone in the graphics department. So he sat there quietly for a few moments. After a while, he said to the receptionist, "Every time I come here, you people are so happy. How do you keep this good attitude?"

He was helping us with one of our printing jobs and came to suggest ways to make it a little easier and less expensive. He'd noticed that Stan, the person he was waiting to see, keeps calm and kind through all the crises that come up in printing.

"I came here to help you," he said, "but maybe I should ask you to tell me the secret for your happiness."

Sometimes people say, when they leave the ECK Spiritual Center, "I'm going out into the real world." At the ECK Spiritual Center it's no different from in the real world. The real world is right where you are.

When people feel they're not in the real world, wherever they are, they're actually out of touch with reality. They should go where they feel comfortable, so they can be in tune with themselves. Or they should be quiet and find out what there is to like about where they are.

My wife, Joan, had a meeting with an outside accountant who comes in to deal with some of our financial matters. This person also said, "You people are always so happy. Why is it?"

Joan said, "The reason we're happy is that we love what we do."

PURPOSE OF LIVING

God's love is a wonderful thing. It shows up in people we love, in the animals, birds, and other pets we have that we love. It shows up in all different ways in what we love. In case you haven't discovered it, the whole purpose in living, the whole purpose of God's plan, is so each of us—you and you and you— learn how to love. That's it.

As a creation of God, you are Soul. You are of the substance of the divine Holy Spirit, the Voice of God. We call It the ECK.

And love begins where? It begins with those who are near and dear to us. If we can't love them, how are we ever going to love God? And before you can love those who are near and dear to you, you've got to learn to love yourself.

That's why Christ said to love your neighbor as yourself. He didn't say more than yourself or less than yourself, which is hate or anger. But love your neighbor *as* yourself. As a creation of God, you are Soul. You are of the substance of the divine Holy Spirit, the Voice of God. We call It the ECK.

A LARGER LOVE

A farmer in Scotland had a large herd of cows. He and his wife treated these cows like their children. Every morning they'd come out to feed and milk them.

They would call each cow by name and give them little treats. They'd pet them. The cows loved the farmer and his wife, and the couple loved the cows.

One day the farmer got on his tractor and drove out into the field. He was going to check on a newborn calf. This was risky because a neighbor's bull had been brought over for breeding purposes and was loose in the field.

When the bull saw the farmer, he charged the tractor and knocked the farmer off and began to gore him. The farmer went unconscious. When he woke up some time later, he found that his herd of cows had made a tight circle of protection around him. The bull was furious, and he charged the cows trying to break through that circle. He charged again and again, and some of the cows died from internal bleeding. But they gave their lives to protect the farmer. They stayed until someone was able to come and help him.

God's love is larger than just a love for humans.

As he was telling his story later, he was crying. He said, "People who say that cows are stupid don't know what they're talking about."

It's true. God's love is larger than just a love for humans. It stretches between humans—to each other—of course, but also from humans to animals, and to birds, and to fish, and to a lot of other things—even, let's say, to a herd of cows.

GIVING TO OTHERS

Selena, an ECKist, was out at the neighborhood park for a walk, and somehow she got talking to a woman with a large dog, a boxer. The woman said, "My dog has arthritis. He's only four years old, and it's causing him a lot of pain. I just don't know what to do for him."

Selena went home, and for two days she thought about this dog again and again. Cassius was the dog's name. She wanted to find something to ease his arthritis.

On the third day, she happened to notice that her husband was reading an article on a new supplement. It was a breakthrough, supposed to get rid of the pain of arthritis in animals, at least dogs. Selena wondered how she could get this information to the woman. Would it be considered meddling?

On the fourth day, in the morning, she opened the door of their home and in the door ran Cassius. His owner was calling to the dog, "Come back here, Cassius. Come back."

Cassius came in the house, lay down at Selena's feet, and looked up at her with great big eyes of love.

Cassius came in the house, lay down at Selena's feet, and looked up at her with great big eyes of love. He just stayed there. He wouldn't listen to his owner. He came for help because he knew that Selena would be able to help him. Conveniently, Cassius came after her husband had read the article in the newspaper.

The woman outside kept saying, "Cassius, come out here," and then she'd say, "I'm so sorry. I'm so sorry." Because they didn't know each other. Selena said, "It's all right. I've got something for you."

Her husband handed her the article, and Selena gave it to the woman. "Thank you so much," said the woman. "This is just what I've been looking for."

Sometime later, down at the ocean, Selena saw the woman with Cassius and two children. Cassius was playing in the surf just like a young dog. Selena didn't know if the owner took the advice and got the supplement, but Cassius seemed to be fine. And whether or not the experience helped the dog, it helped Selena. Every time she thinks of Cassius coming to her home, running in the front door, lying down, and just looking at her with those eyes of love and trust, she says she's been repaid a thousand times. This was a gift for Selena that keeps on giving.

Giving God's love to others is the reason we're all here. God's love comes to us directly from God and through others. Part of Soul's lesson is to learn to somehow give this love back to life and to everything living. Give it back to every living thing.

JOY AND LAUGHTER

We give according to our capacity to give. Our capacity to give depends upon our state of consciousness.

We give according to our capacity to give. Our capacity to give depends upon our state of consciousness.

Some people see a dog who exhibits some very high characteristics of sensitivity, and they say, "That dog will come back in the next lifetime as a human." My question is, Why would a dog want to come back as a human? Many people practice inhumanity on each other. I would say some of those people would probably be better off if they came back as dogs. My pardon to them, but I think the world would be a better place. Just a whimsical little thought.

There should be joy and there should be laughter in a life of love. If someone claims to have love and can't laugh, especially at himself or herself, it would tell me something about them.

But there's no way to suggest to such a person that maybe there's a greater capacity for love and compassion that they might attain. Sometimes if they're of another religion where they feel superior, they may feel they're in the center of love, and you aren't. Which is fine. Let people be what they want to be.

States of Consciousness

God's love shows itself through letting each person find the path to God that is right for that individual. Often people feel that they belong to a superior religion or a superior race. But God has provided a path to fit every person and every group, because we're speaking of states of consciousness.

You are a state of consciousness, and the group you belong to is a state of consciousness.

Sometimes you want to say you *have* a state of consciousness. But the state of consciousness possesses you rather than you possessing it. In the same way, some people say, "I have a soul." You *are* Soul. The Soul consciousness—meaning who and what you are in your true self—has a certain influence, or lack of it, on your behavior in everyday life. Even if you aren't aware of your behavior, other people are.

We know the ins and outs, the ways, thinkings, and feelings of our neighbor, but we suspect he doesn't know ours. We think we know exactly where he's coming from. Of course, the neighbor might be thinking the same thing. It works both ways.

God's love shows itself through letting each person find the path to God that is right for that individual.

Spiritual Awakening

Amy was sixteen years old, and she began to doubt her faith. She was a Christian. At the age of seventeen her mother died. Her mother was the religious one in the family. Right after her mother's death, Amy had an out-of-body experience while she was riding on a bus.

Above the bus in this other sort of reality, closer than right here, she saw a golden Buddha sitting in the lotus position. It was looking down on all the passengers seated in the bus.

Amy had a feeling that this meant something very important for her spiritually. The experience was responsible for her leaving the church. She couldn't understand what it meant, and she heard nothing in the church to explain it. At times she thought, because of the Buddha-like person, maybe she was to become a Buddhist. She talked to some Buddhist friends, and she decided that wasn't for her.

For the next thirty years she was searching. But after that experience on the bus she began having experiences with the Blue Light.

How the Sound and Light Come

Those of you in Eckankar are very familiar with the Blue Light. This is a sign of the Holy Spirit, the Sound and Light of God speaking to the individual. Sometimes It comes as Light and sometimes It comes as Sound. Sometimes It comes as both.

The Inner Master is the matrix that the Holy Spirit forms. The Mahanta is the Inner Master, the inner side. The Living ECK Master is the outer side. People often see the Inner Master first come to them as the Blue Light. This is very common, because they're not yet ready to see the face of the Inner Master, the Mahanta. It would shock them too much.

In some way the Holy Spirit, the ECK, speaks to the individual through Light or Sound. The Light may be any color, but when It shows up as the Blue Light, It's very definitely the Mahanta.

Sometimes the Light is yellow, which is a high spiritual color, and white, even higher. Or it may be a pink or orange light, and sometimes a violet or a purple light. Orange is the Causal Plane—the past-life memory area. But to see the Blue Light is a special blessing.

The Blue Light is a sign of the Holy Spirit, the Sound and Light of God speaking to the individual. The Inner Master is the matrix that the Holy Spirit forms.

Whenever a person sees any of these lights inwardly, either during contemplation, in meditation, or in a dream, this is very important. The Holy Spirit is uplifting them spiritually. The Light doesn't just come. It's not just a colored filter put in front of some sort of lightbulb. It's there for a reason.

It's to uplift that Soul into a higher state of consciousness.

GOOD FORTUNE

So thirty years after leaving the church, Amy finally found Eckankar. She'd run into a library—there wasn't much time before closing—looking for a certain book. She looked through the shelves but couldn't find it. Then she just happened to see *ECKANKAR—The Key to Secret Worlds,* by Paul Twitchell. She flipped through it quickly, and some of the things in there seemed to answer her experience with the golden Buddha figure. She took the book home and read it.

The next Wednesday night there was an introductory talk at the local ECK center. She found the location of the ECK center in the phone book and went to the lecture, listened, and liked what she heard. She liked the people. She decided she would go to the ECK Worship Service that Sunday.

Amy went to the worship service, and she liked that too. So she called the Eckankar Spiritual Center in Minneapolis and said she wanted to become a member.

Back then the receptionist gave her a choice: "Would you like to study *The Easy Way Discourses* or *The ECK Dream 1 Discourses?*" The ECK discourses are letters either I or Paul Twitchell have written to explain different facets of Eckankar and the spiritual

Whenever a person sees any of these lights inwardly, in contemplation, meditation, or a dream, the Holy Spirit is uplifting them spiritually.

life—how to live it. They include some of the more interesting things about the spiritual techniques, places to go and things to do, but mainly what you can do to help yourself spiritually to make this a worthwhile lifetime.

When Amy heard she had a choice, she said, "No, I'd better not take the dream discourses. I don't dream."

The first month of her membership, she saw the Blue Light with yellow lights. Then there was an array of bright white light in the form of little squares—like tiles on a floor—except they were the whitest white she had ever seen. She wondered about them. One of these squares seemed to catch her up and pull her right in.

She soaked herself right into the square, or the square soaked her up, and she saw twelve ocean-going ships, and some of them were sinking. Her point of view seemed to be up in the sky, as if she were an airplane looking down at these ships.

When she woke up, she wondered what that was all about. Now remember, Amy doesn't dream. But this doesn't stand in the way of the Inner Master, the Mahanta. Once an individual becomes a member of Eckankar, an agreement is formed with the Holy Spirit.

Basically, the agreement is this: Show me thy ways.

Before you can see what the Holy Spirit's ways are, you have to open your state of consciousness.

Soul's Schooling

The Holy Spirit begins to show the individual who he or she is. Before you can see what the Holy Spirit's ways are, you have to open your state of consciousness.

Often the Holy Spirit has to open it. This is often

done through the agent of the Inner Master, because people relate better to people. The Master is simply the matrix, or a form created out of this substance and stuff of the Holy Spirit, the same as you.

The only difference between the Master and you is that appearing to people and helping them spiritually is his job. It's his divine calling. That's why the Holy Spirit has put him in that place. God, or Sugmad—which is our name for God—has put this individual there to help Souls who are tired of karma and reincarnation.

Karma means doing things that help you or hurt you. But whether it's good karma or bad karma, both tie you to this world.

Karma means doing things that help you or hurt you.

When people pass on, they generally go to the next heaven just above the earth plane. They go to school there. It's sort of a debriefing for their life on earth. Other people in the spiritual hierarchy are classroom instructors. When the person is settled in, they let them rest awhile, if they deserve it. If they don't, they come back to earth real quick.

The instructors say, "Let's go over the record and see what you've done."

They look in the big book. They say, "Well, you gained here spiritually, but you slipped here because of such and such. So, we're going to have to polish that up in the next lifetime." Then the individual begins a period of instruction on the Astral Plane, sometimes on the Causal or Mental Plane. It depends upon the state of consciousness of the individual.

The person has to learn certain things before they come back, but most of the lessons will come in the next lifetime. Maybe it's not a lesson about something that they needed to learn from the most recent lifetime, but from six, seven, or a hundred lives back.

But it's all one Soul that just had different personalities in different lifetimes, and each one of these personalities came up with different experiences. Some helped, some hurt.

LEARNING ABOUT POWER

Often people in leadership positions are learning the exercise of power. And the higher they go on earth in these positions, they're having to learn more about the use and misuse of power. Sometimes these people make big mistakes. Other times they do much good.

One of the songwriters of the forties and fifties refused to let any negative thoughts cross his mind because he felt it would detract from the creative flow of his songwriting. He said that he didn't hate anyone. Because they're going to harm themselves more than anyone else ever could. But he didn't want anger of that sort to get in the way of his work, of his songwriting.

This is an excellent attitude. Don't hate anyone because they make decisions that you don't agree with or because they do things that you feel are wrong. Let them be.

Anger burns. It consumes like a hot fire. Put your attention to better use.

Karma is an exact law. Karma is simply the Law of Retribution, the Law of Cause and Effect, that's all. For every action there is an opposite and equal reaction.

Some people who know about karma and reincarnation say, "Boy, I can't wait for them to get their due right now." Well, it may be another lifetime or two. So don't waste all your good energy burning yourself up with anger. Anger burns. It consumes like a hot fire.

Put your attention to better use. Put your attention on God's love. You'll be better off for it, and so will everyone around you.

When you come to that school in the first heaven, the Astral Plane, between lives and go over the ledger with your instructor, this whole world and all its aims will seem so petty. The accumulation of power at all costs—it's not worth it. The gathering of money, of a good reputation as a top financier, or some such thing—it's not worth it. Not if you sell your soul, if you will, to the devil. And many people do.

Practice love. Look at life straightforward.

Practice love. Look at life straightforward.

REMEMBERING PAST LIVES

So the first month Amy saw a blue light and twelve ships in her dream. Some of the ships were sinking. The second month, she saw bright squares again. This time she noticed they were like minimovies. Each one of these squares was a superbright white light. She heard the roar of engines, and in front of her she saw a panel of airplane instruments. She said, "What's going on here? Probably just another puzzling dream."

Remember, Amy didn't dream.

The third month, she saw a boy running through a wheat field, and overhead there was a flock of migrating Canada geese. He was trying to stay ahead of them, just running. Another puzzling dream.

The first three dreams with clear scenes all came the night after she read her monthly ECK discourse.

Then she had a realization. The first three dreams with clear scenes all came the night after she read her monthly ECK discourse. It's for this reason that those of you who are members of Eckankar should read only one discourse a month. You may get all twelve, but you're not going to get the meat out of more than one at a time.

You need time to absorb each discourse. Each discourse has a vibration and a rhythm. It fits you at that time. If you try to read two or three because you just don't have the self-discipline to hold back, that's all right. The name for it is spiritual gluttony. You only hurt yourself.

The fourth month, Amy saw in a dream a line of soldiers on horseback. These warriors were getting ready to attack an enemy. The scene again was filled with a background of bright white light, the white light from this little square where it started. She fell down into the little square. It was a very vivid experience.

After receiving the fifth discourse, on karma and reincarnation, she realized the dreams of the four previous months were playbacks of past lives.

The ocean ships, some of them sinking, and then the instrument panel in front of her, meant she was a pilot in World War II with the Royal Canadian Air Force. She knew this. She even knew her name. In the third scene she saw herself as a little boy in that lifetime. As a little boy, she wanted nothing more than to fly faster than a bird. So she fulfilled this dream of her childhood and became a pilot.

The fourth scene was from an even earlier lifetime where she had been a warrior. She realized that in each one of these two lives—as a pilot and as a warrior—she had harmed people. The reason she was back in this present lifetime was because of those and other past lives.

She remembered her name as the pilot, and after a series of coincidences, plus some research on her part, she ended up with some of the government offices in Canada doing research on the pilot. One day she went to Saskatchewan, to the little town

You need time to absorb each discourse. Each discourse has a vibration and a rhythm.

where she grew up as that pilot in the previous life-time. When she got there, she found the town very easily. She found the homestead. The wheat field was there as she remembered it. She looked at the same wide-open clear sky and the migrating birds. The homestead was right in the path of the migrating birds.

She decided she would go out to the cemetery to visit the graves of her parents from before. She knew right where the cemetery was—out of sight of town. She went there and found the grave site of her pre-vious folks. It came to her that, as a young aviator in the Royal Canadian Air Force, this man had promised his mother to come home again. He never had. So in this lifetime as Amy, she had come back. She put flowers on the grave.

This chapter of her life began to make sense; the dreams had a physical verification.

This chapter of her life began to make sense; the dreams had a physical verification. She could check things out, and she did.

LOVE'S INSIGHTS

You might say, "Amy really had some great ex-periences. If I had those, I would be a member of Eckankar for the rest of my life."

I've seen people who had good experiences like Amy's leave ECK. Why? Because they were not grounded in divine love. They were not satisfied with what they had.

Love for her mother brought Amy back in another body, just because she had made a promise. God's love is a wonderful thing. Love gave her all these insights into herself and led eventually to the spiri-tual way that is right for her.

PAST LOVE REGAINED

As a young girl Danielle liked stories about Peter Pan and Mary Poppins. These characters could fly. Flying was important for her because she had a little friend she met in her dreams who would come to her house. It was a little Indian boy; he always wore a headband.

They would go off flying together in the Astral body. Sometimes they'd go out just around the yard and play. Then Danielle's sister, in her Astral body, would come out and say, "You come down from there, you two. If you don't come down, I'm going to pound you." Then the little girl and the little boy would fly down just like birds trying to chase someone away. They would do that just to aggravate the older sister. They'd buzz her. That made her angry, and she'd swat at them like pesky flies. They'd keep out of reach, and they'd laugh and laugh up there where the air was rare.

Some of their astral experiences were different. They went on far adventures. When they went on a long trip, the Indian boy brought along his dog, Sam. At times like this they might visit Alaska and other parts of the world. The dog went along to protect them and did very nicely.

Then the kids would come back home again, fly around the neighborhood, and land. Back home, each would then go off to sleep in their astral forms to wake up later in their own physical bodies. They always remembered these experiences.

As time went on, the experiences became less and less frequent, until they finally stopped.

Years later, Danielle met a young man who was Indian. She loved the color of his skin, and she loved his hair. She just loved him. Pretty soon they were

As a young girl Danielle had a little friend she met in her dreams who would come to her house.

going steady. Even on their first dates, she felt very comfortable with him. So she said to him, "You remind me of an Indian boy who used to be my very best friend. I used to meet him in dreams."

He said, "You remind me of a little girl I met in my dreams. But she had blond hair. Your hair is brown." She said, "When I was a little kid, my hair was blond."

They began to compare notes. He began to describe what he remembered. "Right near your home, train tracks ran past. I remember your garden," he said. She said, "I remember your headband. You always wore a headband. And your dog's name was Sam."

So they made a connection. They got married, and now they have two children.

Divine love brought them together from two different races. When their hearts met, their hearts knew. Divine love is that strong.

When their hearts met, their hearts knew. Divine love is that strong.

Sometimes people who will come together later in life are born at literally opposite ends of the earth. But it is not beyond the capacity of the Law of Karma to bring them together. If they're to be together, no force on earth can keep them apart. Love is the tie that binds. Through this love Danielle found her husband, and he found her.

TEACH YOUR CHILDREN

Danielle sometimes worries about their two children. She says, "They're not having the dream experiences my husband and I did. They go to the ECK Satsang class for children, and we teach them about ECK." They try to make ECK interesting for the children. But she's worried.

She says, "What if they don't want to stay with the ECK teachings?"

This is the hardest thing for a parent of any religion. When the child comes of age and the parent has finished the social and spiritual instruction that is necessary for the child's education in this world, then the child makes its own decisions. The child is no longer a child.

All I can say to the mother is, "Let your children be. Love them." They may leave ECK, but if they're supposed to find it again, they will, because that's how love is. That's how life is.

If your destiny is to move forward spiritually because you've earned the right, that information was made known to you between lifetimes.

If your destiny is to move forward spiritually because you've earned the right, that information was made known to you between lifetimes. Although this information is known between lifetimes, it's forgotten when people are born in the human body. The human must forget, otherwise the past would be too much to carry sometimes. Because we, in our love for our habits, tend to do the things that hurt us.

A Close Call

One day, a couple, Diane and Phil, decided to go out of town on a short vacation. For a while Diane hadn't been very well, and she and her husband, Phil, had the habit of going to the sauna in their apartment complex.

There was a sauna for men, and a sauna for women. Phil didn't feel comfortable leaving Diane alone in her weakened condition. So they tried to figure out how to approach the problem. ECKists are very smart. They think things through. They said, "Who goes to the sauna at one o'clock in the morning?" Answer: practically no one.

So they said, "All right, now it's just a question of which one to go into—the men's or women's sauna." They decided they'd go into the men's sauna. If a man happened to walk into the sauna, he wouldn't scream if he saw a woman in there; a woman might if she came into the women's sauna and saw a man. So just for peace and quiet, they decided to use the men's sauna. This became their regular practice, because Diane needed it for her health.

One weekend, suddenly for no reason at all, they got this very strong feeling: Get out of town.

It was the Inner Master speaking to them—the voice of the Holy Spirit coming through the matrix of the Inner Master, the Mahanta.

So they said, "OK, we'll drive to a small town about forty miles away." They live in the Minneapolis area, and so this put them just into Wisconsin. So they went there, but as soon as they got to the motel, Phil began to get sick. The place was drafty and cold and just miserable. One night of this sort of vacation was enough. "We're going home," they said.

When they got home, the maintenance man came up to them and asked, "Did you hear what happened?"

They said, "No, we've been out of town."

He said, "Last night, after one o'clock, the sauna blew up. There was an electrical short in there. It blew up the whole place. All the exercise equipment, the windows—the whole place was demolished."

Phil and Diane said, "Wow, that was a close call. The Mahanta watched out for us and helped us."

One weekend, suddenly for no reason at all, they got this very strong feeling: Get out of town. It was the Inner Master speaking to them.

God's Love Is a Wonderful Thing

Diane was wondering then about love and the nature of love. She had heard that the African ECKists have such love for the Mahanta, the Living ECK Master. She wondered why. And the answer came back to her.

*Why did
Diane and Phil
have this
protection?
Because of the
love bond
between them
and the
Mahanta.
It's basically
their love for
God and the
Holy Spirit.*

The Master said, "Because the African members of Eckankar put their love for the Mahanta first, and everything else comes second. Because that's the order in which they have their love, the quality of love for everything else becomes different—becomes of a higher, better, cleaner, purer nature."

And why did Diane and Phil have this protection from the explosion? Because of the love bond between them and the Mahanta.

They had this strong love bond because it's basically their love for God and the Holy Spirit. And the Mahanta, being the chief agent for the ECK, appears to them as their spiritual guide and can offer them protection when necessary. It will offer protection to those who have the ears to hear.

God's love is a wonderful thing.

*ECK Springtime Seminar, Washington, D.C.,
Saturday, April 3, 1999*

A test of an experience is: if it helps you to open your heart to divine love, to God's love, then it's a real experience.

13

INSIDE A CIRCLE
OF FRIENDS

I live, move, and have my being at the grace of the ECK, the way you do. I enjoy life as you do. This is what an ECK seminar is about. It's a celebration of life.

Something hard to explain to people not familiar with the ECK teachings, whether they are formal members or not, is that there is a circle of spiritual protection afforded them because they are devotees of the Holy Spirit. Our name for the Holy Spirit, of course, is the ECK.

The message that each ECK Master, each Living ECK Master, and each Mahanta, the Living ECK Master will bring is to tell Soul about God's love— God's love for each Soul.

That means God's love for you.

GOD'S LOVE FOR EACH SOUL

God's love for each Soul includes you, and it even goes down to your pets—to the dog, the cat, the canary, and the fish. Indeed, to all living beings.

God has provided a way for all creatures to draw

The message that each ECK Master will bring is to tell Soul about God's love— God's love for each Soul. That means God's love for you.

closer to divine love. Everyone can, and we all express love simply because we exist.

You may say, "The behavior of some people doesn't reflect that." No, the behavior doesn't. Sometimes Soul goes off on the dark path of power and the psychic forces. It's with the intent to control others.

This is against the principles of ECK, or the Holy Spirit. We in Eckankar are interested in spiritual freedom, both for ourselves and for other people. That means if someone chooses to become a Catholic or a Jehovah's Witness, or even belong to a group that practices one of the primitive religions, that's fine.

The test of any true religion is this: Does it help people into a greater state of consciousness and does it help them find love?

There are two kinds of ECKists: ECKists and the practicing ECKists. This holds true for all faiths. Among Christians, there are Christians and there are practicing Christians. It would be a better world if more people of every religion, including Eckankar, would be practicing members of their religion. But this is earth. So things are not always as they should be.

> The test of any true religion is this: Does it help people into a greater state of consciousness and does it help them find love?

Sing HU for Help

One of the pillars in Eckankar is the HU Song. I'd like to give you an example of how powerful it is—not just to the members of Eckankar, but also to members of other faiths.

A friend of ours was trying to help her friend with a real-estate problem by long distance. Her friend had a house she needed to sell, but she was worried that if it didn't sell quickly she was going to lose it.

So Katie, our friend, said, "If you want some help, just sing the word *HU*."

HU is an ancient name for God. In Eckankar, we sing it. It doesn't tell God, "God, I want to sell my house." But it says, "Let what will be just be." You're saying that you're agreeable with whatever is the will of the Holy Spirit. You're not about to dictate terms to the supreme intelligence about your very small, commonplace, daily affairs.

Some time later they were on the phone again—Katie and this friend in another state—and the friend said, "I've had some offers, but I'm still concerned. The house hasn't sold, and I'm worried about the pool inspection."

Katie said, "Keep your fingers crossed."

Her friend, who was not an ECKist, said, "I think I'll sing HU."

This caught Katie completely off guard. She had told her friend about singing HU, and now her friend was reminding Katie. It struck Katie as funny that the ECK would use someone who wasn't familiar with the ECK teachings to remind her about the sound of HU. But this is how the Holy Spirit works.

To Katie's credit, she recognized the gentle reminder as coming from the Master and the Holy Spirit, the ECK.

When you're with the Master, you're inside a circle of friends—inside the circle of the Mahanta's friends.

When you're with the Master, you're inside a circle of friends—the Master's friends. Katie was, and the friend who was trying to sell her home was too.

Inside the circle of the Mahanta's friends.

Red Clay

In the following story, I'm going to give another name to our lead character and call him Jason. I don't want to embarrass anyone; I don't want him to get a big head.

This is one of the big problems we find on the spiritual path. People will make very good progress for years, and then gradually they'll slip off the path. The spiritual path becomes like a raised trail one foot wide that runs along with a deep ditch on either side. The dirt this individual's walking on is red clay, and it's raining. Some of you have experience with red clay when it's wet. It's as slick as ice.

Jason had been a member of Eckankar for twenty-seven years. He'd heard the warnings of the ECK Masters, of Paul Twitchell, the founder of Eckankar, and of myself saying to keep away from psychic things. They'll just get you into trouble. You'll end up walking on this clay path. On either side is a sharp drop-off into a ditch. As soon as you take your attention off the Sound and Light of God, it's going to start raining in your life. Your footing is going to get very slippery.

But his awakening came like this. Jason was at an ECK class with his wife and other ECKists. On this particular Friday night, a new person came to the class. They welcomed the new individual very warmly. Jason's wife is a hugger. She hugs everybody, so the newcomer got a hug.

The guest had no idea there was such a circle of love. The guest was on the outside of it standing at the doorway. Whether or not she chose to step through was her decision.

As the class progressed, the guest said she had been running into a lot of harassment from a former mate. She went into several examples of how this had happened.

Jason was listening, and he realized he had this sense of peace and reassurance. He felt good. And then he realized it was because he was inside a circle of friends. And that the guest had no idea there was such a circle of love. The guest was on the outside of it standing at the doorway. Whether or not she chose to step through, whether or not she became a member of Eckankar, that was her decision.

Jason had gone down a rocky road himself. He'd heard the warnings of the ECK Masters to stay away from the psychic arts. He was a Higher Initiate; he knew better. But he was also a healer. People came to him. They wanted his counsel, both for physical as well as emotional and other ailments.

He looked at the standard methods of diagnosis, and he thought, *You know, these things seem just too pat. There must be a better, more direct way.*

He began to look into things like acupuncture. This wasn't the psychic area, just one of the skills he learned. Next he learned homeopathy. But then he went to a teacher who had worked with acupuncture and knew how to open the psychic center with needles. He treated Jason with some needles, and opened his psychic eye.

After this experience, there was such a blurring of his vision Jason didn't know what to do. It cleared up after some days, but then he began to see auras. He saw the auras of animals and also of plants. When patients came to him and they were about to express a thought, Jason would put the words in their mouths because he could intuitively tell what was on their minds.

PATH OF LOVE

Pretty soon Jason found this was an awful burden to carry. It's no fun seeing auras. It's a skill that comes to some people along their path. But it's not something that an ECKist would want to seek out, because they should be past that stage. Yet there are some Higher Initiates today who still feel the teachings I give are too low-toned, too commonplace. And I'll have to agree. They certainly are.

Except when I talk about Soul Travel. About dreams. About out-of-body experiences.

It's no fun seeing auras. It's a skill that comes to some people along their path.

Most of the time, though, you'll find anything sensational is like a flash in the pan. It'll last for a little while, but the real substance—especially in ECK—will revolve around the issue of divine love.

A path must demonstrate divine love if it's to be a true path for its followers. This is what I try to impress upon you.

Psychic Detour

As Jason went on his psychic detour, he didn't even realize he'd lost his deep spiritual connection with the Mahanta, the Living ECK Master. When this happens, an individual also loses the connection to divine love.

To break the hold of the psychic powers on him, he went on a long fast. I've gone on that sort of thing myself, and it can be very helpful to break the power of something, or to get one back in alignment spiritually. But it can also play havoc with the physical body. I've learned that too. I've learned a lot of things in these years that I've been here. Some things I just wouldn't do again. When you get older, you say, "Now I've got wisdom, but I don't have youth." That's the nature of life. Some people get old and never even end up with wisdom. If you can say, "Now I've got wisdom," you've got something—if you're speaking true.

Jason's ability to see auras went by the wayside. No longer does he pick up the thoughts of other people. He likes the simple things in life—like a sunset, or the sunshine and the rain, the love of his wife and his son. These things mean something to him. The other things don't mean so very much anymore. He realizes now that he is fully back inside the circle of the Mahanta's friends.

A path must demonstrate divine love if it's to be a true path for its followers.

BEING CLOSER TO GOD

Marie is a very busy mom. She teaches some ECK classes and is active at the ECK center. But at home, her first devotion is to her husband and her three children, some of whom are teens. And Marie now has the feeling she's coming close to an understanding of who and what she is.

This is what everyone should be looking for: to find out who and what you are.

Why are you here? What is your purpose? Is it just a random walk in time and space without a reason for the beginning and the end of this cycle? What's it all about?

One day, Marie did a spiritual exercise. It was an imaginative technique. She imagined seeing a bright, bright light like a sun. Coming down from the sun was a rope ladder. Marie said, "I want to be closer to God. That sun is God, so I will climb the ladder." As she was ascending it, she wondered, *If sparks come off the sun, are they going to burn me?* But the light was soft, warm, and soothing. So she continued to climb upward and upward until she came to this circle of light.

Actually the circle of light was protection, or divine love. In another sense, it's a circle of friends.

She came into this circle of light. When she arrived, she said, "I belong here. I am an heir to this throne. I have earned the right to be here." She didn't feel arrogant about it or superior, as if she'd done something others hadn't. She just felt it was her birthright as Soul to be there.

When she ended up in the circle of light, the experience had turned from imagination into reality. It had become real. Or had it?

This is what everyone should be looking for: to find out who and what you are.

CONFIRMATION

You're going to have many different experiences on the path of ECK. Some of them will be as dynamic as anything you've ever experienced. Others will be like a dream. And some will be simply like figments of your imagination.

A test of an experience is: if it helps you open your heart to divine love, to God's love, then it's a real experience.

Sometimes people say, "I'm looking for Soul Travel, and I want the big experience." Well, maybe first you move into a higher state of consciousness beyond the physical body through the imaginative techniques—through the imaginative or emotional body, which is the Astral body.

A test of an experience is: if it helps you open your heart to divine love, to God's love, then it's a real experience.

If you can imagine a thing, you can make it so. It can become real.

Later, Marie got confirmation of this experience. Her ECK discourse for that month was on the topic of the mind. It said to stay in the position of Soul. This means to get above the problem—get above the mind. Because all problems are of the lower worlds, and the lower worlds include the mind, emotions, and physical body. This is the source of fear, apprehension, and all cousins of this sensation. So she got this confirmation: Stay in the position of Soul.

This is what we mean when we speak of the detached state. *Detached* does not mean apart from the concerns or the feelings of other people. It does not mean when people are suffering, to stand back and say, "I am detached." We help each other. We give compassion to those who need help and love. We give help and love where we can, because it's the nature of Soul to do so.

God is love. Soul is God's creation. Therefore, Soul is love too. That means you are Soul, and you are love.

OVERCOMING SHYNESS

Someone I'll call George is a quiet person, and he finds social interaction with people difficult. He doesn't have the social skills due to past-life problems. But in this lifetime, before he went to the ECK Springtime Seminar in Washington, D.C., this year, he set a goal.

He said, "I want to be more open to people." He wanted to rise above his fears.

This is very difficult for someone who has a problem in social groups. I know, because that's where I once was too. You walk into a room full of people, and you feel inadequate. You feel they're all smarter and better dressed. You think, *Look at how smart they are. They're all chatting along just as easily and comfortably as can be.* Gradually I would find a very comfortable place along the wall.

On his way to the seminar, George got bumped from his flight. As he was waiting for another flight to Dulles International Airport, the Inner Master said to him, "Go to your gate early."

So George went to his gate an hour before the flight, before anybody else had shown up.

George ended up at the front of the growing line of people, standing in front of an empty gate waiting for their new flight. Being at the front of the line made him some sort of an authority for those who came later. People came up behind him and asked questions like, What time is it? Is this the flight to Dulles? "Yes, this is the flight to Dulles," George would say. Another person asked, "Do I need a boarding pass for the next flight?" George happened to

God is love. Soul is God's creation. Therefore, Soul is love too. That means you are Soul, and you are love.

know because he overheard someone else talking about that very thing. So George had the answers.

The Master had told him get to that gate early, and this put George at the head of the line. Shy people like to be anywhere but the head of the line.

Suddenly a problem arose in the line next to theirs. The desk clerk was asking a very elderly couple from another country basic security questions, Did you pack your own luggage? and that sort of thing. The couple had no idea what he was saying. So they smiled and nodded, and the desk clerk was getting very upset. Other passengers said, "Let them go. They don't understand what you're saying."

This was a very stubborn clerk. He said, "They must answer these questions."

George, standing in the nearby line, suddenly remembered to chant HU quietly to himself. All he was doing was saying to the Holy Spirit, "Let this situation be as it should. Bring harmony to it."

> All he was doing was saying to the Holy Spirit, "Let this situation be as it should. Bring harmony to it."

Very soon, everything worked out. The elderly couple was ushered through, and the line began to move again. George saw how the Mahanta had prompted him to sing HU silently within himself. Because George was inside the circle of the Mahanta's friends.

When he got to Dulles, he went out to get a shuttle. When the shuttle bus came, due to the late hour he was the only passenger. The Mahanta said, "Sit near the front."

George usually sat way in back. But he sat in front, and he and the driver had a very pleasant conversation. They just had a good time—a good visit. George was so grateful he gave the driver a big tip.

During the seminar, George happened to go to a Chinese restaurant. When he opened his fortune cookie, it said, "You will always be at the head of the line, never at the end." A nice side note from the Holy Spirit to confirm this experience for him.

George was inside the circle of friends of the Mahanta. His goal before the seminar was to overcome fear and learn how to interact with people. For the rest of the seminar he made an effort to be among people and socialize with them and learn how you have to be in a group. He's learning. He's unfolding. This is what spiritual unfoldment is about. He's begun to love other people more than his own fears.

WAKE-UP CALL

Martin from Ghana had a wake-up call twenty-six years ago as a young student in a prep school. He began having pains in his stomach, and he ended up at the hospital. The doctors looked him over, then the pain suddenly went away. This happened several times.

After a number of visits, the doctors finally said, "This time you stay. We're going to take a look inside and see what's going on in there."

They took out his appendix. The operation was a success, except the doctors couldn't understand the complications that followed. The stitches were letting go. All kinds of problems came up. They operated again, and the same thing happened after a lengthy recuperation. The operation was a success, but infection set in. So during a third operation, Martin was on the table and again the doctors were busy working on him. Suddenly the room began to change in appearance. It became lighter.

A bright, bright light drew him away from the body. At the same time he heard a sound which was very loud to his ears.

This is what spiritual unfoldment is about. He's begun to love other people more than his own fears.

He found himself far away from his body. In the distance he heard someone call his name. This brought his attention back to the operating room. He found himself hanging like a light fixture from the ceiling. He could see in all directions. He was all-seeing and all-knowing, a wonderful state of bliss. He looked down and saw the doctors and nurses busy sewing him back up.

Martin watched this spectacle for a while. But as his attention went more and more to what was happening to the physical body, he became concerned. He followed his physical human self as it was wheeled to the recovery room. Then he was out, unconscious for thirteen hours.

Martin required a fourth and a fifth operation to make everything absolutely right. But during the next two operations, he found he'd lost his fear of pain and of passing on. The world was suddenly a different place for him. He didn't worry about the mundane things that used to take up so much of his day. He was just happy to be alive.

I've heard this before from some other people who have been very sick. After they're over the greatest part of the crisis, they say, "It's a gift to be alive." Not to be rich, not to have friends, not to have influence or power—none of those things.

> "It's good to be alive, it's good to love." These are the important things.

Just, "It's good to be alive, it's good to love." These are the important things.

Martin had a lot of questions about his experience. He was a member of the Catholic Church, but the priest had no answers for him. Martin was very unsettled for the longest time. Eventually he left the church, simply because it didn't give him the answers he needed to his near-death, or out-of-the-body, experience.

This is not to say that the Catholic Church has lost relevance for the rest of the world, because it has not. It is a relevant religion. It, as well as the other religions, is God's gift to humanity.

A long time later—at the right time and in the right place—the Mahanta appeared. The old saying "When the student is ready, the Master appears" had come into play in Martin's life. He had now entered the circle of the Mahanta's friends. He found ECK. Mainly, he had found the Light and Sound of God. Those were the two aspects of the Holy Spirit he had experienced in the operating room as a young man so many years ago.

The old saying "When the student is ready, the Master appears" had come into play in Martin's life.

IN SERVICE IS YOUR REWARD

Some months ago, Mercedes got a letter from Eckankar inviting her to give a talk at a major ECK seminar.

Mercedes had never given a talk before. The letter said, "You will be speaking from 7:05 to 7:10 p.m. on Friday night." She said, "I can handle five minutes." Time went on, and things got busy. It was almost time to pack her bags and get ready for the flight, and Mercedes was wondering, *Will there be time to prepare for this talk?* She was worried. But she got an impression of the Mahanta, the Inner Master, saying, "Everything will be all right, Mercedes. Don't worry."

The night before she left for the seminar, she did a short contemplation. The Mahanta, the Inner Master showed up and handed her a set of keys. She wondered, *What do I need keys for? What's this all about?* She forgot about the keys, but a feeling of calm reassurance remained. The Master had assured her that her talk would go fine.

Once she got to the seminar, she prepared for her talk. She gave it everything she had. On Friday morning an idea came to her. Give a gift to the audience. Give a gift from the Mahanta, the Living ECK Master. She thought it was a great idea. So she talked about the book *The Spiritual Exercises of ECK.* She was excited about the talk, and the audience gave her a good round of applause.

After that talk and the good reception of what she had to say about *The Spiritual Exercises of ECK,* Mercedes understood the statement In service is your reward.

She understood it because she got so much out of the experience. She had opened her heart to the Holy Spirit and to the people she was to deliver that message to. She knew it wasn't Mercedes's big speech. She was just a channel, a vehicle, an instrument of the Holy Spirit. How can you take credit for that when the words are given by the Holy Spirit, sometimes through the agency of the Mahanta, the Living ECK Master, sometimes via the Inner Master, or the Dream Master? How can you take credit for what the Holy Spirit gives you?

How can you take credit for what the Holy Spirit gives you?

INSIDE A CIRCLE OF FRIENDS

Back home after the seminar, Mercedes was to help someone with a book discussion class on my book *The Living Word,* Book 1. But she hadn't read it yet. She wasn't going to begin assisting until the third class, and this gave her time to read the book. Being a busy person, she took it on the train to work with her.

In chapter 5, she learned the meaning of the set of keys which the Inner Master had given to her during the contemplation the night before she left for the seminar. The Master tries to tie up loose ends.

Mercedes read that the key to the worlds of heaven is the Light and Sound of God.

The Mahanta gave her the set of keys because of her love for God, and that love had qualified her to be a speaker at that seminar. There and everywhere, she was inside a circle of friends.

ERASING TECHNIQUE PLUS

I'd like to mention a spiritual exercise. It's from Ray Kroc. He was the founder of the McDonald's hamburger chain, the franchise that's all over the world. He began a new life with the hamburger line when he was fifty-two. He had had all sorts of health problems. Most people would have figured, "My life is pretty much on the ropes now." But not Ray Kroc. He said, "It's just beginning." Since he had to keep tension down, he had this little thing he did to help him go to sleep at night.

He would imagine a blackboard. And he had an eraser in his hand. Whenever a message or some writing appeared, like a thought about a worry or a concern of the day, he'd start erasing it until it was gone.

Another image would come on the blackboard, and he would erase it. You can use this as a technique to get to sleep. But you can do something else too.

Put a colored crayon in your hand. And dream. Draw the dream that you want.

Or draw the state of something that you're striving for. For instance, if you want God Consciousness, draw a very basic scene of an ocean. Because the home of God is the Ocean of Love and Mercy. This is one way to put your attention on God Consciousness. Sometime later I'll speak or write more about

You can use this as a technique to get to sleep. But you can do something else too. Put a colored crayon in your hand. And dream. Draw the dream that you want.

some of the realizations that people had about the need to keep that goal in mind.

God Consciousness—how to become a better channel of divine love. How to love yourself more and to love others more because you love God more. And God loves you completely because you are Soul.

1999 ECK Summer Festival, Anaheim, California,
Saturday, June 5, 1999

"God, I want to be your assistant."

14

IF GOD IS GOD, THEN WHO ARE YOU?

✳

*G*od is God—beyond words. I don't have the words to describe the Supreme Being.

Symbolically you can say the home of God is the Ocean of Love and Mercy. In this highest, highest region, all is light. There are no shadows. There is a hazy sun in the sky you can't quite see, but you can. That's God, or Sugmad.

REALMS OF THE SPIRITUAL WORLD

Many religions of the world have their heavens established at different places. Some heavens are on the Astral Plane. Spiritualism and the very emotional religions like to be on the Astral Plane because it's the place of emotions. The Causal Plane is actually the basement of the Mental Plane. Both are part of the same house. The Causal Plane and the Mental

Symbolically you can say the home of God is the Ocean of Love and Mercy.

Plane generally hold the heavens of the major religions. Christianity is on the Mental Plane, at the ground-floor level, which is a very good area.

*Sometimes
people report
seeing a blue
light and they
ask, Who is
that? What is
the blue star or
the blue globe?*

The color often seen on the Mental Plane is blue. This is the color of the Mahanta appearing to people who have the consciousness of the mental area. Sometimes people report seeing a blue light and they ask, Who is that? What does the light mean? What is the blue star or the blue globe?

It's the Mahanta, the inner form of the Living ECK Master showing up in the mental regions for those people who can reach them.

There are other heavens. Right above the Mental Plane comes the Etheric. Then the Soul Plane, which is the first of the true spiritual regions. This simply means it is pure. It's the dividing line.

The heavens that come before have a little bit of material element mixed in with the spiritual element. But as you go into the spiritual planes above the Soul Plane, it's just pure spiritual substance. In many of these heavens the light becomes brighter and the substance becomes even finer. I don't have the words to describe what you find here, let alone when you come to the heart of God. Those things are beyond explanation.

So is it hopeless to have an understanding of God?

This is where the area of realization comes in. One must realize God, which is called God-Realization.

How do you do this? You go through life and life's experiences. And through these experiences of pain and pleasure and happiness and all the contrasting things in life—good, evil, and the like—a person very slowly unfolds spiritually. As one unfolds, he is able to move into higher realms of the spiritual world.

YOU ARE OF THE SUBSTANCE OF GOD

If God is God, then who are you? You are Soul. You are of the substance of God.

When God speaks, Its Voice, or Its Word, is known in religions as the Holy Spirit. This is the creating element. If you could separate God and God's characteristics, the Voice of God is the part that creates.

When we hear someone speaking, we usually say, "So-and-so said . . ." You put the speaker and the voice together. Yet there are two distinct elements, if you're going to break things down.

The same is true of God. God and the Voice of God. God is God. The Holy Spirit is the Voice of God, or the Word.

If God is God, then who are you? You are Soul. You are of the substance of God.

TWO ASPECTS

The Holy Spirit has two aspects. These are Sound and Light. This is what the Holy Spirit is—Sound and Light, the creative principle.

When God said, "Let there be the lower worlds," it was the Voice of God speaking. When the Voice of God spoke, the lower worlds formed. Why? So that there would be a place for people to go through pain. There was a lot of pleasure in the high worlds of God. But Souls there were just enjoying it and learning nothing.

This will sound like heresy, but one of the secrets of spiritual doctrine is that God learns through you, or through the experiences of Soul.

God creates Soul, creates the place where Soul can have all these experiences, and then watches to see what Souls learn as they run around in this world with free will. Free will was one of the gifts that Soul got.

The Holy Spirit, the Voice of God, at one point came and created Soul. These are the sparks of God, stars of God. You are a spark of God. You are Soul. You are made of the same substance as God, or at least as the Holy Spirit, which is Sound and Light. I've read that people can do very well without a number of things, but take sound and light from them absolutely (if it were even possible to do that) and they would go mad.

Sound is vibration. Even people who are deaf can feel vibration. Sometimes when you're sitting at home and a truck goes by, you can feel the vibration. This is one of the lower vibrations of the Sound of God.

There are all kinds of light: lights in the room, lightning in the sky. These things are all crude manifestations of the Light of God in Its pure form somewhere. I can't say far away because It's as close as right here. It's beyond time and space. Somewhere else—but right here.

TEMPORAL AND ETERNAL

In this earth world, things happen in sequence. We have duration. We say, "Things are near and far," or "The space between now and then is longer or shorter." But in the high worlds there is no time and space. You can't say something is closer or farther away, or something will happen sooner or later. It just is. Things just are.

You are eternal in the Soul body. The human body is temporal.

You are Soul. You just are. You are eternal in the Soul body. The human body is temporal. It's just for the time being. Temporal—that's life here.

If God is God, then who are you? You're Soul. What's your job? To learn to be a Co-worker with God. To work with God. To be God's assistant. To be God's little helper.

GOD'S LITTLE HELPER

A mother was having some health problems. She had fatty cysts on her throat, there was pain in her heart region, and she found breathing very difficult. So she asked the Mahanta, the Living ECK Master if she could have some help in finding better health. Then she let the matter drop.

A few days later she was paying a visit to her sister, who was also in ECK. She brought her little girl along. The little girl has a habit of always finding something to show her mother. This particular time she brought over a book by Ann Wigmore, *Be Your Own Doctor.* The mother thought, *What is this?* The little girl held her hand on the book, looked at her mother, and said with her eyes, "This book, Mommy, is special."

The mother said, "All right, I'll read it." So she flipped through the book, and something jumped out at her. The author was writing about hydrogenation of oils, a process of manufacturing to extend the shelf life.

The mother read this. She asked, "What are hydrogenated oils?"

After she left her sister, she began to research the nature of hydrogenated oils, an ingredient found in many foods. She decided it was a poison to her. At home, she went through her pantry. As she looked at bread mixes, cereals, salad dressings, and mayonnaise, she kept coming across hydrogenated oil in the ingredient list. She said, "Why, this stuff's no good. It's been hurting me."

She threw all these things out. She had to go shopping again, and cook everything from scratch.

Within two weeks' time the mother noticed that the cysts on her throat had gone down to half size.

The little girl held her hand on the book, looked at her mother, and said with her eyes, "This book, Mommy, is special."

Her breathing was normal, the way it should have been. And her heart region didn't hurt anymore.

A little girl, only one and a half years old, was the instrument for the Holy Spirit to bring the information to her mother. To say, with her eyes, "This is special. Here is the answer to the question you asked of the Mahanta, the Living ECK Master."

You're a Giver

Another young girl, about four years old, was a sickly child with all sorts of nervous problems. She'd stutter, and her muscles twitched. As she got older, kids laughed at her. She had a very hard time—few friends and a lot of health problems. Beside that, her parents weren't getting along very well.

The little girl, Diane, was always wondering, *God, what is this life about?*

She went to synagogue with her mother. While she was sitting there, she asked God, "Why? Why such a hard life?"

An answer came to her: "There are takers, and there are givers. If you're looking to get something to make you happy, it won't work because you'll not find the happiness you seek. You're a giver, and happiness will come to you when you are giving and caring for someone else."

The four-year-old girl thought about this. In her prayer, she said, "God, I want to be your assistant."

The four-year-old girl thought about this. In her prayer, she said, "God, I want to be your assistant." She took it for granted that she would be God's assistant. It never occurred to her that God might say, "Hey, kid, you're too small. Grow up first. You're going to change your mind. Anyway, how do you know it will be any fun?"

She didn't worry about it.

When the girl was seven or eight years old, she had one of her first memorable experiences of being one of God's assistants. She lived in New York City at the time, and the state had a program, Camp Sunshine, for kids who were poor. They could get out of the city for three weeks, meet new friends, and do things that they couldn't do in New York City.

The girl's mother looked over the information, and she said, "This looks like a good thing. You don't have any friends here, but you will have a lot of friends there."

Diane's mother was a very religious woman, so she called up the camp officials. "We're Jewish," she said. "Will there be other Jewish kids there so my child won't feel uncomfortable?" They said, "Sure, there will be a lot of friends for her to play with."

When Diane got to Camp Sunshine, she asked how many of the kids were Jewish. There were a thousand kids. But she was the only little Jewish girl.

Diane wanted to eat kosher food. Certain foods were OK, other foods were not. The kids started making fun of her. They said, "Why aren't you eating that?"

"Because I can't. I'm a Jew."

"A Jew! Jews don't believe that Christ saved them." And of course they don't. They've got another religion.

So they started to call her names. They said, "She doesn't believe that Christ will save her." One day when the counselor was away, the children began to beat up on this little Jewish girl. They scratched and pulled at her hair. They hit her. And just then somebody said, "The counselor's coming!"

Now the kids knew they were in big trouble. The

When the girl was seven or eight years old, she had one of her first memorable experiences of being one of God's assistants.

counselor came in the door and said to Diane, "What happened?"

She was just about to tell on the other kids, and then suddenly a voice spoke to her, "Don't get them in trouble. You can be kind and compassionate to them even though they hurt you. If you do this, they can learn to have more tolerance for people that are different from them. You can teach them something very important."

Suddenly a voice spoke to her, "Don't get them in trouble. You can be kind and compassionate to them even though they hurt you."

That's quite a load to put on a little seven- or eight-year-old child. The counselor said again, "So, what happened?"

Diane said, "I was trying to get up a tree, and I fell down."

The counselor knew better, but what could she do?

From that moment on, Diane was everybody's friend. They said, "Hey, come to church with us."

She said, "OK."

So Diane went to church with her new friends. They were all Christian. Nobody cared that she was of some other religion and that she ate different food. It didn't matter now that Diane was different. She had gotten them off the hook. They were friends.

The three weeks passed very nicely. Sometimes the other children would say, "Diane, you can't have that food. It's not on your diet." Because Diane would forget a certain food wasn't kosher. But the other kids would remind her.

This was Diane's first experience being God's assistant. God had used her to teach the other children that being different is not bad.

Diane learned she needed to go beyond her fears, ego, pride, and also her need for revenge. Only then could she serve God.

Live Your Faith

Adults forget this sometimes. They say, "I want to serve God." Then they do all these things during the workweek to the people they work with and to their families that no one of a spiritual nature would ever consider doing. On the weekend, the same people go to synagogue or church, get their once-a-week boost, and say, "I'm a good Christian. I'm a good Jew. I'm a good ECKist."

I respect people who live their faith, whether they are Christian, Jew, Muslim, or ECKist.

ECKists may say we are special. We're special, but so is everyone else. And there are probably just as many people in Eckankar who do not live their faith as there are people in other religions who do not live their faith.

As an individual, we each have the right to say, "This is my space, this is my being. I don't want your advice." You can say it nicely first, but if people keep getting into your space and saying, "This religion is better for you," or "This food is better for you," or "This investment is better for you," you can get tired of it. Sometimes there's a nice way to say, "Well, thank you for your advice. I'll certainly keep it in mind." And then just look blankly back at the people and just blink. It's rather hard to argue with that.

As an individual, we each have the right to say, "This is my space, this is my being. I don't want your advice."

Helping a Sick Friend

Mike in Nigeria had a friend who was very sick with typhoid fever. Mike woke up one morning with the idea to gather three herbs which he knew would help his friend. It was one of the traditional remedies in African medicine.

He said to himself, "It is certainly worth the

sacrifice to go out and look for these herbs, because my friend is sick."

This is the whole point of life. We sacrifice, and we learn to give to others because God is love. If someone wants to become a Co-worker with God, then that individual—meaning you also—has to learn how to have compassion and love when it's needed. And also the discrimination to know when it's not needed.

We sacrifice, and we learn to give to others because God is love.

Mike went out to gather these three herbs. The first herb grew close to home and was easy to get. Now all he had to do was get the others.

So Mike set out through the bush to a place that he remembered—a pretty good walk down paths and through brush—to where these other two herbs used to be. But when he came to the place, he found the area had been cleared for farming. Now Mike had a problem. He had one of the herbs, but he needed the other two so that he could help his friend with the typhoid fever.

As Mike began to walk back home, he asked, "What will I do?"

The only other place he knew of where these other two herbs grew required a trip on public transportation. Mike had been going through some very hard times. He had just enough money to get a bus to the place where these herbs grew. But then there wouldn't have been enough money to deliver the herbs to his friend.

"Maybe I could borrow money from one of my friends," he said, "then I could take public transportation and deliver the herbs."

As he was lost in thought, Mike suddenly realized he had missed the short path home. This was rugged country. The long path was unfamiliar to him, but he hadn't noticed he was on it until he'd gone a ways.

Then he became curious. There was something inside him that said, "Keep going, Mike. See what's at the end of the road."

He did. He came to a compound—a place of dwellings where people lived—and there he found both of the other herbs growing in abundance. He also found that this compound was a lot closer to home than the place that had been cut down for farming. He didn't have to take public transportation. He still had his money.

Mike looked this whole thing over. His mission had been very important—because a friend was sick, and the herbs would be of help to his friend. He was trying to be a Co-worker with God.

If God is God, then who are you? You are one of the lights of God, moving about in this world asking, sometimes minute by minute, sometimes day by day, "God, what can I do now? What can I do now to learn more about your love and mercy?"

The Holy Spirit, the ECK, will provide an opportunity. Believe me, there are lots of opportunities.

You are one of the lights of God, moving about in this world asking, "God, what can I do now? What can I do now to learn more about your love and mercy?"

Open Consciousness

The Mahanta is the Inner Master, the matrix of the ECK, or the Holy Spirit, in human form so people can have someone to work with that is more than just Sound and Light in the pure sense.

Sometimes the Mahanta appears as a blue light, and the ECK Masters may also have a sound associated with them when they're near. Sometimes people perceive them either by a light or a certain sound, like bells. A certain Master may have the sound of bells accompany him. Or it may be flutes, or the music associated with one of the heavens in the other worlds.

The Sound and Light are connected to a state of consciousness, and this state of consciousness exists whether people are looking toward a heaven of a particular religion, or an individual who has that state of consciousness.

ALLOW ME TO SERVE TODAY

Shelly worked in Spain. She wanted to be a helper for the ECK, the Holy Spirit. One day as she was out driving, about to turn onto the main road, she declared herself a vehicle for the Holy Spirit. She said, "Allow me to do thy will today. Give me a chance to be your Co-worker." She meant it from the bottom of her heart.

As she was about to turn onto the main road, she looked off to the side and saw a man hitchhiking. He had his hand out trying to stop cars by flagging them down.

Shelly caught his attention and said, "Come on, get in."

The man got in, and as they drove down the road he told her he was going to a certain town. She said, "I can take you part of the way, to the town where I work."

He said, "Fine."

When she got to her town, she dropped him off and went to work. At work that day things were very slow. Nothing was happening. So, rather than put up with boredom for the rest of the day, Shelly asked her boss, "What if I go to our office in the next town and straighten out some paperwork there?"

Her boss said, "Good idea. Off you go."

She said, "Allow me to do thy will today. Give me a chance to be your Co-worker." She meant it from the bottom of her heart.

Shelly began thinking back to having picked up the hitchhiker. As she approached the main road on the way to work that morning, she had declared herself a vehicle for God. And less than a minute later this man had needed a ride. "Boy, that was quick!" she said to herself.

Two miles down the road, who does she see? This very same hitchhiker she had picked up before.

So, of course, she pulled over. He got in. He said, "I don't know what I would have done without you. I've got to be in court in ten minutes." They were eight minutes from court.

As they drove, the man told Shelly his story. He said he was from the Sahara. He had brought his family to Spain and had travel papers for all of them. Now the only person left was his daughter. She was still in North Africa waiting for a visa so she could come join the family. The hitchhiker said, "Today I plan to do something about it in court."

With only two minutes to spare, Shelly dropped him off at the courthouse steps. Then she said, "I guess I'm your angel today."

He said to her, "Allah is good."

Shelly was thinking, *It must either be very important for this man to get to the courthouse, or that I have a chance to be a Co-worker.* As a matter of fact, both of these things were true.

If one wants to be a Co-worker with God, one must also have an open state of consciousness. One must be open to the Inner Master, the Mahanta, or to whoever your inner master is, and to the needs of others. Otherwise, you can't be of help. Why not? Because you aren't recognizing the need that's right there within arm's reach.

If one wants to be a Co-worker with God, one must also have an open state of consciousness.

All Religions Have a Place

A Nigerian ECKist wanted to renew his membership in Eckankar. So he went to a bank where the local ECK members had set up a special account at the foreign exchange desk. They could take their currency there and get the United States dollar equivalent.

A woman was seated at the foreign exchange desk. "How can I help you?" she asked.

The Nigerian told her he wanted a certain amount of money put as a donation into the Eckankar account. "I've been looking for someone in this organization," the woman said. "What is this Eckankar? Is it like a church?"

The man said, "Yes, it's a religious organization."

Right away, the conversation changed. She said, "In my church salvation is free. What are you sending this money off to some foreign trickster for?"

The ECKist was caught totally off guard; he had no idea what to say. He realized the woman was a born-again Christian. We have born-again ECKists too, and they are very fervent, to put it kindly. Sometimes they're all over other people's space telling them how to run their spiritual life, when that is actually between that Soul and God.

Sometimes they're all over other people's space telling them how to run their spiritual life, when that is actually between that Soul and God.

The Nigerian was standing there, wondering, *How can I get my transaction done? She's going to pull out some religious tract and give it to me. What am I going to do if she doesn't accept my money and give me a receipt?*

The woman said to him, "The Third World economy is in shambles. It takes the average Nigerian two to three months to get together the amount of money that you're going to send off to this foreign trickster."

Then she looked at him, with the silent question *Why be so stupid?*

The man started chanting HU very softly to himself—HU, a love song to God. Basically, he was saying to God, "Thy will be done. Heaven knows, I don't know what to say to this woman."

The man kept chanting HU. The woman kept sitting there, waiting for an answer.

He finally said, "With all these people walking past this desk, and your bosses, I don't think this is the place to discuss it."

She said, "It's a slow desk. If I'm not complaining, what should it matter to you?" And she smiled at him: *Go ahead, say something.*

Just then, a very old man came up to the desk. He was eighty years old or so, bent over with age, walking with an old walking stick. He was in the traditional robes of a Nigerian chief. Later in the conversation, the ECKist also found out he was a retired defense lawyer. But he didn't know that at the moment.

This old man was cracking jokes with the staff, who respected him because he was someone to be reckoned with—a very astute man who also, apparently, had money. They were standing and nodding to him, as he was joking and having a good time with them. Then the born-again Christian held out one of her tracts. "You are saved," she said.

The old gentleman took the tract, looked at it, and said, "I don't have anything against any religion, but, if you don't mind, I'll tell you what I've learned in my very long life."

The woman was taken aback. She didn't know what to say. The ECKist had stood to the side to give respect to the old chief and let him do his transaction.

The man started chanting HU very softly to himself—HU, a love song to God.

So all three of them were at the desk at the moment, the ECKist off to the side a bit. It was as if this old gentleman had come in by divine will and had gotten center stage.

This old man said, "You know, I've studied a lot of religions. When I was young, I was trained as a Christian. I believed that all people in other religions were going to hell. They were damned because they did not know that Jesus was their savior. I'll tell you what I've learned since."

He said, "Way back then the religion that was the greatest opposition to Christianity was the Islamic religion, so I thought the Muslims would go to hell. But in the years that followed I studied the Koran." Not only had he studied the Koran, he had gone through the holy books of some of the other religions too. At great length, he mentioned the Cabala, the Sufi writings, those of Buddhism, and those of the Rosicrucians. He went right into the traditional religions of Africa. He spoke at length about what he had found in these religions.

When he had begun singing HU, he had opened himself to help from the Holy Spirit, from the Mahanta.

His conclusion was that Christianity—which he still belonged to—did not have a monopoly on God. From all his years of experience, he was now wiser to the fact that all religions are talking about the way back to God.

The ECKist felt joy. When he had begun singing HU, he had opened himself to help from the Holy Spirit, from the Mahanta, who is the matrix of this spiritual power in form. And the Mahanta just that quickly had sent this old gentleman.

The old gentleman was being a Co-worker with God. He was an assistant of God, going to the defense of all religions.

Eventually, the old gentleman, having finished

his transaction, shuffled out the door. The woman behind the desk was so confused, she didn't know what to make of it. She said to the ECKist, "Here's your receipt. We'll talk another time." She gave up the floor to the lawyer, to the ECKist, and, mainly, to God.

LISTEN TO GOD'S VOICE

If God is God, then who are you?

You're either a conscious or unconscious child of God. A lot of people are unconscious children of God when they presume to inflict their religion upon other people. It's the big head that says, "My God is bigger than your God," or "My religion is better than yours."

There is one fact about religion, though: Your religion is best for you right now. That's basically all you can say about any religion. All you can speak about is your religion, and all you can say is that it's either the best for you right now or it is not. If it is the best for you, then you should be growing spiritually and enjoying life.

You should be learning things that help you develop more love and compassion for other people in your family, and those you meet when you're out and about in your daily life. That's if your religion is working for you.

If you're not doing these things, then find another one. Or leave religion entirely and maybe listen to the voice of nature.

No matter what religion you belong to, or whether you belong to no religion at all, ultimately you are listening to the divine Voice of God within you— either by intuition, dreams, or direct experiences of the reality of the spiritual worlds.

You're either a conscious or unconscious child of God.

God's love is with you all the time. It's up to you to recognize it through the hard times and the good times.

God's love is making you more of a spiritual being so that you can better understand the conditions and situations that other Souls, other lights of God, are going through too. In doing so, you are able to serve them and all life better.

ECK European Seminar, The Hague, Netherlands,
Saturday, July 24, 1999

The birds know and recognize the sound of HU just like
their human family.

15

THE LAW OF LOVE

✴

*E*verything revolves around love. It always does. No matter how much we rush about in this world and how harried, ambitious, or sorrowful we become, the world stays together for some reason. This reason is God's love.

God's love is the fabric that draws us all and keeps us here. It makes the whole work, even though sometimes it looks like nothing is working at all.

God's love is the fabric that draws us all and keeps us here. It makes the whole work.

THE FABRIC OF LOVE

The Shariyat-Ki-Sugmad, which means Way of the Eternal, is the holy scriptures of ECK. Book One refers to the Law of Love like this: "The law which all seek to know is the great principle of life. Its simplicity is amazing for it is summed up in this statement: Soul exists because God loves It. In other words, all life exists because God so wills it. This is the very foundation of life, the whole of the philosophy of Eckankar. There is nothing more and nothing less."

There are many different aspects to Eckankar: dreams, Soul Travel, the ECK-Vidya—which is prophecy—and then all the healing aspects. These are all part of the teachings of Eckankar. But the thing that binds them all together is love. It all starts with you existing because God loved you, and God loves you. For that reason was the beginning of Soul.

We are made in the image of God, and inwardly we have the creative spark which makes us godlike. But the creative spark must be turned to doing good.

CARRIERS OF GOD'S LOVE

Love brings us together. An ECK couple from Sweden has a family of three budgies. They're little parakeets, Australian parrot-type birds. The husband said he has learned a lot about love from these three budgies.

When you get into a relationship, you learn a lot about love.

When you get into a relationship, you learn a lot about love. But people would do well to remember that the pets in our lives are also carriers of God's love. Pets are Soul in another form.

Some of God's highest, most love-filled creatures exist in the animal world; there are even some in the human world. There are a lot of people who are full of love and understand love rightly. Understanding love rightly means not doing a thing for a person that they can do for themselves. That's a form of selfishness. But we help others who want to be helped. We do what we can.

BIRD PERSONALITIES

The three budgies each have a distinct personality. Number one is Oscar. He's the chief, a nice green bird. Oscar is a very bluff fellow. He blusters and makes a big show of his self-importance. When he's confident, he fluffs his feathers up and makes himself real big.

But Oscar has another side. He's also a very fearful bird. He's afraid of the dark. He'd rather have light around him. Oscar likes music, but he's also a little stupid and clumsy.

Gullen is the only female in this family of budgies. She's a very shy bird unless the topic of food comes up. Gullen is right there when it's mealtime, and the other two birds scatter if they value their feathers.

Gullen also likes to sit exactly where one of the other birds is sitting. The birds may be loose in the room; one may be sitting on the couch. Gullen will go over and start taking the feathers out of the bird sitting on the couch. That bird leaves, and Gullen sits there, quite pleased and contented. Gullen is generally in the background, watching, but if people neglect her too long, she goes inside herself. And it takes much loving and coaxing to bring her out.

The third little bird is Chico. Greenish blue or turquoise, he's the most social and highly intelligent. He's a newcomer. He had a previous owner, and he also had a mate, but when his mate passed on, the owner gave Chico to this ECK couple. So Chico joined Oscar and Gullen and became part of the family.

Oscar and Gullen are a couple, and Chico is on the outside of the circle, so he's more sociable. He has to be more sociable. Chico can also do something the other birds can't. Chico can talk.

When he came to his new owners, he'd say things like, "Washing machine," just out of the blue. Then he'd say, "Skating." His new owners were puzzled. What was this bird talking about? They really wondered when he said, "Whiskey"!

Chico has been places, seen things, and done things. He is a bird of the world.

Chico likes everybody; sometimes he puts his little beak out for a kiss. Since he's the only one who

Chico has been places, seen things, and done things. He is a bird of the world.

can talk or imitate, he goes around the room and chatters. He will see Oscar and say, "Kiss, kiss?" Oscar always looks rather puzzled; he doesn't know what to make of Chico. Oscar can't talk, and anyway, he is the chief. So what's this "kiss, kiss?" An example of puzzled love. Oscar doesn't get it.

So Chico tries it with Gullen, the female. He puts a big smile on his little beak and says, "Kiss, kiss?" Gullen chases him away. She will have none of that from him, a bird of the world. Spurned love.

At night, when it is time for all the good little birdies to say good night to the day, Chico goes to the top of the cage on a perch and stands in front of a mirror. He stands there, looking in the mirror and saying, "Good night, Chico. Chico sweet. Kiss, kiss?" It's lonely at the top.

Way down at the bottom of the cage Oscar is on his perch, trying to get some sleep. Chico keeps talking and talking on into the night. Oscar looks up, ruffles his feathers, and stares at Chico, but it doesn't do any good because Chico is always looking in the mirror. Oscar pulls himself together—because the chief has duties—and begins his slow, laborious way up the cage. Finally he gets up there where Chico is, puffs himself real big, and stares down into the eyes of little Chico. Then Chico makes himself small, stares back, and does not talk anymore.

Oscar, still in his enlarged state, then makes his way back down to his perch, sits down on it, and looks up very satisfied. He has done a good thing. The chief's duties are done for the day, and now all in his little village can rest.

Chico is a good little bird. He likes to clean and trim and groom the mustache and the beard of his owner. The owner is always watching the three little

Oscar can't talk, and anyway, he is the chief. So what's this "kiss, kiss?" An example of puzzled love. Oscar doesn't get it.

birds, and in the meantime all the little lessons of love are rubbing off on him.

He and his wife do the spiritual exercises at night by chanting HU—this beautiful love song to God—very quietly, and Chico always joins them. In the last year, Oscar has finally come closer. He sits behind the sofa on a picture, listening. The birds know and recognize the sound of HU just like their human family.

LEARNING THE LAW OF LOVE

The sister of someone I'll call Adele passed on, or translated, five years ago. Adele often wondered, *Does my sister still remember me? Why doesn't she come, even in dreams?*

Adele teaches art. She lives in a quiet suburb. One day one of her students looked out and saw a kitten nearby that had apparently been struck by a car. It looked as if it wouldn't be able to live much longer. The student ran outside and tried to catch the little kitten but wasn't able to. For the next week Adele worried about the kitten. She put out food and water because it would need some help in getting fed. But the kitten never showed up.

One Saturday morning, Adele had a very clear dream with her sister.

One Saturday morning, Adele had a very clear dream with her sister. It was a very vivid dream, like they were actually together, because they were. Her sister said to her, "I can take care of the kitten for you if you'll give me some food." So Adele gave her sister a saucer with some food on it.

When Adele awoke, she had this feeling of love: two concerns were taken from her heart. First of all, the kitten was cared for, probably in the other worlds. And even more important, her sister had not forgotten her. This was another demonstration of the Law of Love.

Loving Yourself as Soul

Dreams, Soul Travel, and prophecy gain their power through God's love. It's the love God has for you as Soul. That's why centuries ago Christ said to love your neighbor as yourself. That principle is based on divine love.

Some people have a habit of putting themselves down. They look in the mirror, and they see that somehow the mirror isn't giving the same reflections it used to ten, fifteen, or twenty years ago. There seems to be more of a grainy surface to the mirror—it doesn't look as good. So people are hard on themselves.

It's simply because they've forgotten that we are not this body—this thing that looks more grainy in the mirror every year, every decade.

We are Soul, and Soul wears the human body like a suit of clothes, a dress, or an overcoat. It was new once, then it gets comfortably worn. One day it gets old, then it's time to get rid of it. So Soul does. Soul is the eternal part.

Inside the body is where you, Soul, are. Our bodies are very important. They're like our buildings, our temples. We do the best we can to keep them in working order because we would do this out of love for ourselves—because of our love for God, because of God's love for us.

Dreams, Soul Travel, and prophecy gain their power through God's love.

In Time of Need

A woman in the United Kingdom lost her husband in a highway accident. All the cares of this large family were suddenly upon her shoulders, and she wondered what to do.

When her husband was alive, child care was not an expense because they could share the duties. They would juggle their schedules so that someone was always there for the children. But suddenly she was faced with this new expense. When the children came home from school, they needed a place to be until she came home from work. The woman looked at the cost of child care and asked, "How am I ever going to afford this?"

The people at work had been wonderful to her after her husband's death. They had given her a lot of time off to let her heal. Now she felt it was time to get back to work full-time, but she didn't know how to manage it.

She sat down to contemplate. She wanted to meet with the Mahanta, her spiritual guide, and ask for guidance.

She sat down to contemplate. She wanted to meet with the Mahanta, her spiritual guide, and ask for guidance.

Just as she sat down, somebody knocked on the door. It was her next-door neighbor. This neighbor, it just happened, took care of children professionally. The widow had asked for help from this neighbor a long time ago, but at that time there were no places open in the child-care home. But suddenly there was room for her children. They worked out a fair price, and child care was taken care of.

The next concern was her yard. It was in terrible shape; it needed to be weeded and reseeded in certain places. She asked, "How will I be able to do this in my weakened state? And what about the cost?"

She got three bids from professionals; one would do all the work for a whole lot of money, the second would do medium amount for medium amount, and the third would just put in new sod. That cost the least.

One day she was speaking to several friends on the phone, mentioning the different things that had come up to deal with, including her backyard. The next thing she knew, an ECKist came over and said,

"I can help. He started cleaning up the backyard. Soon another friend came over; he was not an ECKist, but he loved gardening. These two were busy working on the backyard, and she was busy making drinks and food for them.

After this was done, she called the least expensive of the professional caretakers who came and put in sod, then she and her children put grass seed in the other places. Every day she watered her backyard, and soon the lawn was looking pretty good.

As soon as the grass came in, the next big expense arose: a lawnmower.

Just that day, a free local paper came. In the classified ads was a lawnmower for exactly half the price of a new one. One of her stipulations had been that the lawnmower would have a guarantee. She didn't want to buy a lawnmower, have it break, then have to figure out how to get it repaired and come up with money for that.

This lawnmower did have a guarantee; it was good for two more years. She bargained a bit and got it for even less than half price.

She missed her husband, but sometimes she saw him in her dreams.

ALL THE MIRACLES

Through all this she was grateful—grateful for the blessings of the ECK as It had come to help her in her time of need and trouble. She missed her husband, but sometimes she saw him in her dreams. She and her husband would go dancing, and suddenly she would feel herself lift from the floor, go higher and higher toward the ceiling. It was a most wonderful feeling to be in the arms of her beloved, dancing ever higher and higher toward God.

There were white lights of God, very near the high ceiling. "Oh, no! No higher. I'll burn," she said.

So very gradually they settled back down, and she awoke.

She looked back at all the miracles: the child care, the backyard taken care of, and the lawnmower. Meeting her husband. Seeing the lights of God, the manifestations of the Light of God, part of the Voice of God. She realized that the Law of Love does work.

REMEMBER TO SING HU

Someone I'll call Ellen has been an ECK member for a while. She renewed her membership some months ago, and she asked the Eckankar Spiritual Center to please send the eighth discourse of the study lesson for the previous year. It just hadn't come—it was probably lost in the mail. So the ECK staff sent out the missing discourse to her.

It arrived shortly before what was to be the last weekend she would see her father in this world. Just three weeks earlier he had been diagnosed with a serious illness and had been given only a month to live.

Years ago when Ellen had first heard about Eckankar, she was so very excited about it. She had heard about the Sound and Light of God. Those two aspects of God are simply God's love in action—the Voice of God. She wanted to share the news with the two people she loved the most—her father and mother—but her father didn't very much care about it. He loved his daughter, and Eckankar was fine for her.

After looking through some of the ECK materials, the mother said to her daughter, "I wish you wouldn't bring it into our home." It wasn't that the mother had anything special against Eckankar; she just wondered about it. She said, "Maybe it's a cult. I don't want my daughter mixed up with this."

Ellen respected her family's wishes, and she never

She had heard about the Sound and Light of God. Those two aspects of God are simply God's love in action—the Voice of God.

spoke about Eckankar in their home again.

Since she'd last seen her father, his appearance had deteriorated a lot. She knew he would leave soon. The missing discourse she had just got in the mail said to share the ECK with those you love. So Ellen decided to do that.

She spoke to her dad very earnestly. "Dad, when I was sick, this name of God, a special spiritual healing sound, was able to help me. Maybe it can help you."

A Special Healing Sound

Ellen had to return to her own home soon after, but during the week she got a call that her father had become very ill and they were going to move him from the hospital to a hospice. Ellen called her sister, who was at the hospital. She said to her sister, "Would you remind Dad to sing HU?"

A little while later her sister called back. "He has been singing it all along. He's been singing HU all the time."

Ellen's dad was a very down-to-earth person. He didn't do what she called "odd" things—like chanting HU just for the fun of it—simply because one of his daughters asked him to. Ellen believed he was doing it because it was helping. It was giving him some sort of comfort.

He was taken to the hospice, heavily sedated, and while in the sedated state, he passed over to the other side in peace, without fear.

Ellen was so grateful that the ECK teachings had allowed her to share this ancient name for God with her beloved father. He certainly wouldn't have used it unless it had helped him. As it apparently must have.

Ellen concluded that in one's daily job and routine, sometimes little things can end up having a

Ellen was so grateful that the ECK teachings had allowed her to share this ancient name for God with her beloved father.

very significant result. So she sent a thank-you letter to the Eckankar Spiritual Center for sending the missing ECK discourse so promptly. She also thanked the Mahanta for being there, for helping her father and her at this very difficult time in their lives. This is the Law of Love in operation.

WHEN THE TIME IS RIGHT

Sometimes people hear about Eckankar many years before they're ready to take that spiritual step.

Ray is a member of Eckankar from New York. Just recently his father told him he was interested in joining Eckankar. Back in 1992, Ray had first found the ECK teachings and was very excited about them. He wanted to share them with someone special, someone he knew would understand, his father.

Sometimes people hear about Eckankar many years before they're ready to take that spiritual step.

Ray's father had come here from Jamaica in the midseventies. He had been a minister, and he had also studied the Eastern religions: Buddhism, Hinduism, and many others. Ray had always looked at his father as being an expert on religions. His father was, in theory. But trying to live all these different philosophies was very difficult.

Back in 1992 when Ray first told his father about Eckankar, his father said, "Oh, I know Eckankar."

Ray said, "You do?"

His father led the way into the basement, where there were mountains of books on spiritual subjects. The father dug around and finally came up with a battered copy of *ECKANKAR—The Key to Secret Worlds* by Paul Twitchell. His father said, "Yes, I know about Eckankar."

So now, seven years later, Ray's father is thinking of taking that spiritual step. Maybe he will join ECK, maybe he won't. There's no hurry.

Boundaries of Free Will

One of the blessings, and perhaps curses, of this world is that Soul can do what It wants to. It has free will.

Of course, there's a saying that my freedom ends where yours begins. And your freedom ends where mine begins. If people understand love correctly, they will understand that.

So many people who pass themselves off as disciples of love today do not understand that simple relationship—that my freedom ends where yours begins. And vice versa. That's how it works.

Do-Gooders

People who are the do-gooders in life cause so many of earth's miseries, whether in religion or science. They always say they're doing something for other people. But they forget that they've crossed the line. They've gotten into the space of other people, the area of personal freedom. They're trespassers.

Since they don't know the Law of Love, they somehow feel that they are God's chosen people. They are actually God's blight on the earth. They wouldn't believe it, because most of the words they use are to get praise from people and the applause of the crowds. And so with all this sound and fury in their eyes and ears, they are deaf and dumb to the law of God's love. But in time they'll come to understand that law too. God doesn't care when.

All the so-called innocent victims of these do-gooders have their own karmic debts to pay—past and present—of when they too were the do-gooders. Sometimes people are do-gooders on a grand scale. And boy, do they reap the karma. It takes a long time

So many people who pass themselves off as disciples of love today do not understand that simple relationship—that my freedom ends where yours begins. And vice versa.

to work that stuff off. But this earth is going to be around a long time.

ELECTROMAGNETIC ILLNESS

The Law of Love also led an individual we'll call Robin to the teachings of ECK. She's a new member of Eckankar, but it took a serious change in health for her to get ready for the ECK teachings.

Robin was in the fast lane in the business world for many years. She was always so busy. She'd known about the ECK teachings for a long time, but she never quite had the time for them. There were things to do, places to see, rungs on the ladder to climb— all these things that were so important.

Six years ago Robin bought a condo. She called it the condo of the dark forces. She was probably too gracious. I would have just called it the condo from hell.

This condo was in a very strong electromagnetic field; it also had geopathic stress. The pipes leaked water, which caused mold. For those of you who have an immune system that's been weakened by electromagnetic fields and geopathic stress, all you need is mold and other toxins. It can be very, very hard trying to regain your health.

The doctors diagnosed her with fibromyalgia and chronic fatigue. So she had an answer for what was wrong with her. It took three more years to find out about the electromagnetic radiation.

SLOW ROAD TO HEALING

As this illness took hold of Robin, she began to sleep more. The more she slept, the sicker she got. She believes that this malady, which has several other phases too, is going to be the illness of the twenty-first century. In fact, it is already responsible

The Law of Love also led an individual we'll call Robin to the teachings of ECK.

for many of the illnesses that are popping up. Science works so fast to heal one illness, and then suddenly another strain pops up here, there, and everywhere.

At some point in our life—say when we reach the half-century mark or so, maybe before, later if we're lucky—we realize that we are always in the presence of God. At a certain time you come to the realization that you are always in God's presence. That this is really a mortal coil, a mortal shell, and that it is a gift to be here.

Of those people who have become very, very ill—and I know I said it myself at the time—when you finally come out of the darkest and the deepest shadows of this long valley, you say, "Life is good. Life is very good."

This is as profound as it gets. Other people will look at you a little bit strange. They won't understand unless they've been there.

That's where Robin was.

Her illness prepared her for the ECK teachings. She'd just moved to a new city, and she went with one of her friends to an ECK discussion class.

This friend had been in Eckankar for fifteen years and had told Robin about these teachings for so long, but Robin simply wasn't ready. It took this serious illness to cut through the ambition and the joy of living too much on the material side, which we've all done. And many of us still do. It took this serious illness for Robin to become softened up enough. Life does that.

Life has a saying: You can come easy, or you can come hard, but you're coming. And that's how God's love draws us.

When Love Calls Us Home

Life has a saying: You can come easy, or you can come hard, but you're coming. And that's how God's love draws us.

We can kick, fight, and resist. But God's love says, "You can come easy, or you can come hard. But I love you." Gradually Soul becomes refined through Its many experiences on this earth and in many of the other worlds that exist beyond here.

So when Robin came to the ECK discussion class that night, she was ready. Now the ECK teachings—the books and the tapes—suddenly clicked for her. They made sense. She said, "Well, of course. Why didn't I see that before?" Simply because she wasn't spiritually ready.

We've all been there, and we thank God that we are here today. Because there are many more people who have never heard of the ECK teachings, and they won't be ready for them for many lifetimes.

Robin counts many miracles since coming to ECK: heightened awareness, dreams, and waking dreams, but especially the HU, this sacred name of God. This spiritual healing Sound.

When we're ready for the ECK teachings, nothing can stand in our way. Love calls us, and then love brings us home.

Soul becomes refined through Its many experiences on this earth and in many of the other worlds that exist beyond here.

TRUE LOVE

While Robin was so ill, she was learning about true love. One of the teachers sent by the ECK, or the Holy Spirit, was her cat, Gizmo.

Gizmo had been Robin's cat for thirteen years; just this summer, he passed on. Throughout Robin's illness, Gizmo had shown her how to have patience: "Hey, slow down. Don't be a type A. Relax. Don't worry about things." Worry is one of the things that goes along with sensitivity to electromagnetic radiation and that sort of illness.

Robin was learning about unconditional love. Love

*She realized
God is love,
God is mercy.
The Ocean of
Love and Mercy
is God's home,
the place where
God dwells.*

is worth more than many treasure chests full of gold. If you have all the gold in the world and not love, you have nothing.

This summer Gizmo suddenly became very ill, and he had to be put to sleep. Robin said, "Can I do it? Should I do it? Should I not?" Back and forth, all the questions.

As she was asking these questions, suddenly the word *mercy* came into her mind, and she realized God is love, God is mercy. The Ocean of Love and Mercy is God's home, the place where God dwells. Maybe it was to be done.

Two days after the passing of her cat, Robin and a friend were sitting on the porch, talking about Gizmo and remembering. Along came this young orange cat. He ran along two neighbors' lawns, right up onto the porch. He ignored Robin's friend and went right into Robin's lap. He just sat there. Robin had never seen him before, but he made himself right at home. He wanted to play. He wanted to make her laugh. He ran out on the grass, did acrobatics, chased a grasshopper, and just had a great time.

This little orange cat just wanted to play. It was almost as if Gizmo was there, telling Robin through the cat, "Look at this young cat body. I got rid of my old one, and I'm going to get a new healthy body."

The next day this orange cat came again; he came right into the house. He searched the counter, nosed around, and found Gizmo's toy mouse. He played with that for a while. Then Robin lay down, as she had often done with Gizmo, and this orange cat plumped down on her chest and put his head underneath her chin. He went to sleep for an hour. Robin was thinking, *Wow, just like Gizmo.* Gizmo used to do the very same thing.

The third day the cat came back to make friends with her husband and look around outside a bit. After this third visit, Robin was very curious. She asked some of the neighborhood kids, "Is there an orange cat around here—a young orange cat?" They said, "Oh, yeah, two blocks over."

But the cat never came back, and Robin never saw him again.

It was a sign to her that Gizmo was sending love and comfort. Gizmo was saying, "Hey, Mom, I'm OK. I'm going to come back in a young, healthy body, and there will be many more good times, if you want."

That's how love works. It knows no bounds.

The Law of Love. *The Shariyat-Ki-Sugmad,* Book One, again says that it is "the great principle of life. Its simplicity is amazing for it is summed up in the statement: Soul exists because God loves It. In other words, all life exists because God so wills it. This is the very foundation of life, the whole of the philosophy of Eckankar. There is nothing more, and nothing less."

These are the blessings of love.

These are the blessings of love.

We blunder around; sometimes we take a good step, sometimes a clumsy one. But what difference does it make? It doesn't make a bit of difference. That was then. This is now. We do the best we can. We love because God first loved us.

ECK Worldwide Seminar, Minneapolis, Minnesota, Saturday, October 23, 1999

His contract was with the Holy Spirit—with the Law of
Life—to do the job as well as he could. What other way could
you do it if you've got a contract with the Holy Spirit?

16
WHAT'S IT
ALL ABOUT?

A few months ago, a woman sent me a very nice thank-you letter for mentioning the book *Your Body's Many Cries for Water* by Dr. Batmanghelidj. This woman had had asthma, bronchitis, and a hacking cough for years. Trying out Dr. Batmanghelidj's theories about water, she found she was dehydrated. Now, when she gets up in the morning, she drinks three eight-ounce cups of water. She's gotten rid of all these health conditions—bronchitis, asthma, and that hacking cough.

She said she didn't want to be like one of the nine lepers in the Christian Bible. Ten lepers came to Christ, and all ten were healed. Only one came back to thank him, though. He was the lowliest of the low in the eyes of the society in those days, a Samaritan. But the Samaritan thanked him.

And Jesus said that the Samaritan's faith had made him whole.

Jesus said that the Samaritan's faith had made him whole.

Who Does the Healing?

Anyone who is a channel for healing for the Holy Spirit doesn't take credit for these miracles himself. Because Divine Spirit does the healing. The individual is only a channel for it.

The more clear a channel is, such as Christ, the more likely these healings are. I would like to recommend to this woman that she thank the Holy Spirit and Dr. Batmanghelidj. Because she knows that the gifts and the blessings of life come from the single source on high.

The doctors and alternative healers are just channels for this healing power that knows better than anyone else what you need.

Anyone who is a channel for healing for the Holy Spirit doesn't take credit for these miracles himself. Because Divine Spirit does the healing.

Gifts from Spirit

I'd like to mention a book I came across through an ECK coincidence, because these things happen even to ECK Masters—especially to ECK Masters. The only reason I say these things happen even to ECK Masters is that they happen to everyone. The difference is that not everyone is aware of these coincidences that occur.

My wife, Joan, and I were at our chiropractor's for a treatment. As we walked in, the chiropractor mentioned a book on her desk. It was *The Metabolic Typing Diet* by William Wolcott.

While she was treating Joan, I scanned the book to see what was in it. We have so many books on health at home, some of which you have been so kind to send. We bought many of the rest ourselves, looking here, there, and everywhere, seeing how—as our health improved step-by-step—to pass on some of this information to you as a thank-you.

I recognize that the Holy Spirit is the healer. It may come through a book that you sent, it may come through a treatment by our chiropractor. These things all work together. It's up to us to accept the gift and the love that's so freely given. We must have the awareness to do so. Often it takes pain and dire necessity before we even come to the point where we say, My eyes are open. I'm looking, I'm looking. Then when the blessings—the different methods of healing—show up, we recognize them as the next step.

This book is good in that it recognizes the differences in people, the same way that we in Eckankar spiritually recognize the difference in each person's state of consciousness. We're all different. We are all made in the image of God. We are created from the same divine substance. But outside of that, we are all different—even to health.

We are all made in the image of God. We are created from the same divine substance. But outside of that, we are all different—even to health.

LEVELS OF HEALING

In this book, *The Metabolic Typing Diet,* William Wolcott speaks of three metabolic types—the protein type, the carbohydrate type, and the mixed type. He provides a number of different foods that he says will help if an individual happens to be of one of these three types. But he leaves a lot of room for times when even his method doesn't work. He'll say, It's due to the differences, and here's what to try next. So there are a number of fallback positions. In that sense it's useful.

For many of you dealing with the struggle to improve your health, this may be another step. It may not work for you. Or a little piece may work for you, and a different piece may work for me. Then we wait until the ECK, the Holy Spirit, brings us to the next stage of healing.

Because each level of healing is a teacher. It teaches us something about ourselves. It teaches us something about our relationship with God.

RIDDLE OF THE QUESTION

The talk for this evening, "What's It All About?" is in three parts: the riddle of the question, the gift of change, and the riddle of God.

In the Eckankar bible, *The Shariyat-Ki-Sugmad,* Book Two, the chapter called "The Eternal Dreamer of ECK," reads:

> The release of the chela [student] from the wheel of life when he enters Eckankar is that point when he begins to accept, and stops all his questions. The riddle of the question is forever plaguing the neophyte, for he never understands that no question can be put without an answer. Yet all questions are on the mental level; but the answers are always available before the question. In other words, there are always the answers to the problems of life, without the questions existing. It is the doubting in the mind of man which leads to questions. This doubt arises when there is a lack of confidence.

What's it all about? The riddle of the question. There are all levels of questions.

HUMOR

To wind down in the evening, I may listen to ECK music or the radio. Sometimes classical, sometimes talk radio. But at night it's often a radio station that plays taped shows hosted by John Doremus, a man with a quiet voice. Between light music, vocal, and instrumental selections, the host tells little stories with his very quiet humor—words to think on, little points to ponder.

Each level of healing is a teacher. It teaches us something about ourselves. It teaches us something about our relationship with God.

One night he said a lot of people believe that the Austrians have no sense of humor. But it's not so. As an example, he said, a wife asks her husband, "Don't you think it's time to take our son to the zoo?"

The Austrian husband says, "They'll come and get him if they want him bad enough."

So, quiet humor. This level question tickled my funny bone as I was sitting there, half paying attention to the radio.

HONORING AGREEMENTS

An ECKist named Bernard came to the United States from another country. He needed to find work in a hurry so he could eat and rent a place to stay. It was a hand-to-mouth existence; he earned just enough money for basic food, rent, and carfare to get to work. I know this situation well, having been in it a number of times. Many of you have too.

Sometimes we put ourselves into it through a lack of planning. And sometimes it's the Holy Spirit's way to bring us some lessons about ourselves that we could not learn in another way.

Bernard went to work at a warehouse that ships for a mail-order company. He was sent to work in the giftwrapping department. Thirty or forty other people were in there, all wrapping packages very carefully. When there was a delicate item, they used fine paper and taped it very carefully.

His first day on the job, Bernard stood near one of the workers to learn how he was wrapping.

His first day on the job, Bernard stood near one of the workers to learn how he was wrapping. The coworker boxed the gift, wrapped it up, put a mailing label on it, then remembered he had forgotten to put the invoice into the box. The man didn't want to open up that box again, so he just gave the box a sharp punch with his fist, caved it in, and was able to slip the invoice into the crack.

Bernard just looked at him. He was appalled. *This is not a good gift anymore,* he thought. He asked his coworker questions of a different level.

Bernard asked the fellow, "Have you ever placed an order by mail?"

"No," said the man.

"So how would you feel if one day you place an order and it arrives looking like this? Would you be happy?" asked Bernard.

"No, I would not be happy."

"Then why are you doing it to others' gifts?"

The fellow thought a bit, then he said, "I'm a selfish person. By doing it like this the unhappy customer will return the gift. Then we will always be called in to work by the company." And he appeared to be very satisfied with his reply to Bernard's question.

Bernard didn't say anything, but he noticed a difference in his coworker's work from that moment on. The man began treating the packages very carefully. Something had occurred to him: This package might be coming to him someday. And he began wrapping each package as if it were.

Bernard realized that the Holy Spirit had a lesson in this for him. He'd made an agreement with the company to do a certain job (wrapping gifts) for a certain amount of money. But Bernard's real contract was with the Holy Spirit—with the Law of Life—to do it as well as he could. What other way could you do it if you've got a contract with the Holy Spirit? You would always want to do your best.

Bernard's real contract was with the Holy Spirit—with the Law of Life—to do it as well as he could.

OPEN TO ECK

The riddle of the question is that no question can be put without an answer. The answers are always available before the question.

Michelle from Maryland got the book *ECKANKAR—Ancient Wisdom for Today*. A sentence in chapter 8 caught her attention. It provided the opening to introduce her to some of the coincidences of the Holy Spirit at work in the life of a person whose state of consciousness has begun to open.

The sentence read: "If you are open to the Holy Spirit, you will find truth coming to you through the actions and words of other people."

The next day Michelle went to the grocery store to pick up some things. Being in a hurry, she ran around the store, collected her groceries, and rushed up to the checkout stand, only to find an empty shopping cart in the checkout lane.

She said to the clerk, "Are you open?" He said, "Yes, I'm open," offering no more. "Well, whose cart is this?" Michelle asked.

Just at that moment, the woman who had checked out just in front of her turned around and came back for the cart. This woman realized she was going to need the cart to take her bagged groceries out to her car.

As she retrieved the cart, she said, "I have so many things on my mind I can't remember everything."

Michelle just nodded to the woman, and that was it. That was the encounter. Michelle went home.

When she got home she went to the mailbox and got her mail. Inside was an official-looking letter. She opened it, and there was an accusation that she had not correctly filled out some important form. She

The riddle of the question is that no question can be put without an answer. The answers are always available before the question.

wondered, *What do I tell them?* Then she remembered the woman in the grocery store and her words, "I have so many things on my mind, I can't remember everything." Michelle said, "That's perfect. That's exactly what's true in my case."

She had forgotten to include a date on this document, and so she sat down and wrote a reply. When she finished, she was awed by the timing of it all, and she wrote me about it, saying in a joking way, "I am not superstitious." She drew a little smiley face then wrote: "Awesome." She had had a firsthand experience with the workings of the Holy Spirit.

This spiritual phenomenon is called the Golden-tongued Wisdom, when the Holy Spirit speaks to us through the words or actions of other people.

This spiritual phenomenon is called the Golden-tongued Wisdom, when the Holy Spirit speaks to us through the words or actions of other people.

Spiritual Help

The riddle of the question. Although the answer is always there, sometimes we don't realize it fully for many years.

A woman's grandchild had died, and this left her distraught. So this woman's son came up to one of the ECKists and asked, "Do you have grief groups in Eckankar?"

This ECKist said, "No, but we do have ESAs. These are ECK Spiritual Aides." They simply listen to the problem of an individual, pretty much the same as the confessor in the Catholic Church, except people are not expected to confess here. Whenever they have any trouble, they can request an ESA session to simply air it. The ESA does nothing—just listens. If the Holy Spirit wants to change something in that person's life, It does so in Its own way at Its own time.

After she had an ESA session, the woman felt much better. Years later, she said, "It saved my life."

It was the answer for her at that particular time.

She and her son began to go to some of the ECK Worship Services. In fact, they went quite regularly. Then she joined a four-week class, "Getting Answers from God through Past Lives, Dreams, and Soul Travel."

The death of her grandchild had happened several years before, but she was still carrying the pain. In all the time that she went to the ECK Worship Services, she hadn't become a member of Eckankar. She was still waiting for the spiritual leader, myself, to drop the other shoe.

She wondered, *Is this guy going to try to coerce people? Is he going to try to deceive them? Make them members?*

No, because then I carry your load for you. I like spiritual freedom, so I won't carry the load of an unwilling person. Whenever you trick a person into following your path, you take on part of that individual's burden. I don't want to do that. I'm into spiritual freedom.

I like spiritual freedom, so I won't carry the load of an unwilling person.

TIME FOR HEALING

At the class, "Getting Answers from God through Past Lives, Dreams, and Soul Travel," the facilitators showed a video of a talk I'd given some time ago, "The Right of Choice." In it I told the story of an African father whose child had died in a hospital. Hearing this story finally released the woman from her grief.

It gave her an understanding of the reason for the death of her grandchild. The healing came through a back door, years after the tragic event in her own life.

The Holy Spirit knows when you're ready to handle the information of why something happens. It may be a few days, it may be a moment, it may be a couple years, or many years. It may come very directly, and very often in a way that is totally unexpected.

The Gift of Change

What's it all about? This part is the gift of change.

The Shariyat-Ki-Sugmad, Book Two, chapter 1, "The Eternal Dreamer of ECK," reads:

> When man cannot understand his problem or something which is unfamiliar to him, he is doubtful and asks questions. He must live by established traditions and forms. He must follow out a unified pattern of behavior and live with others who do likewise. Otherwise, his whole pattern of life is upset. If he is not living close to the source of the divine ECK, he might think in terms of not being able to do anything. This is because he is still living in the patterns and binds of society and not yet able to break through the boundaries of liberation.

The *Wall Street Journal* yesterday, in the Weekend Journal section which is special in its Friday edition, had a very good article on religion, "Redefining God." People in churches today, in a form of religion as it was taught in their youth, are restless. They're looking around for something else.

So ministers are doing what they can to fit the scriptures to the people, because every scripture has something in it for everyone within that religious body.

The article mentioned a Presbyterian church in New York. The minister started talking about God. He said, "O burning mountain. O chosen sun. O perfect moon." And then, "O fathomless well. O unattainable height. O clearness beyond measure." He was trying to reach the outer boundaries of everything within his mental realm he could think of to touch the

People in churches today, in a form of religion as it was taught in their youth, are restless. They're looking around for something else.

farthest end of God possible.

A Methodist minister in Evanston, Illinois, says that on Easter he plans to compare God to a gardener. He's doing this to appease the growing theological diversity in his small church. He says, "I don't want anybody to feel left out."

This is the nature of it. Everyone's understanding about God is different, in the same way that everyone's need and understanding of health is different. These ministers and many others are trying to break out of the established traditions and forms of their religious societies. They are making a very honest and creative attempt to serve the spiritual needs of their congregations.

Several years ago people were trying to decide whether or not God was a woman, a man, or just It. In ECK, of course, we say God is. There isn't much else to be said about It.

You can give God a whole stream of attributes—God is this, God is that, God is not this, God is not that. But the most we can say is that this being, God, or Sugmad, lives in the Ocean of Love and Mercy, and Its Voice is the Holy Spirit. This Voice we call the ECK. And that's all. It's no great mystery.

But the gift of change is what brings spiritual unfoldment to us. It pulls us out of the routines of society, takes away everything familiar, and puts us in a strange place. And we become afraid in a strange place.

God, or Sugmad, lives in the Ocean of Love and Mercy, and Its Voice is the Holy Spirit. This Voice we call the ECK.

A CLOSE SHAVE

An ECK gentleman had felt concern for some time about his beard. He had carefully grown the beard over seven years. Some of the other ECKists were saying to him, "You look like an ECK Master."

That was very flattering, but he knew himself better than they did, and he figured that was at least a couple of years off. So this gentleman asked the Mahanta's help. He said, "Please help me in some way. Let these people see that I'm not an ECK Master yet. In some way, help them change their attitude."

As it had been growing more than seven years, by now his beard was quite long. So he got out his electric trimmer. It had a number of settings on it. He figured he'd use the first setting, which would just take a little bit off. He figured if he cut back on his beard just a little, the people would slowly and gradually get over their impression of him as an ECK Master.

He figured if he cut back on his beard just a little, the people would slowly and gradually get over their impression of him as an ECK Master.

So he was starting to shave, and five seconds later the trimmer cut out. He shook it, cleaned it with his little brush, and tried again. But the trimmer stopped again. He wondered, *Now what do I do?*

He cleaned it again and then it came to mind: Oil it. So he oiled it, and it began to work really well.

But while he was fiddling around, trying to get it to run, he moved the switch from the first setting, which was a very light shave, to a clean shave—position number five. And as he ran the trimmer over his face, it looked like it was clearing a path running through a dark woods.

"Now what am I going to do?" he asked. Because he couldn't go out with a big gash out of one side of his beard.

"Well, I've always wanted a mustache and a goatee," he said. So he picked up his trimmer again, and because he didn't have any real experience at this sort of thing, pretty soon there was no more goatee. Pretty soon no more mustache.

Finally he ended up with some very short sideburns.

This man is not a fool. He thought this would be a good time to call his wife at work—prepare her. He didn't want her to recoil in shock when she came home and saw this stranger standing in their home.

At the next ECK Worship Service, he was rather curious. He wondered, *What's everybody going to think now that my beard is gone?* One of the people who had been identifying him with an ECK Master came up to him and said, "You look sort of different today." She looked at him again. She said, "Oh, your beard's gone. You shaved it off. You don't look like an ECK Master anymore." Then she left.

He said, "Thank you, Mahanta. I wanted a way to help these people change their attitude about me and my beard. You gave the answer in a way that left no doubt."

This was a gift of change.

EMBRACING THE UNEXPECTED

Susan, one of our dear friends at the Eckankar Spiritual Center, had come to that point in her life where she could appreciate the quietness of being in this silence within her state of consciousness. She was so grateful for it. About that time, an invitation came to her: Would she speak at the ECK regional seminar that's going to take place in town? This terrified her because she hadn't ever given such a talk before.

She wanted to say no; then the person inviting her said, "The title of this talk will be 'Embrace the Unexpected with Grace.'" *With a title like that, how can I say no?* she thought.

Susan was very nervous. She went about preparing the talk notes; her husband, Rich, gave her an idea for a story. Then a number of waking dreams

He said, "Thank you, Mahanta. I wanted a way to help these people change their attitude about me and my beard. You gave the answer in a way that left no doubt."

began to occur in her life. These are events that happen in the outer, daily life that are actually some message from the Holy Spirit. The waking dreams came in quick order, and soon she had her basic talk. Now she had to capture it. She wanted to put it in writing and polish it.

So she got the whole talk down on paper, then she began to rewrite it. She rewrote it, and rewrote it, and rewrote it. Then she went to people who are good speakers to get tips on how to make this talk most effective, so it could help people in the audience.

She put all her talk notes on little index cards. Just about that time, someone said, "I went to an ECK seminar one time, and the speaker had all his notes on these little index cards, and they fell out of his hand and scattered all over the floor." Susan's no fool. She took a hole punch and punched a hole in those cards. Then she put a key ring through the hole. They weren't going to get away from her.

Next she began to practice in front of the mirror. She practiced all the time. She carried the little cards with her everywhere. When she went to sleep at night, they were right by her bedside. When she went out during the day, those cards were in her purse. She wasn't letting them out of her sight.

Most speakers who have given a talk in ECK, and a lot of other people too, have gone through the same torment. I know I have. I have punched holes through some of my talk notes and run a key ring through them too. It works.

Finally the day of the seminar came. In her preparation she had asked the Mahanta, the Inner Master, "What should be in this talk? What points are important? What points need to be said?"

The Inner Master is the inner side of myself. As

spiritual leader of Eckankar, I serve as the Outer Master. There are two parts. This is one of the unique features of Eckankar: The spiritual leader of the times is able to work with you first as the Outer Master and then later as the Inner Master.

Susan was wondering, *How am I going to keep my mind off this talk?* It was scheduled a little later in the day. So she offered to be a volunteer. She volunteered wherever she could, just to keep herself busy and her mind off the talk. But finally the moment of the talk came. All she remembers is that she kept talking for the allotted time. And she tried to put in all the points that were important, that might help someone who was seeking an answer spiritually.

Later, as people came up to congratulate her, Susan was still rather in a daze. Rich said, "I know you had the notes, but you didn't actually really look at them."

Finally a young man came up to her, someone she didn't know. He shook her hand and said, "I had a nudge to come to this seminar today, and throughout this whole day I haven't heard what I needed to hear. But your talk told me what I came for. I could have been working. Heaven knows I need the money. But I came, and it was to hear your talk. Thank you very much." He beamed with love.

A gift of change is always a gift of love.

This is a gift of change. And a gift of change is always a gift of love.

THE RIDDLE OF GOD

What's it all about? The third part is the riddle of God.

The Shariyat-Ki-Sugmad, which means "Way of the Eternal," says this in Book Two, chapter 1, "The Eternal Dreamer of ECK":

Once the chela steps onto the path of Eckankar, his karma begins to resolve and his reincarnations become fewer.

All the ways of liberation offered by the various orthodox religions generally must take Soul through the endless cycle of reincarnation until It becomes awakened to Its true self. But ECK gives the chela a concise way which is not known in any other path to God. Once the chela steps onto the path of Eckankar, his karma begins to resolve and his reincarnations become fewer. When he is initiated, it means that never again will he have to return to this physical and material world. From the moment he steps upon the path of ECK, his spiritual life is under the protection and guidance of the Mahanta, the Living ECK Master.

The initiation referred to here is the Second Initiation in ECK. If someone takes it, he no longer has to return to this physical, material world again.

I would also like to mention here a good book to answer some of your questions about the Mahanta: *The Rosetta Stone of God* by James Davis. It's available in bookstores and from the Eckankar Spiritual Center. You may find it very helpful.

Now, let's go back to that article from the *Wall Street Journal*, "Redefining God." A number of professionals and religious leaders were interviewed. The question was, What is God? An outfielder for the Texas Rangers, a Christian, said, "my creator." A minister for an American Baptist United Church of Christ congregation from New York said, "A force field of positive energy." A Jewish man, a CEO of a record company, said, "Pure love, intense feelings of love." That was his understanding of God. A novelist, a Catholic woman, said, "It may be a sexless being, but it's a being who cares very much about us as fleshly creatures."

Another Christian preacher said, "I don't need to see Him to believe Him. I don't see heat, but I know it's hot." Another person, the cofounder of a computer company, reduced God to a gene. He said, "As scientists we can say God is part of our genes. The desire to believe in God is built into us as a species." In a way, not faulting his view of God, it's a reflection of his state of consciousness.

What is science on the threshold of doing today? Manipulating genes. So then, basically, who becomes God? Man becomes God—if God is part of our genes. Maybe it's a stretch, but everyone sees God in a unique way.

Another minister, a Southern Baptist, said, "I think people who put a face on God are making a big mistake."

So what is the riddle of God? In *Stranger by the River* by Paul Twitchell, in the chapter by the same title, "The Riddle of God," Rebazar Tarzs says this:

> The riddle of God is this.
>
> God is what ye believe It is. No man is wrong about the existence of God, and yet no man is right about his knowledge of God. There is no mystery in God except that It is what each Soul believes that It is. So the riddle is that; but all men will quarrel and argue about the greatness of God and their own knowledge of Him.

No man is wrong about the existence of God, and yet no man is right about his knowledge of God.

It's in Your Hands

One evening, to wind down from the day's work, I listened to the John Doremus Show on the radio. He told the story of some clever village boys. They set a snare, and they caught a game bird.

These boys were full of mischief, and they decided they were going to play a joke on the wise man of the village. They would take this game bird to him. They would hold it in front of the old wise man and ask, "Is this bird living or dead?" They were going to trap him. They were going to catch him in a wrong answer.

If the wise man said, "Why, the bird is living," the boys intended to prepare the bird for the cooking pot right then and there. But if the wise man said, "Why, the bird is dead," they were going to take this live bird and throw it into the air and let it fly away.

So they were very sure of themselves. They came up to the village wise man, and they posed their question to him. They said, "Is this bird living or dead?"

The wise man looked at them a long time, and then he looked at the bird. After a long silence, he said, "It is in your hands."

What's it all about? It's all about spiritual liberation. That means unfolding to the state of being a clear channel for divine love and service.

That's exactly how it is with your spiritual destiny. It's in your hands. What you do today, what you do tomorrow, what you've done in the past—everything added up makes you who and what you are today. And what you do today and tomorrow determines who you will be tomorrow.

So with this talk, I've tried to give you an overview. The title is "What's It All About?" in three parts: the riddle of the question, the gift of change, and the riddle of God.

Now what is the answer to this question, What's it all about? It's all about spiritual liberation. That means unfolding to the state of being a clear channel for divine love and service.

That's all that it's about. May the blessings be.

ECK Springtime Seminar, San Diego, California, Saturday, April 22, 2000

GLOSSARY

Words set in SMALL CAPS are defined elsewhere in this glossary.

ARAHATA. *ah-rah-HAH-tah* An experienced and qualified teacher of ECKANKAR classes.

CHELA. *CHEE-lah* A spiritual student.

ECK. *EHK* The Life Force, the Holy Spirit, or Audible Life Current which sustains all life.

ECKANKAR. *EHK-ahn-kahr* Religion of the Light and Sound of God. Also known as the Ancient Science of SOUL TRAVEL. A truly spiritual religion for the individual in modern times. The teachings provide a framework for anyone to explore their own spiritual experiences. Established by Paul Twitchell, the modern-day founder, in 1965. The word means "Co-worker with God."

ECK MASTERS. Spiritual Masters who can assist and protect people in their spiritual studies and travels. The ECK Masters are from a long line of God-Realized SOULS who know the responsibility that goes with spiritual freedom.

GOD-REALIZATION. The state of God Consciousness. Complete and conscious awareness of God.

HU. *HYOO* The most ancient, secret name for God. The singing of the word HU is considered a love song to God. It can be sung aloud or silently to oneself.

INITIATION. Earned by a member of ECKANKAR through spiritual unfoldment and service to God. The initiation is a private ceremony in which the individual is linked to the Sound and Light of God.

LIVING ECK MASTER. The title of the spiritual leader of ECKANKAR. His duty is to lead SOULS back to God. The Living ECK Master can assist spiritual students physically as the Outer Master, in the dream state as the Dream Master, and in the spiritual worlds as the Inner Master. Sri Harold Klemp became the MAHANTA, the Living ECK Master in 1981.

315

MAHANTA. *mah-HAHN-tah*   A title to describe the highest state of God Consciousness on earth, often embodied in the LIVING ECK MASTER. He is the Living Word. An expression of the Spirit of God that is always with you.

PLANES.   The levels of existence, such as the Physical, Astral, Causal, Mental, Etheric, and Soul Planes.

SATSANG. *SAHT-sahng*   A class in which students of ECK study a monthly lesson from ECKANKAR.

SELF-REALIZATION.   SOUL recognition. The entering of Soul into the Soul Plane and there beholding Itself as pure Spirit. A state of seeing, knowing, and being.

THE SHARIYAT-KI-SUGMAD. *SHAH-ree-aht-kee-SOOG-mahd*   The sacred scriptures of ECKANKAR. The scriptures are comprised of twelve volumes in the spiritual worlds. The first two were transcribed from the inner PLANES by Paul Twitchell, modern-day founder of ECKANKAR.

SOUL.   The True Self. The inner, most sacred part of each person. Soul exists before birth and lives on after the death of the physical body. As a spark of God, Soul can see, know, and perceive all things. It is the creative center of Its own world.

SOUL TRAVEL.   The expansion of consciousness. The ability of SOUL to transcend the physical body and travel into the spiritual worlds of God. Soul Travel is taught only by the LIVING ECK MASTER. It helps people unfold spiritually and can provide proof of the existence of God and life after death.

SOUND AND LIGHT OF ECK.   The Holy Spirit. The two aspects through which God appears in the lower worlds. People can experience them by looking and listening within themselves and through SOUL TRAVEL.

SPIRITUAL EXERCISES OF ECK.   The daily practice of certain techniques to get us in touch with the Light and Sound of God.

SRI. *SREE*   A title of spiritual respect, similar to reverend or pastor, used for those who have attained the kingdom of God. In ECKANKAR, it is reserved for the MAHANTA, the LIVING ECK MASTER.

SUGMAD. *SOOG-mahd*   A sacred name for God. Sugmad is neither masculine nor feminine; It is the source of all life.

WAH Z. *WAH zee*   The spiritual name of Sri Harold Klemp. It means the Secret Doctrine. It is his name in the spiritual worlds.

For more explanations of Eckankar terms, see *A Cosmic Sea of Words: The ECKANKAR Lexicon* by Harold Klemp.

INDEX

FOR FURTHER READING AND STUDY

Autobiography of a Modern Prophet
Harold Klemp

Master your spiritual destiny. One man's journey illuminates the way. Venture to the outer reaches of the last great frontier, your spiritual destiny! The deeper you explore it, the closer you come to discovering your own divine nature as an infinite, eternal spark of God. This book leads you there.

The Art of Spiritual Dreaming
Harold Klemp

Dreams are a treasure. A gift from God. Harold Klemp shows how to find a dream's spiritual gold, and how to experience God's love. Get insights from the past and future, grow in confidence, and make decisions about career and finances. Do this from a unique perspective: by recognizing the spiritual nature of your dreams.

Our Spiritual Wake-Up Calls,
Mahanta Transcripts, Book 15
Harold Klemp

When God calls, are you listening? Discover how God communicates through dreams, the people you meet, or even a newspaper comic strip. Learn how you are in the grasp of divine love every moment of every day. The Mahanta Transcripts are highlights from Harold Klemp's worldwide speaking tours.

35 Golden Keys to Who You Are & Why You're Here
Linda C. Anderson

Discover thirty-five golden keys to mastering your spiritual destiny through the ancient teachings of Eckankar, Religion of the Light and Sound of God. The dramatic, true stories in this book equal anything found in the spiritual literature of today. Learn ways to immediately bring more love, peace, and purpose to your life.

Available at your local bookstore. If unavailable, call (952) 380-2222. Or write: ECKANKAR, Dept. BK33, P.O. Box 27300, Minneapolis, MN 55427 U.S.A.

There May Be an
Eckankar Study Group near You

Eckankar offers a variety of local and international activities for the spiritual seeker. With hundreds of study groups worldwide, Eckankar is near you! Many areas have Eckankar centers where you can browse through the books in a quiet, unpressured environment, talk with others who share an interest in this ancient teaching, and attend beginning discussion classes on how to gain the attributes of Soul: wisdom, power, love, and freedom.

Around the world, Eckankar study groups offer special one-day or weekend seminars on the basic teachings of Eckankar. For membership information, visit the Eckankar Web site (www.eckankar.org). For the location of the Eckankar center or study group nearest you, click on "Other Eckankar Web sites" for a listing of those areas with Web sites. You're also welcome to check your phone book under **ECKANKAR**; call **(952) 380-2222, Ext. BK33;** or write **ECKANKAR, Att: Information, BK33, P.O. Box 27300, Minneapolis, MN 55427 U.S.A.**

☐ Please send me information on the nearest Eckankar center or study group in my area.

☐ Please send me more information about membership in Eckankar, which includes a twelve-month spiritual study.

Please type or print clearly

Name _____
first (given)   last (family)

Street _____ Apt. # _____

City _____ State/Prov. _____

ZIP/Postal Code _____ Country _____

ABOUT THE AUTHOR

Sri Harold Klemp was born in Wisconsin and grew up on a small farm. He attended a two-room country schoolhouse before going to high school at a religious boarding school in Milwaukee, Wisconsin.

After preministerial college in Milwaukee and Fort Wayne, Indiana, he enlisted in the U.S. Air Force. There he trained as a language specialist at Indiana University and a radio intercept operator at Goodfellow AFB, Texas. Then followed a two-year stint in Japan where he first encountered Eckankar.

In October 1981, he became the spiritual leader of Eckankar, Religion of the Light and Sound of God. His full title is Sri Harold Klemp, the Mahanta, the Living ECK Master. As the Living ECK Master, Harold Klemp is responsible for the continued evolution of the Eckankar teachings.

His mission is to help people find their way back to God in this life. Harold Klemp travels to ECK seminars in North America, Europe, and the South Pacific. He has also visited Africa and many countries throughout the world, meeting with spiritual seekers and giving inspirational talks. There are many videocassettes and audiocassettes of his public talks available.

In his talks and writings, Harold Klemp's sense of humor and practical approach to spirituality have helped many people around the world find truth in their lives and greater inner freedom, wisdom, and love.

International Who's Who of Intellectuals
Ninth Edition